'This book is a landmark text that is set to become a fundamental read for forensic students and researchers. Sarah Brown and Emma Sleath have done a fantastic job of putting together a text that explains the process of conducting forensic psychology research from start to finish. This is the first UK textbook to specifically grapple with the "real-world" problems experienced by forensic researchers which mainstream texts are unable to address. I only wish such a text had been available when I was conducting my own PhD!'

Theresa A. Gannon, Professor of Forensic Psychology,
CORE-FP, University of Kent, UK

'Comprehensive, accessible, detailed, and practical – a gem of a book for anyone researching in a forensic setting. From formulating your research question to disseminating your findings, everything you need to know to plan, conduct, and present your research is right here. A "must-have" for all students and budding researchers in criminal justice.'

Jo Clarke, PhD, Programme Director,
MSc in Applied Forensic Psychology,
University of York, UK

'I am delighted to endorse this book. I have been involved in delivering postgraduate forensic psychology training for almost 20 years and this is *the* book that we have been waiting for. It is clear and concise and focuses on all the main issues that plague any early researcher in the forensic field. I will be putting this on my required reading for our postgraduates and would recommend that postgraduate students, early researchers, and all other course directors buy a copy too.'

Liz Gilchrist, Professor of Forensic Psychology,
Glasgow Caledonian University, UK

Research Methods for Forensic Psychologists

Research Methods for Forensic Psychologists is an accessible and comprehensive textbook that introduces students to the research process in forensic psychology. Adopting a problem-based learning approach, this book offers a 'how-to' guide to the whole research process and empowers readers to develop their own programme of research, from initial vague ideas, to developing a research question, to carrying out a methodologically rigorous research project, to disseminating the findings.

The text is centred on five case studies, sufficiently different in nature to address the most common research methodologies. Each case study is linked with a specific research question that will be used to illustrate the research process throughout the rest of the book. Topics covered in the book include:

- **Design and planning**, including a literature search, a discussion of different sorts of data, practicality and feasibility issues, research ethics, and developing a research proposal.
- **Conducting research**, including the submission of ethics proposals and responding to feedback, collecting data, and dealing with the problems and challenges of analysing data.
- **Dissemination of findings**, including an overview of the different types of papers, with examples listed and other methods of disseminating findings discussed, such as conference presentations and the use of social media.

Throughout, issues of common difficulty or confusion are highlighted and activities are provided for readers to consider and apply the information discussed further. Additional reading sections and summaries are also provided at the end of each chapter. This book is essential reading for advanced students in forensic psychology, as well as for trainees and practitioners within relevant forensic psychology organisations.

Sarah Brown is a professor, chartered psychologist, Associate Fellow of the British Psychological Society, a forensic psychologist, and Fellow of the Higher Education Academy. She has developed and led forensic psychology master's courses and taught both quantitative and qualitative research methods. Professor Brown has over fifteen years of experience in supervising numerous undergraduates and teaching postgraduate and doctoral research projects in forensic psychology using a range of research methods and types of data analyses. She has published peer-reviewed literature reviews and empirical papers from many of these projects with master's and doctoral students, and many of these studies have been presented at national and international conferences.

Emma Sleath is a senior lecturer in psychology, registered HCPC forensic psychologist and Fellow of the Higher Education Academy. Dr. Sleath has taught postgraduate forensic psychology courses for over ten years, and she has a range of experience in both quantitative and qualitative research methods. Her research interests focus on police practice in relation to victims of crime, and she has published numerous peer-reviewed journal articles in this area.

Research Methods for Forensic Psychologists

A guide to completing your research project

Sarah Brown and Emma Sleath

LONDON AND NEW YORK

First published 2016
by Routledge
2 Park Square, Milton Park, Abingdon, Oxon, OX14 4RN
Simultaneously published in the USA and Canada

by Routledge
711 Third Avenue, New York, NY 10017

Routledge is an imprint of the Taylor & Francis Group, an informa business

© 2016 Sarah Brown and Emma Sleath

The right of Sarah Brown and Emma Sleath to be identified as authors of this work has been asserted by them in accordance with sections 77 and 78 of the Copyright, Designs and Patents Act 1988.

All rights reserved. No part of this book may be reprinted or reproduced or utilised in any form or by any electronic, mechanical, or other means, now known or hereafter invented, including photocopying and recording, or in any information storage or retrieval system, without permission in writing from the publishers.

British Library Cataloguing in Publication Data
A catalogue record for this book is available from the British Library

Library of Congress Cataloging-in-Publication Data
Brown, Sarah, author.
   Research methods for forensic psychologists : a guide to completing your research project / Sarah Brown and Emma Sleath.
      p. ; cm.
   I. Sleath, Emma, author. II. Title.
   [DNLM: 1. Forensic Psychiatry—methods. 2. Research
Design. 3. Data Collection—methods. 4. Ethics, Research. W 740]
   RA1148
   614'.15—dc23
   2014049467

ISBN: 978-0-415-73242-0 (hbk)
ISBN: 978-0-415-73247-5 (pbk)
ISBN: 978-1-315-84915-7 (ebk)

Typeset in Bembo
by Apex CoVantage, LLC

Printed and bound in the United States of America by
Edwards Brothers Malloy on sustainably sourced paper

SB – To Steve and all the students and early career researchers who have provided the inspiration for writing this book. To students and researchers embarking on your research projects, I hope this makes your progress as smooth and stress free as possible. Good luck!

ES – To Viren. A special thanks to all friends, colleagues and collaborators for always providing excellent support, advice, inappropriate jokes and cake whenever necessary.

Contents

List of figures	xi
List of tables	xii
Acknowledgements	xiii
1 Introduction	1

SECTION I
Designing and planning | **5**

2 Searching the literature	7
3 Methods	31
4 Types of data	63
5 From research question to research design	79
6 Practicality and feasibility issues in research	96
7 Ethics in forensic psychology research	117
8 Research proposal	138

SECTION 2
Conducting research | **159**

9 Gaining ethical approval	161
10 Setting up and implementing your study	182
11 Collecting data	193
12 Data analysis	207

x Contents

SECTION 3
Dissemination of your research findings 223

13 Purpose of dissemination 225

14 Literature review papers 237

15 Empirical papers 253

16 Conference presentations 272

Index 283

Figures

8.1	An example of a simple Gantt chart	151
15.1	Structure of an empirical paper	260

Tables

4.1	Example of conditions within an experimental design	66
8.1	Example of timetable for planning out the project process	149
8.2	Example risk assessment for case study one	156
9.1	Examples of research situations that require gatekeeper approval with suggested gatekeepers	169

Acknowledgements

We would like to thank Kate Walker and Rebecca Crookes for their speedy, excellent proofreading services, and all our research students who unwittingly helped us write this book. We would also like to thank all those who have advised and assisted us in our research endeavours, and we hope that, although we can no longer name the source of each pearl of wisdom, you are happy that we have passed it on to others to use in their research projects.

Chapter 1

Introduction

Carrying out research in forensic psychology can be a challenging experience for any researcher, whether you are a postgraduate student or an experienced practitioner. Therefore, our main aim in writing this book is to highlight many of the issues that are likely to arise in the course of carrying out your research. Indeed, many of the problems/issues that we discuss in the book are ones that we and our students have encountered. We want this book to be as practical as possible in guiding you through the whole research process, from developing your initial ideas/questions, to carrying out well-designed projects that result in outcomes that develop our understanding of forensic psychology issues. We can never promise that the course of a research project will run smoothly, but we hope that this book will help you to avoid the most common issues that arise in completing forensic psychological research.

As you will see, the book is structured to walk you through a project from start (developing your idea) to finish (disseminating the findings of your study). So if you have a research question that you want to address, we will guide you through the process of developing this idea based upon the current literature in that area. We then examine the many methodologies that you could use and the types of data that could be generated to address research questions, hopefully enabling you to identify the most appropriate approach for your question. At this point, we introduce five case studies to illustrate how an idea is refined into a specific research question and how an appropriate method is selected across a range of forensic psychology topics and methodologies. The aim is to highlight a range of issues that you should consider when developing your own research projects, with the help of some practical examples.

This problem-based learning approach is integrated throughout the book, where we use the five case studies to illustrate the potential for problems and processes that should be followed. We also refer to examples of published studies to illustrate different types of approaches/methods that can be used. We adopted this approach because we want you to understand exactly how to apply the ideas and/or solutions that we are outlining. The different case studies each highlight a range of issues that a researcher may need to address, from negotiating access to participants, to the different methodologies and analyses that can be carried out on the huge range of possible data that can be collected within the course of a project. By highlighting the many potential options and the issues that may arise from these choices, we hope to help you to consider these points before embarking on your own research project.

As we will emphasise throughout the book, often all that is needed is some guidance about the research process *and* some time to consider how this may impact on your own research project. Taking the extra time to think about your project will always be beneficial and is never a waste of time. We hope that you will find this to be a useful approach that will aid you in your own research project.

The basic ideas behind the case studies are outlined in the following box. These are obviously very basic at this point in the research process, but you will see as you progress through the book how these can be developed into fully fledged projects.

Case study examples

Case study one

You are interested in looking at a service provider's response to intimate partner violence.

Case study two

You want to examine how different types of sentencing of offenders impact upon the psychological well-being of victims. This is based upon different theoretical perspectives about the purposes of sentencing.

Case study three

You want to test whether a reasonably large-scale intervention is having an impact on the offenders in line with the theoretical model of change of the intervention.

Case study four

You are interested in exploring how jurors perceive DNA evidence within a court trial.

Case study five

There is an intervention that is being run by a local service provider, and you want to test whether that intervention is having the desired impact on a small group of offenders.

Following the outline of the case studies, we consider a range of practicality and feasibility issues that should be considered in research projects to enable you to design a project that is 'doable' (i.e., achievable). Gathering your data in an ethical manner is important, and the ethical principles and processes that you should consider and take into account in your design are outlined. Section 1 of the book is completed with advice on writing a research proposal.

In Section 2 of the book, we discuss setting up your project, collecting data and analysing your data. The aim of this book is not to cover each and every type of data analysis that could be conducted in detail (there are many other excellent publications you can refer to for this), but to walk you through the steps that you should take in carrying out this phase of your study and the key points that you should consider to try to avoid any problems and difficulties. The case studies are used to illustrate these.

When you have finished your data analysis, we hope you have found something interesting that adds to the knowledge base in the field and that you will want to share these findings. In many instances, you will need to write up your research to fulfil course and/or training requirements. In Section 3 of the book, we outline different methods of disseminating your research, for example, writing literature reviews, empirical papers, conference presentations and posters, as well as other ways (e.g., social media) you can share your findings. The case studies are used to demonstrate key aspects of these presentation methods, and we refer you to published examples.

We hope that you find this book to be a useful guide throughout your research project, and we wish you the best of luck throughout this process.

Section 1

Designing and planning

Chapter 2

Searching the literature

In this chapter, we will outline the importance of conducting literature reviews for any research process. We will highlight the important differences between the types of literature reviews that can be carried out, as well as establish the reasons for carrying out each of these and outline the process of conducting good reviews. The purpose of this chapter is to help you use the literature to establish your own research questions, which will assist you in designing your research study. Once you have read this chapter, you should be able to:

- understand why literature reviews are important;
- distinguish between different types of literature reviews and their purposes;
- conduct a literature review; and
- use a literature review to design a research study.

The reasons for conducting literature reviews

A literature review is a "summary and synthesis of relevant literature on a research problem" (Notar & Cole, 2010, p. 3). Put simply, it is a method by which you can gain a thorough understanding of a particular topic, such as an area of research, a form of intervention/treatment, or a practice approach. Although the focus of this book is research, it is important to be able to conduct literature reviews and draw appropriate conclusions in line with the scientist–practitioner model and/or to employ evidence-based interventions/ strategies in your practice. As such, you need to be able to find and evaluate the empirical evidence for a particular strategy/approach/intervention in order to be able to employ that which is most empirically supported in your practice. (See the Shingler [2009] review listed in the 'Literature review examples' section of this chapter for a good illustration of a review conducted to establish the evidence base for a technique used in practice.) Much of the information in this chapter is relevant to conducting literature reviews for evidence-based practice reasons, as well as for conducting your own research. In fact, these purposes are often combined, in that your research has practice relevance (e.g., you wish to evaluate a particular intervention/approach).

8   Designing and planning

It is beyond the scope of this book to discuss in detail the different theoretical (epistemological) positions in relation to research; however, it is important to note that, generally speaking, research develops incrementally. For example, researchers A conduct research and develop theory A; researchers B conduct research that supports research/theory A; however, researchers C use a different approach and support some of theory A but make some modifications to develop theory C; theory C is then tested by researchers D and so on. Hopefully, you can see that in order for your research to contribute to the development of knowledge in this area, it should be based on the knowledge gained from the research/theoretical developments to date and allows others to continue the developments in the future. Hence, you need to search the literature to identify the research developments in that area and design a study that helps to contribute to the advancement of knowledge in the area.

Common difficulties

Many people decide on a study including its design (e.g., I want to interview 10 sex offenders in XX prison about their attitudes to the SOTP intervention) without any, or a very limited, understanding of what research has been conducted in the area already. Although this might be a good way to identify the general area within which you wish to conduct your research, it is important to conduct a literature review to ensure that your research incrementally builds on the existing knowledge base, as outlined previously. The same principle applies if you have been asked to conduct a study on a particular topic/for a particular purpose. A review is also potentially very helpful because you can identify how research has been conducted in the past (i.e., you do not need to work out how to design the study unaided), the range of methods/approaches you can use, the strengths and weaknesses of these approaches, and common difficulties/issues that might need to be overcome, all of which will aid you in designing your own study.

Searching and gaining a thorough understanding of the current and previous literature is therefore an essential and integral part of any research project that should not be ignored. A literature review can be used to identify your broad area of interest (see 'Common difficulties' on page 8). A more detailed review will then be required to move your general interest in a topic area to the point where you will be able to start the developmental process of a well-thought-out research project. Additionally, there are several other reasons why you should carry out a literature review; these are listed and discussed in more detail later. You may find that a combination of these reasons means it is important that you do a detailed literature review that forms the basis of a report/article; however, the depth of the review will vary according to the reason/purposes of the review and the extent/nature of the literature.

Purposes for conducting a literature review

- To identify theories/strategies/interventions etc. that have (or lack) empirical support and/or that have the most/least empirical support
- To understand the breadth of knowledge on a topic/intervention
- To progress your research idea from a general concept to a specific idea
- To establish a rationale for your proposed study
- To explore previous methodologies that have been used to research the topic area
- To develop the design of a new research study
- To achieve innovation in a proposed research project
- To synthesise (combine) empirical research findings

Common difficulties

Be wary of starting a literature search, particularly if it is to establish a topic area for your own research, with current or recently published research papers. Depending on the area/topic, it is likely that contemporary papers will be based on a great deal of prior research and theoretical developments, so it might be complex in nature/design and/or written for an audience familiar with the developments and current understandings on the topic. Reading books, book chapters and/or readers will provide an overview of topics/research so that you can (a) identify areas that you are interested in and (b) develop an understanding of the core information/background to the topic area. Note that it might also be a good idea to read the research papers you identify in chronological order (oldest first, starting with the 'core' papers/theories outlined in the books), so that you can understand how the research/knowledge on the topic has developed over time. This should then enable you to understand more easily the latest papers/research on the topic.

To understand the breadth of knowledge on a topic/intervention

It can often be the case that ideas about potential research projects present themselves without any background context. This situation can occur for a

10   Designing and planning

range of reasons, such as questions that arise from teaching/training sessions or from forensic psychological practice. These potential projects might arise because of a gap in our own personal research knowledge. This does not automatically mean that there is a gap is the current research literature. Therefore, a literature search is needed to augment our own understanding of the issue, as potentially there is already a knowledge base available within the literature. Breadth of understanding is important here, requiring a thorough literature searching strategy (see later in the chapter for more on this issue).

Common difficulties

A common question in relation to literature reviews is: 'How many studies/articles do I need?' This question is impossible to answer without a thorough search of the literature to identify the range of studies conducted/published on the topic. A search of the literature on a topic means that you should identify as much of the literature on that topic as you can find, not a specific number of papers/studies on the topic. Look up definitions of *literature* and you should get a sense of the scope of the distinction between this and, for example, 'a collection of studies'. When writing an essay, you may be able to stop searching for empirical evidence once you have found sufficient evidence to support your argument; however, conducting a literature search involves a broader and more exhaustive approach. As you might already have realised, this potentially means a huge number of studies/papers and a great deal of time/effort. First, this should alert you to the fact that literature reviews take a great deal of time to complete – time that you need to build in to your study plans. Second, you might need to consider the breadth of your topic and narrow it to enable a thorough search (there are other ways to narrow a search, as discussed later in the chapter). Searching the literature on eyewitness testimony, for example, is virtually impossible given the sheer number of studies/papers on the topic; however, searching for studies on the relationship between the confidence of adult eyewitnesses and the accuracy of their testimonies is likely to be more achievable.

To progress your research idea from a general concept to a specific idea and to establish a rationale for your proposed study

It is important for your study to have a clear 'rationale' – that is, a clear reason for you to conduct the research. You should develop this reason from your reading of the research and the development of research/theory/ideas on the topic over time. Reading the chronological development of research on a topic should allow you to gain a clearer idea of how each study is designed with a specific purpose or rationale to build on the previous studies/knowledge base. The rationale is often stated in a research paper towards the end of the introduction. Note that it might not be referred to as a *rationale*, but in each paper there should be a reasonably clear outline of the purpose for the study. You will need to be able to outline the purpose for your study. Without a rationale for carrying out a study, there is very little point in completing the research. Essentially, you need to understand exactly why the research needs to be completed. To establish this rationale, it is important that you have a strong grasp of the current literature, as you will use this literature to develop an argument for the proposed research.

Activity

Select five empirical quantitative research papers and highlight the rationales for the studies presented in these papers. Note how the rationales are outlined in the papers and identify how the authors have developed the rationales based on the previous research, which should be discussed throughout the introduction sections.

To explore previous methodologies that have been used to research the topic area

Although at the start of the research process you may have a clear understanding of *what* you want to examine, you may not understand *how* you can investigate this topic. A literature review can assist you in understanding how the topic has been researched previously, the methodologies that have been employed, the reasons (rationales) for the designs employed, and the strengths and weaknesses (look at the limitations of the research identified by authors in the discussion sections of empirical papers). This will help you to develop your thinking about exactly how you are going to implement the research idea that you have. In addition to helping with the design of your project, this search should also help you to identify materials that you may wish to use, such as existing scales/ measures. Using existing scales/measures can save considerable time and energy in the research process because developing a new validated scale/measure can be a time-consuming process. Note that you may need to obtain permission from the authors of the measures/scales to use them in your study.

To develop the design of a new research study and to achieve innovation in a proposed project

Innovation and originality in a research project are highly valued within forensic psychology (and academia more generally), as they usually indicate that the research study will make a contribution to the developing knowledge base

Designing and planning

within an area. As a student, innovation becomes increasingly important as the level of study increases. For example, some level of innovation is expected within master's level dissertations. For PhD programmes of research, innovation is an expected and integral part of the research process, where the proposed research is anticipated to develop and contribute towards the current knowledge. As a researcher, innovation is also important, for example, research publications should be original and make a contribution to the development of knowledge – factors that are also important when applying for funding via research bids. Therefore, to be able to establish innovation in your current project, you need to have a good understanding of how the topic has been researched previously and how your research is innovative in its design or process. A good literature review will enable you to establish this argument.

Common confusion

You will be encouraged to develop an *original* and *innovative* idea (rationale) for your research study. Don't panic and don't be too ambitious. Taking the latter point first: you are unlikely to be able to answer grand questions such as 'why do people commit crime?', 'how can forensic psychologists help the police solve complex cases?' or 'how can you enable a repeat offender to desist from crime?', as the questions are too broad and the answers too complex. That does not mean, however, that you cannot develop and conduct research that has an impact and/or builds our knowledge on a topic. Small changes/developments in research designs/questions can be important; for example, there has been much research that has tended to support the view that there is no relationship between the confidence of eyewitnesses and the accuracy of their statements. Kebbell, Wagstaff, and Convey (1996) considered this research and noted that researchers had generally taken global assessments of confidence and measured this against a single accuracy rating, even though eyewitnesses provided a number of different details, each of which could be accurate/inaccurate and which ranged in difficulty. In a simple modification to existing designs, they asked participants to state how confident they were about each piece of information they provided, with the information requested ranging in difficulty. In addition to demonstrating higher confidence–accuracy correlations than in previous studies, this revealed that when eyewitnesses were 'certain' about specific pieces of information, these details were extremely likely to be accurate. In addition to developing our knowledge on this topic, this finding has clear implications for practice. This sort of modification/development is what is meant by *original* and could also be considered to be fairly ambitious, though not impossible, for master's level projects, where the *originality* might be in the form of testing a theory on a group that it has not yet been tested on, replicating a study in a new area/with a different type of participants, or using a different research design to test a theory/approach. Hence, don't panic – you can be *original* by evaluating the previous research, thinking about how things work in practice, or carefully considering your research design.

To synthesise empirical research findings

Sometimes the purpose of research is to complete a review in itself. Given the breadth of literature that is available within forensic psychology, a good review of the current literature can provide the opportunity for significant new developments in both theory and practice. Therefore, as you will see here, many types of literature reviews can be considered as a research process with the output component being the synthesis of the literature. A research question can be addressed through the amalgamation of the current literature (e.g., in relation to the effectiveness of a particular component of a treatment programme). It should be obvious that in this situation, a thorough literature review is an extremely important part of the research process.

Types of literature reviews

There are several different types of literature reviews that are outlined in more detail below. A literature review can be a stand-alone piece of work that is written up as a full journal article (see the examples section towards the end of this chapter for a list of references of different types of published stand-alone reviews that you can read in conjunction with this chapter) or it can be completed to form the introduction to an empirical journal article or report outlining a new piece of research. If you are carrying out a literature review for the introduction to an article, it is likely that you would want to adopt a narrative review style. This does not mean that you cannot adopt a systematic review approach to searching the literature; however, it would be unlikely that you would decide to complete the full systematic review process, as this would be time consuming and unnecessary for your purposes. The point of an introduction to an empirical journal article is to provide the background literature and to establish a rationale for your study. Therefore, a full systematic or meta-analytical approach is unwarranted; however, your search for literature when conducting any type of review should be conducted in a clear, thorough manner.

Narrative review

This is one of the most common styles of review that you will see in journal articles. Note that such reviews are not always labelled as 'narrative reviews'. A paper/report that indicates a 'review' of a topic is most likely to be a narrative review; systematic reviews, meta-analyses and meta-syntheses (see the following

14 Designing and planning

sections) tend to be labelled more specifically. You can use this review style to establish the rationale for your empirical study and to outline the methodologies that have been used by researchers to explore similar research questions. This approach can also be used for a stand-alone review. The term *narrative* largely relates to the style in which the review is written and, as in any literature review, the search for relevant papers should be conducted in a well-thought-out, thorough, consistent manner. In a narrative review there is no specific way in which the literature should be searched for (advice on conducting a good literature search is provided later in this chapter), as there is for a systematic review. Narrative reviews tend to be discursive in their style of presentation and can look fairly similar to essays, although rather than answering a specific question, as is common in essays, the central argument running through the review is in relation to critically summarising the literature on a specific topic.

Navathe, Ward, and Gannon (2008) used a narrative review approach to explore the theoretical approaches to cognitive distortions (i.e., the different methodologies that have been used to examine cognitive distortions) and then to reflect upon the implications for clinical practice. In this paper, the authors adopted a prose writing style throughout the review; however, some narrative reviews provide greater levels of detail about the articles being discussed. For example, Sandhu and Rose (2012) provided a greater level of detail than Navathe et al. (2008) in relation to their search strategy, and they also summarised the articles included within the review. Both of these approaches typify the narrative review style where the aim is to provide a clear summary of the literature that has been published in one particular topic area. Ideally, it should be clear to the reader of a narrative review how the literature was searched and the types of studies/papers that were included and excluded from the review. The reader should also be provided with a good sense that the review discusses all or most of the relevant literature on the topic. The authors of good literature reviews should convey expertise in the topic area, methodologies used, and so forth, and in many instances, reviews should be used to make recommendations for future developments in research, theory and/or practice. It is important to note that narrative reviews tend to have an argument or purpose in relation to summarising the literature on a specific topic; for example, this purpose might be to assess what the implications of the research are for practice, or it may be to assess a theory or to determine if the research has enabled us to answer a specific question/issue.

Activity

Read the narrative review papers (listed in the 'Literature review examples' section at the end of this chapter) and see how they differ. Identify how the authors searched the literature and determined which papers to include and exclude from the review.

Find five more narrative review papers (tip: there are more in the 'Examples' section at the end of this chapter; journals with review in their title, e.g., *Clinical Psychology Review*, only include review papers; *Aggression and Violent Behavior* is a review journal) and see how they differ in style/approach and level of detail in discussing the studies and identify the search strategies and inclusion/exclusion criteria.

Identify the overall/underlying point that the authors are trying to make about the literature in each paper: the purpose of the review, what conclusions are reached, what recommendations are made, and so on. It is important to note that review papers, like empirical papers, need to contribute something new/original to the literature in order to get published. Have a think about what the new/original point or argument is that is being made in each paper.

Systematic review

A systematic review is, in many ways, very similar to the narrative review. The purpose is still to provide an overview of the literature; however, there is a much more formalised methodology associated with carrying out a systematic review. There are numerous guidelines that you can use to facilitate the completion of a systematic review and learn more about this methodology (e.g., Centre for Reviews and Dissemination, 2009; Torgerson, 2003). As you will see from Tully, Chou, and Browne's (2013) review, there is a much more rigorous methodological approach to systematic reviews. A good systematic review such as this will provide a clear background to the methodology used to search the literature, as well as explicit search terms and inclusion/exclusion criteria to assess whether an article should be included within the review. In addition, there are often quality assessments of the studies/articles and data extracted from them. In comparison with the narrative review, there is a clear difference regarding the depth and extent of the literature review process. This clearly makes it an inappropriate method to use when establishing an introduction or rationale for a study; however, should a thorough and conclusive overview of a topic be needed, a systematic review is an excellent method to establish the current findings in the area.

Activity

Look at the Cochrane Library web site (http://www.thecochranelibrary.com) to identify some more systematic reviews and also learn more about these types of reviews. What reviews can you find that are relevant to forensic contexts? Note how compared to narrative reviews, systematic reviews are much more standardised in their presentations and the sections/headings used, and so on.

Look through the guidance in conducting a review and note how the steps/stages of a systematic review are very methodical and specific. It is important to note that if you wish to carry out a systematic review, you will need to conduct it in the specific, structured way, following every step/stage carefully.

Meta-analysis

Meta-analysis is a statistical approach to synthesise (i.e., pool or combine) the research findings from quantitative empirical studies (Borenstein, Hedges, Higgins, & Rothstein, 2009). The start to a meta-analysis is similar to that of a systematic review in that the reviewers have to decide which articles to include or exclude from the review process. However, whereas in a systematic review the literature is discussed and summarised, in a meta-analysis the data/findings from studies are pooled together using specific statistical techniques. These data are then subjected to statistical analyses to, for example, establish effect sizes across the data from all the studies included in the review. Meta-analyses can be seen as a means of drawing conclusions from a range of studies that have provided mixed results, though care is needed to select methodologically robust studies for inclusion; a study that pools together the findings from a number of poorly conducted studies does not really help a great deal. This means that selecting the studies to include in a meta-analysis can be a contentious issue; if you read the literature and meta-analyses conducted in relation to the evaluation of sex offender treatment programmes, this will provide you with an example of the difficulties in determining the studies that should be included in meta-analyses.

This approach can be used to see how a new or particular study contributes to the knowledge on a particular topic. A cumulative meta-analysis can be conducted retrospectively as a series of meta-analyses in which each analysis incorporates an additional study, so it is possible to see how knowledge has developed over time. Alternatively, it can be conducted prospectively, with new studies (e.g., your study) added to a meta-analysis of the previous evidence base to establish how the new findings contribute or add to the evidence base.

The decision to complete a meta-analysis is not one to take lightly. This process requires significant time and energy in the gathering of the data and also sufficient understanding of statistical analysis to be able to further analyse the data. However, meta-analyses are very useful for establishing a clear understanding of the usefulness of an approach. For example, Snook, Eastwood, Gendreau, Goggin, and Cullen (2007) used meta-analytical approaches to establish the effectiveness of criminal profiling. This analysis showed where there is a lack of difference between self-labelled profilers and comparison groups but also established where the profilers outperform comparison groups. Meta-analyses have proved very useful in establishing where effective practice lies; for example, Singh and Fazel (2010) conducted a mind-boggling meta-review of meta-analyses, presenting a qualitative assessment of the findings from meta-analyses in relation to forensic risk assessment.

Meta-synthesis

Meta-analyses are reserved for quantitative findings. A relatively new type of review is the meta-synthesis, where the findings from qualitative research studies are reviewed and synthesised. This approach was used by Walji, Simpson, and Weatherhead (2014) to pool together the key themes that have emerged from qualitative studies on sex offenders' experiences of engaging in therapeutic intervention. These were synthesised into a summary of the key findings, which is then used to identify implications for practice. While it is clearly a good idea to have an excellent understanding of statistical analyses to conduct a meta-analysis, it is likewise a good idea to have an excellent understanding of qualitative methodologies/analyses in order to complete a good meta-synthesis.

Activity

Read the meta-analysis and meta-synthesis example papers. See how many other meta-syntheses you can find in published journal articles.

Note how what is essentially the same purpose/task (pooling the results of a number of studies) compares/differs when using quantitative and qualitative research studies and approaches – that is, compare the meta-syntheses with the meta-analyses.

How to carry out a literature review

In the following section we will discuss the literature review process that you should undertake when developing your research ideas and/or conducting a stand-alone narrative literature review. If you wish to complete a systematic review, a meta-analysis, or meta-synthesis, we strongly recommended that you consult the further reading section and read some of those resources to assist you in completing this task.

Writing a research protocol

It is good practice to write a research protocol when you are completing a literature review. According to Torgerson (2003), a research protocol is "an a

18 Designing and planning

priori statement of the research questions, aims and methods of the review" (p. 51). The purpose of the protocol is to map out the process that you complete when searching the literature, and it will also act as a research diary for you to record the decision-making process that you engage in when completing the review. It will also enable you to set out exactly what the aims of the review are prior to becoming entangled in the literature. Writing a good and clear research protocol should enable you to maintain clarity through the literature searching process and, therefore, stop you from becoming side-tracked through this process. It may seem like an additional step, but writing a research protocol will save you time in the long run. One final point to make is that the research protocol should not be a static and unchangeable document. It should be adapted as you refine your ideas and methods. For example, you may adapt your search terms once you begin searching the literature when you realise that the terms are too broad. You may also define your research questions more specifically when you realise the body of literature is too large to synthesise using the current framework.

Research protocol headings

Title of review
Aim of the review
Specific research questions
Literature search strategy
Inclusion/exclusion criteria
Data to be extracted from the studies

Title of review

A title of a review may seem unnecessary right at the beginning of the literature search process. However, a title can help focus your thinking on what exactly you want to research. Obviously, this title does not have to be the final title that you use; however, it is good practice to have this established early on. It does not have to be imaginative; it can simply be "A review to examine X in relation to Y". Referring back to this title will help you keep on track when other interesting areas of research may distract you away from your original purpose.

Aims of the review

This section does not have to be a lengthy section; however, it is important that you clearly articulate the aims of the review, to enable you to address the question "Why am I carrying out this review?" This can relate to both the research

Searching the literature 19

(e.g., to synthesise the literature regarding an offender treatment method) and to your purpose in carrying out the review (e.g., to understand the methodologies that will inform your proposed research). It is really useful to get this established early on in the process; as with the construction of the title, writing out the aims will force you think clearly about the purpose of the review. It will also keep you on track because you should continually refer back to the aims should you feel that you are moving away from your original purpose.

Specific research questions

This section is more specific than the 'Aims of the review' section because the research question(s) are much more unique to the review that you are carrying out. Your research questions might be as follows:

1   What extra-legal factors affect jury decision making?
2   What is the evidence for the underlying assumptions of case linkage?
3   What is the evidence that a specific type of treatment is effective at reducing reoffending in violent offenders?

As you can see from the examples, these set out the exact factors that you are going to examine within the review (e.g., extra-legal factors, usually in relation to another factor, such as jury decision making). It is very important that you have these research question(s) set out before you start the research process. Many researchers/students can find it challenging to write out research question(s) at the start of this process; however, it is strongly recommended. You might need to speak to a supervisor/colleague to help you formulate the questions. Starting a literature review without clear aims and research questions will only result in wasted time from researching articles that are not useful to the review. Setting out clear research question(s) means that you are much more focussed on your purpose, which will ultimately save you time in the completion of the review.

Literature search strategy

A literature search strategy needs to be very thorough to ensure that you gain a detailed perspective of the current literature. There are a number of different ways that you can search for papers. One of the main ways is to use electronic databases such as PsycINFO or those available through your library. However, searching using these databases should also be supplemented with 'hand searching' of the literature (e.g., examining the references in papers that are relevant to your research question). This process of searching the literature will be explained in much more depth later on in this chapter. The purpose of this section in the research protocol is to outline how you are going to search the literature. This means that this section should be used to detail what databases you are going

20   Designing and planning

to use and any other methods that you will use to search the literature, as well as to highlight the search terms that you are going to use during the searching.

Search terms are of key importance in enabling you to examine the literature successfully. As you may imagine, there is a significant amount of psychological literature that is available from electronic databases, so having specific search terms will enable you to find the relevant literature to your research questions, whilst hopefully excluding much of the material that is not relevant to you. Therefore, it is important that you are explicit about what search terms you are going to use. As you initially write out the research protocol, you may outline search terms that have to be changed as you go through the research process (e.g., if you have not been specific enough). However, you should continue to document the decision-making process that you go through in adapting your search terms. This will enable you to be able to report your search process thoroughly in any resulting manuscript.

Inclusion/exclusion criteria

Inclusion and exclusion criteria refer to the limits of the research that you are going to include and exclude in the review. Very simply, this is where you identify the articles you will include in the review and those that you will not. Note that the inclusion/exclusion criteria should be justifiable for reasons that relate to your research questions/review purpose, and you should be consistent in applying these criteria to the papers you obtain and read (e.g., it is not appropriate to exclude papers from a review because you find them difficult to understand or because you are not familiar with the method of analyses used). It is appropriate to only include empirical studies in a review, since including review papers is likely to mean that many studies are discussed more than once and this might influence the conclusions drawn about them.

Justifiable criteria may relate to the time span of the articles; for example, if you only want a current view of an area, you may wish to limit the articles from those published in 1990 or even 2000 onwards. It is better, however, to have a specific reason for your choice of cut-off date; for example, choose a date that coincides with the introduction of a new policy/practice approach, or one following a published review on that topic (i.e., so your review adds to, rather than overlaps, the original review). If you are unable to read articles in languages other than English, you may want to set English-only articles as an inclusion criterion. You may want to be very specific about the type of articles that you are searching for; for example, if you are looking to learn about quantitative research designs in a topic area, you would want to exclude all articles that solely adopted a qualitative approach, though you may decide to include articles that use a mixed methods approach (i.e., both qualitative and quantitative methods). If you are interested in treatment methods for a specific type of offender, you would want to exclude articles that include other types of offenders. You may find that some articles contain a combination of different types of offenders, so you will need to decide whether you want to include or exclude these articles.

If you do not have a good knowledge of the area already, it is likely that you will update this section as you search the literature and make decisions about whether to include or exclude certain types of articles. When searching the literature, you may discover issues that you were not previously aware of and therefore have to make amendments to the exclusion/inclusion criteria. This does not matter and does not reflect on the quality of your initial decision making. However, it is important that you document all of these processes. If your ultimate aim is to write a literature review, these inclusion/exclusion criteria should be very clearly specified within the writing of the review to establish that the methods that you adopt in searching the literature are rigorous. Finally, when writing/updating these criteria, make sure that you refer back to the aims and research question(s) of the review. This is a quick check to ensure that you are not moving away from the original purpose of the review.

Data to be extracted from the studies

This section should outline what data is going to be extracted from each article that you are including in the review. Again, this depends upon the information that you want to include within the review. Some common examples of data that you may want to extract from the articles are: the number and type of participants, the methodology (including any measures that are used in the study), the findings reported in the study (these should include both significant and nonsignificant results), and any methodological limitations. A later section in this chapter outlines the process of data extraction in more detail.

Searching the literature

Searching the literature thoroughly has become much easier with the use of large electronic databases that categorise journal articles. It is very likely that you will have heard of many of the large databases, with PsycINFO being one of the most commonly used databases within the area of psychology. Having written your research protocol, you should have a good idea of what databases you are going to use to search the literature. However, these databases should not be considered infallible in finding your literature, as the size of the database can make it challenging to find the exact literature that you need. Electronic searching may not collect all of the possibly relevant articles available in databases or websites. No electronic search process is perfect in managing to select all appropriate articles, so it is important to also use other processes to search the literature. This can involve directly searching through relevant journals (i.e., hand searching) to seek out all potential articles. You should also add to the findings from the electronic searches by using a snowballing process. When you read each of the articles, you may find that there is an article cited that is relevant to your literature review question, but that has not been picked up by the electronic searches. Therefore, searching the reference section of relevant articles can help add additional relevant papers to your search. You can also search for prominent researchers within a particular area; many researchers have lists of their current and previous publications on their websites. This offers another opportunity to find articles that larger electronic databases may sometimes not identify. By using any or all of these additional processes, you are ensuring that you are not just relying on the electronic search process to find every relevant article, thus guaranteeing that your searching is as thorough as it can be.

In searching the literature, Torgerson (2003) suggested that there is balance needed between sensitivity and specificity. *Sensitivity* refers to the need to examine all of the articles that are held within a database to establish whether they are relevant to your literature review. *Specificity* refers to the need for only the most relevant articles to be examined. Once you begin to use search terms, you are immediately reducing sensitivity and increasing specificity in that you will only be examining certain articles (that are returned as search results), not the entire databases. However, the use of search terms is essential to the completion of any literature review. Given the significant body of published psychological articles that is available, it is simply not possible to search through every single article to check whether it is relevant to your literature review. To emphasise earlier points, this means that you need to carefully consider the appropriateness of your search terms and any inclusion/exclusion criteria before deciding to start searching the literature.

Search terms

It is very likely that you will have some idea of the keywords that should be used in a search engine. If you are struggling to identify keywords to use, look at articles that you have identified as relevant to your review and note the keywords listed (they are usually listed after the abstract). Rather confusingly, 'keywords' are not necessarily single words; 'keyphrases' would be a more accurate description. Keywords such as "sex offender treatment" and "cognitive behavioural" would be appropriate to use to search for papers relating to cognitive behavioural sex offender treatment programmes.

When you have identified some keywords, you can start to use these within the database/search engine that you have chosen, to understand whether these keywords will return the literature for which you are searching. You should use two additional processes to ensure that the searching is thorough. The first is the use of a wildcard symbol, which is an asterisk (*). This enables you to include a root word with the asterisk at the end to ensure that all variations of that word are found. For example, if you are searching for literature relating to female offenders, you may wish to use the keywords "female offend*". This will enable the search engine to search for any articles that include variations that may come from the root word *offend* (e.g., offender, offenders, offending).

Using a wildcard will make your search much more efficient, eliminating the need for you to run the search several times for each of these possible variations. Using a wildcard can also account for the differences in US and UK spelling; for example, you will get a different set of results if you search for "behaviour" compared to "behavior", so a search for "behav*" is much more efficient and effective.

You should also use Boolean logic operators in your search. If you are familiar with PsycINFO, you will already have seen these within the search blocks to one side of the search term boxes. The three operators are AND, OR and NOT. The use of these enables you to search the literature more efficiently. You can find out more detail about how to use these search terms in the accompanying box. You can also use these operators in combination with each other to further increase the specificity of your results. For example, if you are searching for treatment programmes for violent and sexual offending but are not interested in child abuse offenders, you can use the following search terms, along with the wildcard asterisk: "treatment program* AND violen* OR sexual NOT child abuse". It is very likely that you will need to adjust your search terms throughout this process with the use of a wildcard and the logic operators. Remember to keep a record of all of the adjustments that you make in your research protocol. This will enable you to keep accurate records of how you have completed your electronic searches. Note that although the principles of searching are similar, each library and database resource has a different look, manner of entering the required information, and so forth. Some databases may, for example, allow you to restrict based on paper type (e.g., only empirical papers), publication year, and so on. Using the full range of options available in the databases is an important skill to develop and will save you time in the long run; it is therefore an extremely good idea to attend classes and advice/drop-in sessions or to follow information links on library/database pages to develop your skills in this area.

When to use AND, OR, NOT

AND

You should use AND when you have two or more keywords that are relevant to your search (e.g., "sex offender AND treatment programme"). The use of AND will enable you to search the literature to find all the articles that contain *both* sets of keywords. For example, "sex offend* AND treatment program*" should reveal articles about sex offender treatment programmes but not articles about sex offenders that have no reference to treatment programmes and vice versa. (Note the use of the wildcard to account for offender, offenders, etc., and for UK and US spellings of programme/program.)

OR

This is used when you want to identify papers with *any* of the terms you include; that is, it will return articles that have only one of your keywords. You can use OR when there may be several different terms that relate to the same thing. For example, if you were searching the literature for articles on police officers, you can use the search "police officers OR law enforcement officers". This means that the search strategy will pick out all articles with *either* the first keyword or the second keyword within it.

NOT

You should use NOT if you want to exclude certain keywords. The use of this operator will therefore narrow down your search strategy. For example, if you wanted to search for treatment programmes for offenders but you did not want to examine programmes for violent offenders, you could use the search "treatment program* NOT violen*".

Bear in mind that people are fallible, and it is people who enter information into computers, write papers, and so on, so papers where the keywords have been misspelled (either in the original paper or in the database entry), for example, will not be identified by a search for the correctly spelt keywords. You might want to search for a common misspelling to take account of this. This relates to the issue mentioned previously in relation to the differences in spellings, so having a good idea of the differences in spelling used in various English-speaking countries will aid your searching. In addition, it is important to note that completely different words/phrases might be used to describe the same/similar things in different countries, cultures, and ethnicities, and you might need to think about this in your searching. For instance, when searching the literature about prisons, you will need to use OR to reflect the different terms that describe prison environments, e.g., "prison OR jail OR gaol OR penal OR detention centre". This is why the hand and snowball searching strategies previously described will also be important aspects of any good literature search.

A final point about the search process is that it would be very unusual for a search process to only select the articles that are relevant to you. It is very likely that you will have search results that returns hundreds and maybe thousands of potential articles. If your search terms are returning thousands of articles, this suggests that your search terms are not specific enough. You may wish to revisit your search strategy to ensure that it is as efficient as it can be. However, it is very likely that you will need to examine a number of articles that may or may not be relevant to your literature review question. You then need to work out how you are going to assess whether an article is relevant to your research question. One of the quickest ways to do this is to first examine the title of the paper. This will normally establish whether the article is relevant to your literature review article. If it is still not clear, then read through the abstract to see if that establishes whether it is relevant for your review article. This is usually sufficient for you to decide whether an article is relevant. However, you may have to read further into the article if it is still not clear.

The culmination of this process is that, via the use of electronic searching and the other methods of searching previously discussed, you should have a number of articles that are relevant to your literature review and that help address your specific research questions. As you might have gathered by now, this takes time. In addition, you might need to wait for some papers to arrive (e.g., papers that you have had to request via your library's document supply/ interlibrary loan facilities). Therefore, it is important that you allow ample time for conducting literature reviews when planning your review/research activities.

Extracting data

Once you have all of the papers/articles/reports identified from your search, you can then start processing the articles via reading, data extraction, and note-taking. It is important to remember that one of the main aims of a literature is to read the literature *critically* (Ridley, 2012). This means that you need to evaluate the paper as you read through it. For example, you could consider the following questions:

1   What is/are the theoretical underpinning(s) of the argument?
2   Is the argument being made within the paper well supported by the current evidence?
3   Are there any methodological limitations?
4   Do the findings conclusively support the argument(s) within the paper?
5   What contribution to theory has been made? Do the findings support current theory?

You must remember to take this approach with each of the papers that you read. This should become easier as you progress through the papers, as you will become more used to adopting a critical approach. Note that the authors of the papers can assist in the process; for example, authors will critique studies in the introductions of empirical papers to make a case for their research, and there should be an analysis of the limitations of the study in the discussion sections of papers. Note, however, that you do not need to rely on others to critique the papers; your own assessments of the methodology, sample size/make up, and so forth are just as worthy and useful as those that are published. There is an element of confidence involved in developing this thinking, but it is a crucial

26   Designing and planning

step in being able to develop interesting/original research projects. If you are initially unsure of your critique of a paper, discuss your ideas with others.

> ## Common confusion: Does critical mean negative?
>
> A critique does not have to be negative; for example, a film critic will outline what he or she thought was good about a film, as well as the areas of weakness or elements that he or she liked less. Think about a film or TV programme that you have seen recently and critique it by identifying the things about it that you thought were good and the things that the less good. A critique such as this, in which you can outline the strengths of a study, the methodological approach used, sample employed, etc., as well as the areas of weakness, and in which you can identify the weaknesses that can be overcome or more effectively taken into account and those that are more difficult to deal with, is a good approach to adopt in reading all research papers, reports, and articles.

Having thought about how to adopt a critical stance to your reading, you should now consider what information you want to extract from the articles. There are several approaches that you can take to achieve this, from taking general notes as you read through each of the articles to using a standardised data extraction form. It is suggested that using a data extraction form is the best approach to take because this generally means that you will gather the same data from each article as you read it. This should save you time in the rereading and rereviewing of articles. A data extraction form usually includes standard bibliographic information about the article as well as information that relates to your research question. Following is an example of a data extraction form.

Author	Country of research	Design	Methodology	Details of participants	Key findings	Methodological limitations

The data extraction form should be adapted according to the purpose of your literature review. For example, if you are reviewing the literature to understand how this issue has been studied before and the methodologies that have been used, you may wish to adapt the form so that it focuses more on the methods used within the studies.

In addition to using the data extraction form, you should also be thinking about the connections within the articles that you are reviewing. An example of these connections would be grouping together papers that use similar methodologies. You should question the findings as you read through each paper. Do all the studies find the same effect? Are there different patterns of significant and nonsignificant findings? Does this reflect differences in participants, settings, locations and design of studies? This will contribute towards your critical reading of the texts and also will assist you in writing up the review. You will begin to see patterns in the findings that you should address when reviewing the papers.

Writing up a literature review, either in full form or as an introduction, will be covered later in the book. In the next chapter, we will consider what you have learnt about the literature review process and how this can inform your thinking about the design that you will use for your own programme of research.

Summary and checklist

In this chapter, we have examined the process of a carrying out a literature review. Hopefully this has highlighted for you the approach that you should take when completing your own literature review(s). Use the following checklist to help you when you complete your own literature reviews:

1 Plan and account for the time involved in conducting a literature review. As you can see from this chapter, there are several stages involved in conducting a good review and all of these take time. This is not something you can do in an afternoon/day, so you need to allow sufficient time for this at the start of a project. Break the review into a series of steps. Take into account that you might need to allow time for some papers/articles to be ordered and arrive, or that you might want to spend a few days doing nothing but reading articles. Plan your schedule accordingly.
2 Write a research protocol so that your review is focussed and well thought out. Remember to record the steps that you have taken, and be sure that you have the information you need for the written report/article.
3 Note and keep all reference information about each article/report. You will need this should you need to find the article again, and you will also need to report this in the reference section. Developing a filing system for your articles is an extremely good idea, and you might wish to investigate resources (such as RefWorks) that can aid in this.
4 Obtain as many of the articles/reports that are identified in the searches as possible. You might need to investigate your university/organisation's resources and support in relation to obtaining articles/reports that are not available within the library resources (e.g., in many universities, students are

able to order articles for a reduced costs, or there may be a free allowance for a specified number of papers). It is not a good idea to rely on others' summaries of a research study. If you do so, you should (a) indicate that you have obtained the information from a secondary source rather than the primary source (note referencing guidelines for secondary sources of information), and (b) do so sparingly – only when it is extremely difficult to obtain the original.

5   Read each article carefully and document details about each study (according to your research protocol) as you read each document. Do not just read the article. Be careful with directly copying and pasting information from papers into your documents: if you do this, consistently indicate the difference between your words/ideas and those from the original paper. Your reports/articles should be written in your words, so being clear in all your note-taking and writing should help you avoid plagiarism in your work.

6   Remember to critically evaluate the literature. There are likely to be contrary or alternative findings that need to be reported and considered.

Literature review examples

Narrative review

Clements, H., Dawson, D.L., & das Nair, R. (2014). Female-perpetrated sexual abuse: A review of victim and professional perspectives. *Journal of Sexual Aggression, 20*, 197–215. doi:10.1080/13552600.2013.798690

Navathe, S., Ward, T., & Gannon, T.A. (2008). Cognitive distortions in child sex offenders: An overview of theory, research & practice. *Journal of Forensic Nursing, 4*, 111–122. doi:10.1111/j.1939-3938.2008.00019.x

O'Brien, K., Daffern, M., Chu, C.M., & Thomas, S.D.M. (2013). Youth gang affiliation, violence, and criminal activities: A review of motivational, risk, and protective factors. *Aggression and Violent Behavior, 18*, 417–425. doi:10.1016/j.avb.2013.05.001

Sandhu, D.K., & Rose, J. (2012). How do therapists contribute to therapeutic change in sex offender treatment: An integration of the literature. *Journal of Sexual Aggression, 18*, 269–283. doi:10.1080/13552600.2011.566633

Shingler, J. (2009). Managing intrusive risky thoughts: What works? *Journal of Sexual Aggression, 15*, 39–53. doi:10.1080/13552600802542011

Systematic review

Tully, R.J., Chou, S., & Browne, K.D. (2013). A systematic review on the effectiveness of sex offender risk assessment tools in predicting sexual recidivism of adult male sex offenders. *Clinical Psychology Review, 33*, 287–316. doi:10.1016/j.cpr.2012.12.002

Meta-analyses

Nunes, K.L., McPhail, I.V., & Babchishin, K.M. (2012). Social anxiety and sexual offending against children: A cumulative meta-analysis. *Journal of Sexual Aggression, 18*, 284–293. doi: 10.1080/13552600.2010.549243

Singh, J.P., & Fazel, S. (2010). Forensic risk assessment: A meta-review. *Criminal Justice and Behavior, 37*, 965–988. doi:10.1177/0093854810374274

Snook, B., Eastwood, J., Gendreau, P., Goggin, C., & Cullen, R.M. (2007). Taking stock of criminal profiling: A narrative review and meta-analysis. *Criminal Justice and Behavior, 34*, 437–453. doi:10.1177/0093854806296925

Meta-synthesis

Walji, I., Simpson, J., & Weatherhead, S. (2014). Experiences of engaging in psychotherapeutic interventions for sexual offending behaviours: A meta-synthesis. *Journal of Sexual Aggression, 20*, 310–332. doi:10.1080/13552600.2013.818723

Further reading

Borenstein, M., Hedges, L.V., Higgins, J.P.T., & Rothstein, H.R. (2009). *Introduction to meta-analysis*. Chichester, England: John Wiley and Sons.

Cochrane Library web site, http://www.thecochranelibrary.com

Lipsey, M.W., & Wilson, D.B. (2001). *Practical meta-analysis*. London, England: Sage.

Paterson, B., Dubouloz, C., Chevrier, J., Ashe, B., King, J., & Moldoveanu, M. (2009). Conducting qualitative metasynthesis research: Insights from a metasynthesis project. *International Journal of Qualitative Methods, 8*. Retrieved from http://ejournals.library.ualberta.ca/index.php/IJQM/article/view/5100/5587

Torgerson, C. (2003). *Systematic reviews*. London, England: Continuum.

References

Borenstein, M., Hedges, L. V., Higgins, J.P.T., & Rothstein, H. R. (2009). *Introduction to meta-analysis*. Chichester, England: John Wiley and Sons.

Centre for Reviews and Dissemination. (2009). Systematic reviews: CRD's guidance for undertaking systematic reviews in health care. Retrieved from http://www.york.ac.uk/inst/crd/pdf/Systematic_Reviews.pdf

Kebbell, M.R., Wagstaff, G.F., & Covey, J.A. (1996). The influence of item difficulty on the relationship between eyewitness confidence and accuracy. *British Journal of Psychology, 87*, 653–662. doi:10.1111/j.2044-8295.1996.tb02614.x

Navathe, S., Ward, T., & Gannon, T.A. (2008). Cognitive distortions in child sex offenders: An overview of theory, research & practice. *Journal of Forensic Nursing, 4*, 111–122. doi:10.1111/j.1939-3938.2008.00019.x

Notar, C.E., & Cole, V. (2010). Literature review organizer. *International Journal of Education, 2*, 1–17. doi:10.5296/ije.v2i2.319

Ridley, A. (2012). *The literature review: A step-by-step guide for students*. London, England: Sage.

Sandhu, D.K., & Rose, J. (2012). How do therapists contribute to therapeutic change in sex offender treatment: An integration of the literature. *Journal of Sexual Aggression, 18*, 269–283. doi:10.1080/13552600.2011.566633

Shingler, J. (2009). Managing intrusive risky thoughts: What works? *Journal of Sexual Aggression, 15*, 39–53. doi:10.1080/13552600802542011

Singh, J.P., & Fazel, S. (2010). Forensic risk assessment: A meta-review. *Criminal Justice and Behavior, 37*, 965–988. doi:10.1177/0093854810374274

Snook, B., Eastwood, J., Gendreau, P., Goggin, C., & Cullen, R.M. (2007). Taking stock of criminal profiling: A narrative review and meta-analysis. *Criminal Justice and Behavior, 34*, 437–453. doi:10.1177/0093854806296925

Torgerson, C. (2003). *Systematic reviews*. London, England: Continuum.

Tully, R.J., Chou, S., & Browne, K.D. (2013). A systematic review on the effectiveness of sex offender risk assessment tools in predicting sexual recidivism of adult male sex offenders. *Clinical Psychology Review, 33*, 287–316. doi:10.1016/j.cpr.2012.12.002

Walji, I., Simpson, J., & Weatherhead, S. (2014). Experiences of engaging in psychotherapeutic interventions for sexual offending behaviours: A meta-synthesis. *Journal of Sexual Aggression, 20*, 310–332. doi:10.1080/13552600.2013.818723

Chapter 3

Methods

In this chapter, we will outline the different methodological approaches that can be used in research studies, including quantitative and qualitative approaches and evaluation techniques. We will highlight the important differences between these approaches, along with the strengths and weaknesses of each, so that you are able to consider carefully which approach is the best fit for your research question. The purpose of this chapter is to build on the knowledge that you have from Chapter 2 regarding the methodologies that have been used in the area in which you wish to research. It is important to remember that there is overlap between the sections in this chapter (e.g., evaluation and qualitative methods), so you should not read any section in isolation. Once you have read this chapter, you should be able to:

- describe the range of methodological approaches that can be used;
- identify the differences between these approaches;
- understand when it is appropriate to use each methodological approach; and
- assess the strengths and weaknesses of each of these methodologies.

Experimental methods

Experimental methods allow you to manipulate chosen variables to understand the effects that they may have upon other variables. In essence, if designed well, they allow you to draw conclusions about cause and effect. This means that you can identify the impact variable A (the independent variable [IV]) has on variables B and C (the dependent variables [DVs]). This is a particular strength of this type of design; however, it can be difficult to conduct experimental studies in applied settings because it is not always possible to isolate and manipulate variables required for a controlled, experimental approach.

If a study is not appropriately designed, one or more variables may also vary, along with the IVs (Hole, 2012). Thus, the level of control (or lack of control) used within these types of studies leads to a frequent criticism; for example, variables that have not been monitored or controlled for could be argued to have had an influence on the DVs in addition to the IVs, thus limiting the validity of the findings. These 'additional' variables are known as *confounding variables*, and you need to try to avoid them having an impact on your study or identify and measure them in your study so that you can include them in your analyses. Thus, in order to be able to make clear conclusions about the impact of your IVs on your DVs, the differences in the IVs should be the only differences between the experimental conditions. For example, if you are asking people to read texts that have been manipulated in line with your IV, you would need to make sure that reading ability was not operating as a confounding variable (i.e., reading ability should be equivalent across your groups and not influencing the DV), perhaps by only including participants with particular reading abilities/levels, or by measuring reading ability and using this as a variable in your analysis. It is not easy to identify all possible confounding variables, but careful thought should be put into the design of your study so that confounds are avoided or controlled for where possible.

In order to maximise control over variables, strict experimental conditions can be applied to data, perhaps by producing mock data or by truncating/simplifying real data. However, whilst this approach might mean that your study has experimental validity, it might be criticised because it lacks ecological validity. This means that the control and conditions implemented within the study are unlikely to reflect real life.

Common confusion

You are probably very familiar with the term *ecological validity* from your undergraduate studies; however, be aware that it is a term that is often overused. Lab-based experimental studies are often criticised for lacking ecological validity, but this might not always be the case. If, for example, we are investigating whether written information (e.g., instructions given to potential jurors about the rules and requirements of jury service) is easily understood by a range of people and/or whether it can be made more understandable, this can be done in an experimental/lab setting. In this instance, conducting the study in a lab setting does not limit the ecological validity of the study (provided it is based on actual information that is given to jurors) because the location of reading the material (e.g., at home, in a lab or elsewhere) should not have an impact on its actual understandability. On the other hand, many juror decision-making studies, in which very short and simple mock case materials are used, lack ecological validity because the mock cases do not very well replicate complex real cases.

If you are going to use an experimental method, one of the first decisions to make concerns whether to use a between-groups or within-groups design, or a combination of the two in a mixed design. A between–groups design means that different groups of participants will complete different experimental conditions within the study. An example of this would be: if you were examining the effectiveness of a treatment, one group would receive the treatment, whereas the other group would not. This design may seem easy to implement by simply dividing your participants into two groups and giving one group the treatment and the other no treatment; however, caution should be taken to consider any possible differences between your two groups that may reflect confounding variables. This issue will be examined in more depth later, when we discuss randomised controlled trials. The within–groups design means that all participants take part in all experimental conditions, for example, asking a group of participants to read two or more different versions of juror information (with the information varied only in line with your IVs) to rate comprehension and the ease of understanding. In a mixed design, you would have two or more different groups of people (e.g., one group reading the information online and another group reading the same information in paper format), with each group reading two or more versions of the information.

The benefits of the within–groups design are that: (a) each participant acts as his or her own control, reducing the likelihood of confounding factors due to differences between the groups (Hole, 2012) and (b) a smaller sample size is required compared to a between–groups design. This may make you think that this approach is easier to implement; however, confounding factors may still arise from issues such as order effects. Order effects result when performance on the previous part of the experiment improves performance on the second or later part of the experiment. In the previous example about understanding information provided to jurors, it may be easier to understand the information presented in the second/third versions of the instructions because much of the information has been read previously. Therefore, you might want to counterbalance the order in which participants are asked to read each set of information. In a design in which there are two tasks, this would mean that half of the sample would complete one task first, with the other half of the sample completing the second task first. This will balance out any order effects within the design. The impact of having done the task once (e.g., reading one version of the information), however, might be so great that you need to use a between–groups design (in which each participant only reads one version of the information).

There are many other issues to consider about the strengths and weaknesses of the between- and within–groups designs that you would have considered in your undergraduate studies. The key point to emphasise is that careful thought always needs to be put into constructing the experimental design so that you can be confident that you will be able to draw conclusions about the impact of your IVs on your DVs.

Common confusion

Different terms are applied to aspects of experimental designs that effectively refer to the same things. For example, a *between-groups design* and *unrelated design* are the same. Likewise, a *within-groups design* and *related design* are the same; another term for this is a *repeated measures design*. It is important, therefore, to understand the underlying principles of these designs so that you can identify the most appropriate for your study and can interpret the design used by others no matter which terminology is being used.

In order to be sure that it was the IVs that had an impact on your DVs, you need to know if the participants noted the key aspects of the IVs that you manipulated in your study; for example, if you ask someone to look at a picture (that has been manipulated in some way in line with your IVs) before reading some information, it is important to check that participants actually looked at the picture. This is known as *manipulation checking* and should probably be used more extensively in experimental forensic studies than it currently is. For example, it has become more common to see manipulation checks in juror decision-making studies (e.g., where questions are asked about the case information to check whether participants read/noted information in the materials that were varied according to the IVs), and eye-tracking is being used more frequently (though it is still rare to find it in published journal articles) to assess how much participants looked at key research materials. This type of checking might not be appropriate in all designs, and it can be done in many ways, but you should consider whether some form of monitoring/checking is appropriate for your study so that you can be more confident in the validity of your findings.

Common difficulties

As you can see from the discussions in this chapter, there are many factors to take into account when designing your study. Some of these factors work in opposition; for example, between-groups designs limit order and fatigue effects but might introduce confounding variables because it is difficult to ensure your groups are experimentally equal, whereas within-groups designs avoid issues of group differences but suffer from order and fatigue effects. Therefore, you will need to decide the approach that is best for your research question. Remember, as discussed in Chapter 2, you should use the previous literature to guide you: it might be that you want to use an approach that is different from the one taken by previous researchers (e.g., if you think the design has led to findings that might not be valid or replicable if a different design was used), or you could use the same type of approach that has become common/standard in a particular area, perhaps because the most appropriate methodology has been established by previous researchers over time with different approaches having been tried. It is important to remember that no research study is perfect; that is, each design that is used has some associated limitations. You need to be aware of these and use the design that you think is most appropriate for your research question, taking account of as many potential difficulties as possible but bearing the limitations of the design in mind when you draw conclusions about your findings. This is why there is usually a discussion of the limitations of the study in reports/journal articles about empirical studies.

Activity

Find four empirical journal articles of experimental studies. (Many jury decision-making, eye-witness testimony, suspect line-up and identification studies use this type of design.) Read the introduction and methods sections of the papers to identify why an experimental approach was used and consider the following questions for each study:

- What type of design (i.e., between-groups, within-groups or mixed) was used?
- What were the IVs and how were these manipulated in the study?
- Were any manipulation checks conducted? If so, do you think these were appropriate? If not, do you think these should have been done?
- What were the DVs in the study?
- Were any potential confound variables taken into account/controlled for in the design?
- Do you think there are potential confound variables that have not been taken into account that potentially limit the findings of the study?

There are many ways to use experimental designs in forensic psychology (see Karlén, Roos af Hjelmsäter, Fahlke, Granhag, & Söderpalm Gordh [2014] and Righarts, Jack, Zajac, & Hayne [2014] in the 'Methods examples' section). One

36 Designing and planning

of the most frequently used approaches – vignette-based studies – is discussed in the next section, whilst the use of randomised controlled trials (RCT) is discussed later in this chapter in relation to conducting evaluation studies. Please note that these are not the only types of experimental studies that you can use.

Vignette-based studies

Vignette based studies involve the use of a short description or scenario (vignette), usually of an event or mock case, after which participants are asked to respond to some questions regarding the content of the scenario/case. The vignettes are manipulated in line with the experimental IVs (e.g., the gender and race of the person included in the scenario/case), and the questions asked about the scenario/case are the DVs. The use of vignettes within forensic psychology research enables you to present participants with a scenario with which they may not have had personal experience and, as such, they can provide judgements regarding that scenario/case. Vignettes are also used because it is very easy to manipulate the material in line with the IVs whilst keeping all the other information the same between experimental conditions (reducing potential confounding variables). This is a common methodology that has been employed for a considerable amount of time (see Alexander & Becker, 1978). It is frequently used within certain areas of forensic psychology research, such as jury decision making, in which the lack of access to real jury members means that researchers need to recreate the environment in which a court case takes place in order to mimic the jury decision-making processes (see for example, the Connolly & Gordon [2013] paper listed in the 'Methods examples' section).

As you can see, this can be a very valuable method to employ because the flexibility of the approach enables researchers to examine a wide variety of topics. For example, Louden and Skeem (2013) used this approach to investigate risk assessments conducted by probation officers and Storey, Gibas, Reeves, and Hart (2011) to evaluate risk assessment training (both publications are listed in the 'Methods examples' section at the end of the chapter). Note too, that vignettes can be used in other types of designs; for example, Edens, Epstein, Stiles, and Poythress (2011) (see 'Methods examples') used them in a quasi-experimental design to investigate voluntary consent in correctional settings. However, some caution needs to be adopted when constructing vignettes for use within research projects. Barter and Reynold (1999) suggested some fairly obvious issues to consider, such as ensuring that vignettes are realistic and easy for participants to understand, as well as presented in an appropriate format. A written format is usually adopted, but other formats have been used such as video or pictures. There has been some discussion regarding the appropriate length of vignettes, with some researchers cautioning against long vignettes (Anderson & Lyons, 2005). Barter and Reynold (1999) also suggested some guidelines about the production of vignettes for participants: vignettes need to have sufficient context but also must be vague enough for respondents to use attributional processes in drawing conclusions about the vignette; it is preferable to include a 'control' vignette to ensure that the differences demonstrated are a reflection of the content of the vignette; and the vignette should not contain overly complex material.

As with all designs, there are some potential limitations to consider. First, as previously noted, in many instances vignettes can lack ecological validity. This is a point that can often be levelled in jury decision-making research, as any presentation of evidence via a vignette is unlikely to mimic entirely the process of sitting in a courtroom listening to a court trial. However, Bornstein (1999), following a review of jury simulation techniques, concluded that there was little evidence to suggest that the findings from mock juror studies would not be generalisable to the behaviour of real jurors.

Second, because vignette studies are relatively simple to use, they can be used with little thought put into them and into the purpose of the study. For example, there are many studies in which vignettes have been used to examine factors that influence the level of blame attributed to rape victims. Perceptions of victims in rape and sexual assault cases have important consequences, and so this is an important focus of research; however, it is common for students to suggest studies that do not build on the understanding that has already been developed in this area and/or do not develop our understanding further. Manipulation checks are also not common in these studies. As was stressed in the previous chapter, it is important when you consider this type of study that you carefully review the literature so that you select variables that will add to the development of the knowledge base.

Common confusion

Should you include a pilot study? The answer to this question will depend on the materials that you intend to use in your study. If you are using materials that have been used previously (e.g., a vignette or psychometric tests with established reliability and validity), then a pilot study might not be necessary. However, if you are developing new materials, or revising materials used in previous studies, then you should conduct a pilot study. Pilot studies are conducted to make sure that your materials are appropriate – for example, that the participants can understand what they are being asked to do and can complete the study as you intended and remain engaged; that the DVs can be measured as you expected; and that there are no floor or ceiling effects in your DVs that might influence your findings (e.g., if all participants rate an offender as extremely culpable in all your experimental conditions, then you might have a ceiling effect).

You must be prepared to make changes to your materials following your pilot study and you might need a series of pilot studies (i.e., if you make significant changes following the first pilot, you may need a second pilot on the revised materials). This stage is generally overlooked and/or poorly considered, but it should be included in the design of your study and in your timetable and planning. A study that includes new materials that have not been piloted is less likely to produce reliable and valid findings. If you find yourself saying in your discussion that a limitation of the study is that participants did not seem to understand the vignette, or got bored/fatigued completing the study, or did not understand what they were being asked to do, then that looks very poor because these are all issues that could have been revised following a good pilot study.

Quasi-experimental methods

Many of the questions that we wish to answer within forensic psychology do not always fit neatly within an experimental method. As such, we may wish to adopt a quasi-experimental approach. Essentially, this approach attempts to employ as much control as possible over the variables that are being used within the study, whilst also taking account of the fact that perfect experimental control can rarely be implemented within the real world and/or it may not be ethical to do so (e.g., it is clearly not ethical to randomly allocate people to two groups, submit one group to some sort of violence and the other to 'no violence', and then measure a range of variables in the two groups to determine the impact of the violence).

Common confusion

What is the difference between an experimental design and a quasi-experimental design? Quasi-experimental designs can look very similar to experimental designs and they can be used as between-, within-, or mixed-groups designs. The key aspect that distinguishes experimental designs is the level of control over the IVs and allocation to experimental conditions. In experimental designs, researchers should control the manipulation of the IVs and the allocation, preferably randomly, of the participants to conditions. It is not possible for a researcher to allocate a participant to being male or female, a particular race or sexuality etc., for example, so the inclusions of these types of variables as IVs mean the study will be quasi-experimental. This is because there could be something about the experiences of these different groups, the way they are treated etc., that has an impact on the DVs, rather than the IVs, and therefore potentially introduces some confound variables. So the quasi-experimental design is regarded as being less methodologically robust than the experimental design because of this. Other practical circumstances might mean that it is not possible to allocate participants to conditions; for example, in an evaluation of an intervention it might not be possible to select who receives the intervention. It is for these reasons that quasi-experimental designs are common in applied research studies. This does not mean, however, that you should worry less about your design if you employ a quasi-experimental approach; you should still aim to conduct the most methodologically robust study possible and reduce the potential confounds/limits to reliability and validity.

Larzelere, Kuhn, and Johnson (2004) stated that the regression discontinuity design is the most robust quasi-experimental design because it specifies the selection processes involved in identifying experimental conditions explicitly, though these are rarely applied in forensic psychology studies. The next most robust approach, according to Larzelere et al. (2004), is the interrupted time-series design. However, this is rarely employed in forensic psychology because given the common focus on long-term outcomes (e.g., reoffending and/or victimisation), this approach would not be appropriate for that type of DV because it is not possible to 'interrupt' these factors. Non-interrupted time-series designs are more common; this approach involves having only one sample (i.e., a within-groups design) but taking measurements of the DV(s) at certain time points (e.g., two or more points). An example of this would be examining the effectiveness of an intervention, taking measures of effectiveness at the beginning, middle, end, and at one or more postintervention time points. This would enable the researcher to establish effectiveness between and across these time points; however, unless a comparison group that does not receive the treatment/intervention is employed, it is difficult to establish if it was the treatment/intervention that led to the changes to the DV, or some other confound variable (this issue is taken into account in the interrupted design by monitoring changes when the intervention is provided, then removed, and then provided).

There are a number of ways of conducting interrupted time series designs, and you should read more about these if you wish to conduct this type of study. As with all designs, this approach also has some limitations, such as testing effects. It is understandable that if you are given the same test on a number of occasions that you naturally improve your performance due to familiarity and practice; hence, this might limit the validity of your findings. This might be reduced, however, if a comparison group is used (and you can test how much the treatment group improved its performance on the tests over the increased performance of the control group). Time-series studies that are conducted over long periods of time will also be subject to participant attrition (i.e., fewer participants take part in later stages of the project due to a variety of reasons), which may reduce the power of the analysis to detect changes in the group and reduce the validity of the findings (e.g., if those who drop out of the study perform differently than those who do not).

The comparison of nonequivalent control groups (NECG) is, according to Larzelere et al. (2004), the third most robust quasi-experimental design. This is a between-groups design that involves comparing two or more NECGs on one or more measures (see Freeman's [2012] study in the 'Methods examples' section). The challenge with using this approach is that variation between the groups can occur due to a range of effects, other than the impact of the study IV(s), such as maturation, selection bias, and history effects. Fife-Shaw (2012) highlighted that it is important to recognise that these effects can work to enhance and/or reduce group differences, so it is near impossible to predict the impact of these effects on the DVs.

There are methods that can be employed to make these designs more robust, for example, by measuring variables that might have an effect on your DVs and controlling for these statistically (an approach used by Palmer, Hatcher, McGuire, Bilby, Ayres, & Hollin [2011]; see the 'Methods examples' section), or by matching participants on important variables and then allocating one of each matched pair/group to the conditions of the study (prospective matching), or selecting matched pairs/groups to include in the analysis (retrospective matching). Exact matching on more than two variables can be difficult and often fails (Hanson & Nicholaichuk, 2000). Most studies use the less-effective method of matching variables retrospectively, which as Friendship, Beech, and Browne (2002) discussed, is poorer because it is often only possible to match participants on a small number of variables due to the lack of information from the comparison group(s) or a lack of similar pairs/groups. The difficulties in finding matches might mean that your sample size becomes small or you end up broadening the matching criteria, which makes the approach less rigorous. Prospective matching, Friendship, Beech, and Browne (2002) argued, is preferred because it attempts to control for extraneous variables in advance of the treatment/intervention, and there is more opportunity to select a range of variables that are likely to impact on the problematic behaviour and to collect relevant data from both the treatment/intervention group and the comparison group. See the study by Zhang, Roberts, and McCollister (2011) in the 'Methods examples' section for an example of a prospective matched quasi-experimental design.

The final type of quasi-experimental design is a combination of the previous two approaches where NECGs are used and testing is conducted over a number of time points (e.g., see the Zalmanowitz, Babins-Wagner, Rodger, Corbett, & Leschied [2013] study in the 'Methods examples' section). If you are using a simple time series approach (i.e., pre- and posttesting), using a comparison group that is tested at the same time points as the treatment group is more methodologically robust than only testing one group. However, some of the challenges previously identified remain, such as participant attrition. It can be particularly challenging, for example, to find appropriate comparison participants willing to be tested on more than one occasion when they are not receiving any form of intervention.

There is a great deal of debate in forensic psychology (and criminal justice more broadly) about the use of quasi-experimental designs and the value of the findings, due to concerns that studies lack methodological rigor. The extent to which groups could be considered comparable and the potential impact that differences in groups have on interpreting the findings are key areas of debate. When designing such studies, therefore, it is important that you think carefully about your design. Consider whether you can adopt the most robust types of design, select your NECGs carefully, and determine whether you can measure/control for potential confound variables and/or use a matched design.

Facet theory

Borg (2005) outlined facet theory as an approach that enables the linking of facets together to provide meaningful mapping of these objects of interest. Facet theory can be considered a very flexible methodology to use because the researcher can use it for either bottom-up hypothesis generation or more traditional top-down hypothesis testing (Brown, 2011). This approach can frequently be found in forensic psychology in studies that attempt to classify offending behaviour. One of the earliest studies in this area was conducted by Canter and Heritage (1990) and enabled the development of typologies of sexual offending. At this point, the term *facet* may seem quite obscure; however, a facet represents a component within the research and generally can be categorised into three different types. A *background facet* (as the name suggests) represents a background characteristic of an individual (e.g., age, ethnicity). A *domain facet* represents content of a particular aspect of the research (e.g., motivation to commit a crime) (Brown, 2011). Finally, a *range facet* relates to the potential responses given in answer to the domain facet (Brown & Barnett, 2000). Statistical methods enable the mapping of facets to demonstrate the closeness of the relationships between them. These techniques include: multidimensional scalogram analysis (MSA), partial order scalogram analysis (POSA), or smallest space analysis (SSA). To give you an example of what this may look like, in an SSA, a map is produced where the facets are represented as points on the map. Points that are closer together represent greater similarity between the facets, enabling the researcher to draw conclusions about the similarity of these facets (Guttman, 1968) and potentially construct categories within this mapping space. This partitioning of facets is one aspect that draws criticism within facet theory due to the flexibility that can be used in deciding where to partition, and questions arise regarding the subjectivity that this may introduce into experimental design (Brown, 2011). However, supporters of this approach have offered best practice in this area (e.g., Hammond & Brown, 2005).

Research that uses facet theory tends to be in the area of behavioural analysis of offenders, so examples of the research published using SSA, MSA, and POSA tend to include categorisations of behaviour (see Porter & Alison [2006] and Salfati & Bateman [2005] in the 'Methods examples' section). The benefits to using facet theory are numerous, in that it is a very flexible approach; as Brown

42   Designing and planning

(2011) highlighted, much of the data that is available to forensic psychology researchers can be messy and difficult to interpret. This is particularly true of data that are gathered within police forces, although this is a criticism that can also be levelled at other criminal justice organisations. However, there are disadvantages to this approach such as the criticisms about the partitioning of facets and the availability of more specialised analysis packages. Looking beyond these issues, facet theory should not be ignored because it can offer forensic psychology a different approach to more traditional methods of analysis and, as such, it is a useful addition to the range of available research methods.

Cross-sectional methods

Cross-sectional and longitudinal methods (see the next section for discussion of the latter) fall into the group of comparison methods within forensic psychology. The similarity between these methods lies in their aim to demonstrate change within a psychological variable or variables (Coolican, 2013). Cross-sectional designs involve collecting data from two or more different samples at one time point. This differs from longitudinal research as it reflects only one time point in participants' lives (in longitudinal research, data is collected at a number of different time points). Therefore, the aim of cross-sectional research is to examine the differences across groups in relation to the variable(s) being measured, which can be used in a variety of ways to ask many questions relevant to forensic psychology. For example, Langevin and Curnoe (2014) used this approach to examine the characteristics associated with weapon use in sex offenders; Lewis, Klettke, and Day (2014) used it to determine factors affecting judicial decision making in child sexual assault cases; and Rosenfeld, Rojek, and Decker (2012) used it to examine factors influencing police searches of motorists (all of these publications are listed in the 'Methods examples' section). The benefit of this approach in comparison to longitudinal studies is that it is more achievable for an individual researcher, particularly if time is limited, whereas longitudinal research requires considerable time and resources. Additional benefits are that because testing is only completed at one time point, you do not have to worry about practice effects that may occur within longitudinal studies or attrition of participants from the study.

The challenges to this approach are similar to those highlighted previously in relation to quasi-experimental designs. The differences identified between the groups may not actually be due to the variables that led you to select the groups. This may be a particular problem when drawing comparisons across different age groups, where differences in the groups may be due to age-related experiences rather than developmental differences (Coolican, 2013). A related issue with these designs is attributing the cause/reasons for the identified differences. Although you will identify your groups in line with your variable(s) of interest (e.g., ethnicity), any differences you identify across these groups are not necessarily because of the key variable. It might be that another, unmeasured variable is a more important factor in causing the identified differences (e.g., poverty, home location, levels of education). This means that you need to think carefully about the variables you include in the study and conduct a thorough search of the literature (see Chapter 2) to determine the variables that should be included. You might, for example, want to record or measure ethnicity, income, location and education, so you can account for all these variables in your analyses. This challenge is inherent within research designs that include group comparisons, so you must be careful in designing your study by building in as much control as possible. However, it is challenging (and nearly impossible) to remove all possible differences between groups, so these limitations must be recognised and taken into account when making conclusions about any significant differences found between your groups.

There are a number of ways in which cross-sectional studies can be conducted and there are many types of data that you can use (e.g., psychometric tests, demographic data, personality and behavioural variables, qualitative data). You may be able to take advantage of data that have already been collected, you may want or need to collect new data, or you might use a combined approach. When using preexisting data, it is important to have a good understanding of the data set, how the data were collected and on whom, how the variables were measured/recorded and so on. When collecting new data, depending on the number of groups that you wish to include in your study, you should bear in mind that you might need large samples for quantitative designs (see Chapter 6 for a more detailed discussion of sample sizes and statistical power). If using quantitative data, since this approach is likely to involve a number of variables and potentially a number of different types of data (see Chapter 4), you need to be confident in selecting appropriate types of analyses and using large quantitative data sets. Using qualitative data to draw comparisons between groups can be tricky, and you need to carefully think through which qualitative approach can be used to do this and which one is most appropriate for your study.

Longitudinal methods

A longitudinal approach is used when a researcher wants to collect responses from a group of participants over an extended period of time. The data that can be gathered can take a variety of formats (e.g., quantitative data from a wide range of variables, survey/questionnaire data, qualitative data). However, the majority of studies gather a range of quantitative data that can be compared across the time periods. As such, this method can be particularly useful when understanding age-related development. Within forensic psychology there are a number of well-known longitudinal studies that have provided very valuable insights into the developmental process in relation to delinquency. For example, in the early 1960s, 411 males were selected from six primary schools in the London area for the Cambridge Study of Delinquent Development. Various data from the original sample of boys, their parents and extended families, as well as the offspring of the original sample and beyond (Farrington, 2003) have been collected at a number of time points. Some longitudinal studies do not have specific forensic purposes but can still provide useful information on forensic-relevant topics; for example, Bowen et al. (2005) (see 'Methods examples section) examined the Avon Longitudinal Study of Parents and Children (ALSPAC) to examine the rates of domestic violence reported during and after pregnancy. For most researchers, longitudinal research is not a viable option given the vast amounts of time and financial and staff resources that are required to set up and continue to administrate these projects. These types of projects can generate huge data sets, and there may be opportunities to access these data sets that should not be ignored. In drawing conclusions from such analyses, you will need to be aware that issues such as attrition or practice effects can impact on the conclusions that can be drawn from these analyses. As noted in the previous section, in order to carry out this type of research, you will need to have a good understanding of the original study and the types of data collected and be proficient at using and analysing large data sets.

Data

It has become increasingly common for data collected for research studies (using a range of research deigns) to be made publically available, enabling others to conduct research using it. Some of these datasets are available via the web, while access to others (e.g., ALSPAC) requires an application/approval process. These datasets can provide opportunities to conduct research studies relevant to forensic psychology, particularly when there is limited time to conduct a large scale study (e.g., as is the case for dissertation projects). Do not assume that finding a dataset is all you need to do to design your study and that this type of study will not take much time; you will need to search around to find a dataset that has data relevant to your research aim/questions (you will have to do the same literature review around the topic area as outlined in the previous chapter), and you will have to investigate the dataset carefully and consider what data is available relevant to your research aim/questions, what type of data (see Chapter 4) are available, what analyses would be possible etc. (and can you do these analyses!), all of which might take a significant amount of time. There are a growing number of web resources that list datasets; a small selection of UK sites is listed below. There are many more, and there are datasets for other countries. You should find a range of datasets by searching the web and/or speaking to your supervisors/colleagues.

UK Government Data: http://data.gov.uk/data/search

Office for National Statistics: http://www.ons.gov.uk/ons/datasets-and-tables/index.html

UK Data Archive: http://www.data-archive.ac.uk/find

UK Data Service: http://discover.ukdataservice.ac.uk/

Economic and Social Data Service: http://www.esds.ac.uk/Introduction.asp

Survey/questionnaire methods

This approach is commonly used within forensic psychology and involves surveying participants for a range of purposes. The Crime Survey in England and Wales and other similar national surveys (e.g., the National Crime Victimisation Survey in the US) are perhaps the most well-known studies using this design, and they can be used in a variety of ways (e.g., to assess attitudes, perceptions and experiences of crime or related issues). See, for example, Barkworth and Murphy's (2014) study of police procedural justice encounters with the public; Melinder and Magnussen's (2014) survey of expert witnesses; and Szlachcic, Fox, Conway, Lord, and Christie's (2014) study of attitudes and cognitions in mentally disordered sex offenders (all of which are listed in the 'Methods examples' section). This approach can be used in the designs previously discussed; for example, you might compare attitudes cross-sectionally, or use a survey in a quasi-experimental design across different locations (e.g., in areas where a particular initiative has been introduced versus areas where the initiative has not been implemented). Surveys can be conducted in a number of ways; for example, participants can be asked to respond to questions read out by the researcher in a one-to-one format; they can similarly be asked questions via the telephone; it is possible to conduct surveys by text and other means via smart phones; or participants can be asked to complete questionnaires themselves via paper or online formats.

Online technologies have facilitated the ease of gathering questionnaire data, with a number of companies now offering services that assist in the construction of a questionnaire/survey. (Note there may be a cost involved in using these services, and you should be mindful of data protection issues.) Participants can submit their responses via an easily accessible URL. Online methods can be used to conduct other types of studies as well (e.g., all of the methods previously discussed could be conducted online with careful thought/consideration of your design). The ease of online and traditional approaches makes questionnaires/surveys an attractive option; however, you need to bear in mind that questionnaire data can be difficult to analyse (see Chapter 4), and you need to have a good reason for using this approach. It is not ethical to use this approach simply because this is an easy method to use! Your study should have a clear rationale/purpose, and it is important to justify why a survey/questionnaire is being used and how this relates to the research question.

Common difficulties

There are a number of terms that are often used interchangeably that can cause confusion. When you are conducting an experimental or quasi-experimental study, for example by asking participants to read some information and then asking them to respond to some questions about the information, these questions are the DVs of the study. Although you may present this information in a paper format, it might be confusing to refer to this as a *questionnaire*; a better term to use is *research materials*. You need to think carefully about how you will measure the responses to your questions (e.g., use the response to each question separately, or add up the responses to two or more questions) and what this means for the type of analyses that can be conducted.

Scales (e.g., attitudes scales) should be developed carefully. They are like psychometric tests in that they should be used to assess a particular construct/variable and should be reliable and valid. Scales normally have a series of questions that are 'scored', with the responses to a number of questions added up to form a subscale or overall scale score. If you have limited time to conduct your research and there are previously developed scales available that are suitable for your study, then it is advisable to use these. If you wish to develop a new scale, there are a number of steps/stages that you should follow to ensure that the scale you have developed is reliable and valid – developing a reliable and valid scale could be a research study in itself.

Questionnaires often have a range of questions that might elicit different types of data (see Chapter 4). You could include one or more scales in a larger questionnaire; however, questionnaires could also include a series of questions for which the responses are treated independently (i.e., scores are not produced or are not appropriate). Questionnaires can also include questions for which written responses are required. In designing questionnaires, you need to think very carefully about the types of data that will be produced and the analyses that can be used (see Chapter 4). There is a tendency to think that questionnaires are easy to design; however, great care is needed in writing questions that, for example, are not leading, biased, or double-barrelled. Questionnaires must be developed carefully and piloted thoroughly.

One of the most common pitfalls with this type of study is that people collect a large amount of data only to realise that they cannot analyse it as anticipated; therefore, you need to engage in careful thinking about your research design and the nature of the questions you will use. If you wish to use this type of design, you should read about survey methods and questionnaire design (see 'Further reading').

Qualitative methods

Qualitative methodology can offer you the opportunity to gather rich, in-depth data about a particular topic area and/or to gather data that are less influenced by prior assumptions/expectations. One of the main strengths of qualitative research is the inductive approach that drives many of the methodologies within this paradigm; one example is grounded theory, in which the process of analysis allows a researcher to generate a theory from the data that have been gathered (Bryant & Charmaz, 2007). Further strengths are centred on the type of data gathered: some researchers argue that qualitative data resembles more naturally occurring data through the use of methods such as interviews and focus groups (Silverman, 2000). Therefore, qualitative approaches may enable you to establish more meaning from your data because it is in context rather than in isolation. For example, as can be seen from the papers in the 'Methods examples' section, Guo (2012) examined female inmates' attributions of responsibility for their crimes; Bourke, Ward, and Rose (2012) developed a model of offence-specific decision making; and Cromby, Brown, Gross, Locke, and Patterson (2010) explored moral reasoning around crime and antisocial behaviour. A difficulty surrounds the issue, which is that many psychologists perceive qualitative methods to be unscientific. This is based upon the perceived lack of control that is so strongly emphasised within quantitative methodologies (Braun & Clarke, 2013). However, a well-thought-out and carefully analysed piece of qualitative research can be just as rigorous in the conclusions that are drawn as any quantitative study.

Braun and Clarke (2013) identified two broad categories into which qualitative research falls. The first is *experiential qualitative research*, which seeks to understand participants' perspectives, experiences, or views. As such, this approach centres on participants being the experts on a particular topic, with their interpretations being the focus of the study and accepted by the researcher. Researchers using the second approach, *critical qualitative research*, take a different standpoint whereby participants' experiences are actively questioned and examined for underlying meaning. Deciding which approach is most appropriate for your research will depend on which is most appropriate for your research questions/aims.

Completing a qualitative project also means that you should attempt to gain some understanding of the importance of ontology and epistemology within qualitative approaches. To summarise very briefly (see 'Further reading' for more information), Braun and Clarke (2013) defined ontology as "the relationship between the world and our human interpretations and practices" (p. 27). This relationship can range from relativism to realism. Along this continuum sits a critical realist approach, within which it is argued that we construct our own understanding of the world via the use of our own perspectives (Maxwell, 2012), and this underpins many qualitative approaches, such as thematic analysis and grounded theory. *Epistemology* refers to theory of knowledge and how and what we can know (Willig, 2013). This can be broadly divided into two camps: realists consider that the world exists independent of our own perception of it (Searle, 1995), whereas constructionists consider that our experiences of the world are not a direct reflection of the world itself but an interpretation through the way in which we experience the world (Willig, 2013). It is important to understand ontology and epistemology so that you can identify the best approach for your research questions/aims.

It is important that you use qualitative methodology for the right reasons; many choose this approach because they do not like statistics or because they simply think it would be a good idea to interview people about a topic. Conducting qualitative research takes a great deal of time and requires good abilities in a range of skills, such as conducting interviews and encouraging people to discuss their views/experiences in detail and being analytical to consider the data in detail and generate themes and link these together. Qualitative research is becoming more common in forensic psychology, and done well it will provide you with a good understanding from the perspectives of your participants, which can lead to important theoretical and practice developments. So when choosing this approach, as with the other methodologies, make sure that it is appropriate for your research question and consider carefully the design of the study and the method of data collection.

Furthermore, how you frame your research questions will impact on the method you will use to analyse your data. When using quantitative methods you are encouraged to consider what would be the appropriate analysis for any data being gathered, and this is also important when using qualitative methodology. There are a number of different methods of analysis for qualitative data (see the following box, in which we have summarised the three most common methods of analysis that have been used in forensic psychology). There are many more approaches that could be used, and you should read about qualitative methodology and analysis carefully in developing the design of your study. In selecting the most appropriate method of analysis, it is often best to consider all the options one at a time; you can probably rule out some quite quickly due to the focus and purpose of your design, and other choices might involve more careful consideration and comparison of the similarities and differences between the approaches and the underlying ontology and epistemology. Note that the choice of analysis should influence how you collect your data and the type of data that is appropriate, so you should think these things through carefully in the design phase of your project. It is not appropriate to say that you are going to interview people and then 'do qualitative analysis', as there are fundamental differences between each of the qualitative approaches that will influence design decisions that need to be made throughout the research process (from the way participants are approached, to the way in which they provide data, the types of questions asked [if indeed questions are asked], the type of analysis, and the presentation of findings).

Qualitative analysis methods

Thematic analysis: This is one of the most common methods used with qualitative data. Braun and Clarke (2006) introduced a clear method for how to carry out a thematic analysis. This analysis method is very useful because it is very broad in its application, so it can be used with many types of data. However, this should not be the automatic choice for your analysis; you need to be clear that this is the most appropriate analysis for your research question, and you need to consider your ontological and epistemological positions in using this approach.

Grounded theory: This is a very useful method of analysis when you wish to build a model/theory 'grounded' in your qualitative data. As such, it is very useful for areas that have had very little research, as this method allows you to build a model that can be tested with future studies. There are some disagreements within the field as to what is the correct method to use in analysing your data; therefore, you will need to carefully read about this to determine the approach most appropriate for your study.

Interpretative phenomenological analysis (IPA): IPA is based in phenomenological psychology and is used when a researcher is attempting to gain an understanding of the participants' experiences and views of the topic being investigated. The researcher is attempting to understand the experiences that the participant has had and how he/she interprets these or has found meaning in relation to that phenomenon. This method of analysis leads to a description of the issue based on what is reported by the participants. Although the researcher does not attempt to impose any of his/her own attitudes or opinions about the issue, it is recognised within this approach that the researcher will have brought his/her own experiences to the study and these are noted and taken into account.

Single case methods

It is important to differentiate between two methods that involve single case designs. The first is a single case (i.e., with only one participant) experimental method in which time series methodologies are used. The second method is a case study of observations of an individual (Wilson, 2006), which we will refer to as a *clinical single case study*, for ease of distinguishing between the two. A single case experimental approach can be very useful for populations where the number of available participants is very small. In this situation, it may be useful to examine the effectiveness of an intervention for a single individual, for example by testing the individual prior to treatment, during treatment, and after treatment (ABA approach) (see Burns, Bird, Leach, & Higgins [2003] in the 'Methods example' section), or by measuring change during treatment (for example, see Campbell-Fuller & Craig [2009] in the 'Methods examples' section). If there are changes present in line with the behaviours you hope to change when treatment is being delivered that reduce when treatment is removed and then return when it is reintroduced (ABAB design), this indicates that the treatment is having an impact.

50 Designing and planning

Rosenfeld, Byars, and Galietta (2011) outlined some of the obvious difficulties with this approach with questionable internal validity and generalizability. However, Wilson (2006) suggests that although drawing conclusions from a single study would be problematic, meta-analyses across a number of single case experimental studies can establish the basis for an experimental effect. Published single case experimental studies are rare in forensic psychology; however, this might be a suitable approach if you are working with an individual with whom you are introducing a new or novel intervention, or if you wish to assess whether your practice with an individual is having an impact.

Clinical single case studies can offer detailed insights into specific cases that might have important implications for practice and theory development. As such, they can answer questions regarding the how and why of a particular situation (Yan, 2013). In forensic psychology, this approach can offer a rich and in-depth analysis of an individual or a very small number of cases. For example, Lad (2013) reported a single case report where cognitive behavioural therapy (CBT) was used to addressed posttraumatic symptomology associated with an offender's commission of murder, and Burgess, Wollner, and Willis (2010) reported on two cases of educator sexual abuse, one that involved a female student victim and one that involved a male student victim. Although this approach may seem attractive, there is a substantial amount of information that is needed to complete a rigorous case report, and it is easier to write if you are the person working with the individual or are working closely with others who are working with the individual. There are considerable challenges to writing a report that is both sufficiently descriptive and analytical, and there should be a strong rationale for why a single case report is merited. Its use can be justified in cases of rare phenomena. It is likely that this type of research design would be more appropriate via your practice, or that of your colleagues, but it is unlikely to be suitable for dissertation (or similar) research. (If you do use this approach, see Gillham [2000] in the 'Further reading' section.)

Evaluation methods

If you want to carry out an evaluation of an intervention or treatment programme, many of the methods described within this chapter will be appropriate for you to adopt (e.g., experimental, quasi-experimental). However, it is useful to consider these approaches specifically in relation to evaluation techniques.

Randomised controlled trials (RCTs)

RCTs are often viewed as the 'gold standard' of research methods in enabling a researcher to draw clear conclusions about cause and effect. With a high level of control of experimental conditions and the random allocation of participants to experimental conditions, it should be possible to ensure that all possible confounds are removed from the design and that firm conclusions can be drawn about the impact of the IVs on the DVs. The benefits of adopting this approach are therefore very apparent; however, as you will learn later, there are considerable challenges to using this approach, which often means that it is just not feasible (particularly for dissertation research). In addition, there are ethical issues that need to be carefully considered. These difficulties mean that there are relatively few RCTs conducted in forensic psychology (some examples have been listed in the 'Methods examples' section).

In essence, this design requires the researcher to randomly allocate participants to each experimental condition (other methods of randomisation are available, e.g., to 'cluster' participants based on a service being offered in randomly allocated areas; see Boruch, Cecil, Turner, Victor & Hyatt [2012] in the 'Further reading' section and Troquette et al. [2013] in the 'Methods examples' section). True random allocation needs to be used, such that each participant has an equal chance of being placed in any of the experimental conditions. It is important that all participants are appropriate for the treatment; for example, all potential participants should be assessed for their suitability for the treatment prior to random allocation, and only those that are suitable should be randomly allocated. It is important that all groups are treated identically with the exception of the experimental manipulation, to ensure that no confounds are introduced to the study. For this reason, rather than not receiving any treatment, the control group should receive a placebo treatment. Ideally, the participants, treatment providers (for both the treatment and placebo) and the researchers should be 'blind' (i.e., unaware of the conditions to which participants have been assigned) to reduce the likelihood that the participants in the different experimental conditions will be treated differently. Following the implementation of the experimental condition, the outcome variables should be measured in the same ways in all groups. The high degree of control in a well-designed and conducted RCT enable the researcher to directly attribute change to the experimental manipulation rather than to any other factors.

At this point, you may be thinking that RCT seems like an ideal approach to adopt; however, you might have noted some issues that would be difficult in forensic settings. Is it possible to have a placebo intervention that looks/feels like the real treatment but has no intended treatment impact? Brown (2010) highlighted the difficulty of implementing a placebo when evaluating offending behaviour programmes. Whilst it is more achievable in medical research to give participants a placebo pill, the practicalities of attempting to provide a placebo treatment programme are challenges that may be impossible to overcome. Furthermore, would it be possible to have treatment providers and participants who are blind to the condition in which participants have been placed? Further issues remain, such as when the individuals who know they have not been selected for treatment may engage in more negative behaviour due to decompensation (Campbell, 2003) and/or may seek some other form of intervention, which limits the validity of the RCT design. In order to take account of this, researchers might have two different types of intervention and randomly allocate people to treatment A or B; however, this design will only enable them to identify if one is better than the other but not if treatment is better than no treatment (and if both treatments are equally effective, it is difficult to assess what this means – they could be equally good or equally bad). When compromises such as these are made to an RCT, the design does not fulfil the gold standard criteria because potential confounds are introduced.

It is important to also consider issues such as the ethical implications associated with random allocation. In essence, the random allocation of participants means that one group of participants will receive no treatment/intervention. Given the beneficial impact that a treatment/intervention may have on an individual (and perhaps on others, such as future victims), some people argue that it is unethical to withhold treatment (e.g., Marshall & Pithers, 1994). An equally important but opposing view (for example, see Quinsey, Harris, Rice & Lalumière, 1993) is that there is an ethical duty to show conclusively that an intervention is effective (as it may be harmful if ineffective interventions are used), and because RCTs are the best way of demonstrating effectiveness, they should be used to evaluate interventions. Hollin (2011) argued that it is only ethical to use an RCT approach where there is a degree of uncertainty in the effectiveness of the intervention. In some areas of forensic psychology, this is difficult to judge and can be an area for debate in itself. The arguments surrounding this can become entrenched, with some contending that effectiveness cannot be determined without RCTs and others arguing that RCTs are not appropriate due to ethical issues. In many instances this is a moot point, since a number of issues relating to practicality and feasibility mean that it is not possible to employ an RCT (many offenders are court ordered to complete an intervention, for example, and here an RCT might simply not be legally possible). There is, therefore, a great deal of debate about the use of RCTs in forensic contexts (e.g., whether focussing on impact with RCTs is the most appropriate area of research). See Gendreau, Goggin, and Smith (1999), Hough (2010) and Section 2 of Bowen and Brown (2012) (all listed in the 'Further reading' section) for more information on these issues. If you wish to conduct an RCT, you should consult this literature and fully explore the techniques required to conduct a good quality RCT. Hollin (2008, 2011) summarised many of the issues in relation to RCTs and also the practicalities associated with implementing this approach (see also Asscher et al., 2007).

Quasi-experimental methods

Given the challenges discussed in the previous section regarding RCTs, you may decide to use quasi-experimental approaches instead. In the area of evaluation, the practicalities of carrying out this research often mean that the less robust quasi-experimental approaches tend to be used more frequently (see Larzelere et al., 2004). Selecting a group for comparison with a treatment group can be a challenging experience, as Brown (2010) noted in relation to comparison groups in sexual offender treatment evaluations. There are a variety of different comparison groups that can be available (e.g., offenders who are waiting to complete a treatment programme, offenders who served their sentences prior to an intervention being introduced, or offenders who are unwilling to complete a treatment programme). Finding good comparison groups can be difficult, but try to find groups that are most similar on key aspects; for example, comparing a group that was deemed suitable for treatment with a group that was not deemed suitable for treatment has a significant weakness in that these groups have obvious differences that might impact on outcome variables. Comparing the treatment group with a group that is deemed suitable for treatment but has yet to receive it (a waiting list comparison group) is likely to be more robust, although it would be important to investigate how people are allocated to treatment/waiting lists. If this is done due to priority/assessment of need (i.e., the most needy receive treatment quickly), then this makes the comparison group less valid. The basic advice is to minimise as much as possible any differences between a treatment and a comparison group. Obviously, you will not be able to remove all differences, but the more these other factors can be minimised, the more confident you can be that any differences that are found are due to a treatment effect rather than any other factor.

Single-case designs

Should neither experimental nor quasi-experimental approaches be possible due to the number of individuals who are receiving the treatment/intervention, it is possible to use single-case designs. There are a number of terms that refer to this type of methodology, such as *small-N, N-of-one* or *single-subject*. The method used within this type of study does not vary significantly from those described in either the experimental or quasi-experimental approaches, in that the usual method includes pretesting and the use of an intervention, with testing at certain points (e.g., postintervention, three-month follow-up) (Freeman, 2003). Although we are often taught that sample sizes need to be large to establish generalizability, some researchers argue that single-case studies can be considered more generalizable due to the fact that the issue of group differences is not relevant in single-case designs (Wilson, 2006). This argument does rely upon the rigour involved within the experimental design. This challenges the usefulness of this approach because, as Rosenfeld et al. (2011) suggested, the variations in this design can affect the degree of experimental control within the study. Thus, if you choose to utilise this design, you need to determine whether you will be able to employ the appropriate level of experimental control.

Qualitative methods

Other approaches are also relevant in evaluating interventions. There is still some debate about the usefulness of qualitative methodologies in evaluation research

(Lösel, 2008); however, qualitative methods such as IPA enable us to gain a rich understanding of participants' experiences of a particular phenomenon (Smith, 2004). An example of where this may be useful in evaluation techniques is that it could give you an understanding of how participants experienced an intervention (see the 'Methods examples' section). Qualitative approaches are becoming more common in evaluation research (and are often used in process evaluation, discussed later), and new approaches are being developed (for example, see Barnard [2012] in the 'Further reading' section). These methods may give you a greater understanding of the process of change and what it was about the intervention that led to the change, rather than simply indicating that change has taken place. Your choice of methodology depends upon your research questions. Should you wish to simply assess whether a programme enacts change in an individual, then a quantitative approach is likely to be most appropriate. However, should you wish to understand how a programme facilitates change, then a qualitative methodology may be most appropriate.

Cost–benefit analyses

The previous discussion has focussed on whether treatment/interventions are effective or not; however, trends in policy and politics towards more evidenced and accountable practices have increased the awareness of, and requests to examine, whether the benefits of the interventions can be justified relative to the costs of delivering them (see Bergin [2013] in the 'Further reading' section for more information). This requires cost–benefit analysis, which is a comprehensive economic evaluation technique derived from economic theory (see Cohen [2000] in the 'Further reading' section). It requires an estimate of all the costs of an intervention and should include both fixed and incremental costs (e.g., see Shanahan and Donato [2001] in the 'Methods examples' section). This is then offset against an estimate of all the benefits of the intervention.

Some of the costs and benefits may be relatively easy to calculate (though it might be difficult to access the relevant data); however, determining the exact costs and benefits of an intervention can be difficult. For example, how much of the costs of running (heating, lighting etc.) a prison should be included in the cost of delivering an intervention in prison? Estimating the benefits depends on the effectiveness of the intervention, which can be a difficult and contentious issue, as we have previously discussed. Even when assumptions are made about intervention effectiveness, estimating the value for all the benefits is difficult. Some benefits may have clear tangible costs, such as avoiding the cost of reconvicting an offender, but some assumptions must be made about whether just one reoffence or more reoffences were prevented for each recidivist, the number of victims and/or level of damage, value of losses and so forth for each offence. In addition, calculating a monetary cost for intangible benefits, such as the cost of harm to the victims and/or society, is difficult. However, there are precedents for some of these calculations (e.g., payments for damage in criminal and civil law) that can be used. Some researchers have looked at the cost-effectiveness of an approach, with the analysis less focussed on financial outcomes (e.g., to determine if a practice produces benefits) (for example, see Block, Foster, Pierce, Berkoff, & Runyan [2013] in the 'Methods examples' section). In reality, gaining access to all the necessary financial data can be difficult, particularly if you are external to the relevant organisation; however, this approach might be useful to consider if, for example, you are working for small-scale organisations wishing to evaluate the costs of their interventions and/or considering the introduction of new interventions.

Process evaluation

Process evaluation allows us to examine whether a treatment/intervention is being or has been implemented as planned/expected and is being given to appropriate individuals (see Cherner, Nandal, Ecker, Aubry, & Pettey [2013] and Stead et al. [2014] in the 'Methods examples' section). It is not uncommon for programmes to 'drift' away from the original plan, for example, as treatment providers adjust the programme with each delivery. It has become increasingly common for interventions to have detailed manuals and for treatment delivery to be monitored carefully to improve adherence to treatment regimes, although there has been debate about the use of manualisation (see Mann, 2009; Marshall, 2009). It is important to build process evaluation techniques into programme implementations and to use these to assure quality treatment, though this is not always given as much focus as it should. Where such techniques are not present, or when a new intervention is about to be implemented, there may be an opportunity to conduct a process evaluation. Process evaluations can be conducted in a formative manner, where the intervention is monitored, feedback is provided and revisions are made as the intervention is being delivered; or in a summative manner, where an intervention is monitored/evaluated in terms of the process of implementation/delivery and the feedback on this provided at the end. The latter is more likely to be useful for a dissertation/research project, though the former should be considered in practice during the delivery of interventions. Ideally, programmes/interventions should be evaluated for process and outcome (and perhaps cost-effectiveness). They should be constantly revised in line with these findings and reevaluated, although such rigorous ongoing assessment of forensic interventions is rare.

Summary and checklist

In this chapter, we have summarised the range of methodological designs that can be used in a forensic psychology study. Space limitations mean that we can provide only a brief overview of each design; we would encourage you to read

56 Designing and planning

more about each approach if you are considering it for your research and to look at published studies in which the approach has been used to understand the design in practice. In considering the design of your study, the following checklist is important to bear in mind:

1 Plan and account for the time involved in selecting the design of your study. As you have seen in this chapter, there are many issues to consider, and you may need to read about several designs, look at the relevant literature of published studies and so on in order to select the design that is the most appropriate for your study. It is important to remember that time spent at this stage will be worthwhile, as it should avoid difficulties later in the study.
2 Consider a number of designs and 'rule out' or 'rule in' designs in line with decisions you make about your research questions and research aims. At this stage, you might have a number of designs that might be appropriate for your research questions, but considerations discussed in the next chapters in this section of the book will help you determine which design you are able to use.
3 Update your research protocol and your study diary/notes to record the decisions you make in selecting your design, and ensure that you keep the references for all the studies/sources of information that you use in your decision making. You will need much of this information for your report/article, and it will save you time if you keep good records and notes throughout the project.

Methods examples

Experimental methods

Karlén, M. H., Roos af Hjelmsäter, E., Fahlke, C., Granhag, P.A., & Söderpalm Gordh, A. (2014). Alcohol intoxicated eyewitnesses' memory of intimate partner violence. *Psychology, Crime and Law*. Published online. doi:10.1080/1068316X.2014.951644

Righarts, S., Jack, F., Zajac, R., & Hayne, H. (2014). Young children's responses to questioning: The effects of delay and subsequent questioning. *Psychology, Crime and Law*. Published online. doi:10.1080/1068316X.2014.951650

Experimental methods: vignette-based studies

Connolly, D.A., & Gordon, H.M. (2013). He-said-she-said: Contrast effects in credibility assessments and possible threats to fundamental principles of criminal law. *Legal and Criminological Psychology, 16*, 227–241. doi:10.1348/135532510x498185

Louden, J.E., & Skeem, J.L. (2013). How do officers assess and manage recidivism and violence risk for probationers with mental disorder? An experimental investigation. *Law and Human Behavior, 37*(1), 22–34. doi:10.1037/h0093991

Storey, J.E., Gibas, A.L., Reeves, K.A., & Hart, S.D. (2011). Evaluation of a violence risk (threat) assessment training program for police and other criminal justice professionals. *Criminal Justice and Behavior, 38*, 554–564. doi:10.1177/0093854811403123

Methods 57

Quasi-experimental methods

Freeman, N.J. (2012). The public safety impact of community notification laws: Rearrest of convicted sex offenders. *Crime and Delinquency, 58* (4), 539–564. doi:10.1177/0011128708330852

Zalmanowitz, S.J., Babins-Wagner, R., Rodger, S., Corbett, B.A., & Leschied, A. (2013). The association of readiness to change and motivational interviewing with treatment outcomes in males involved in domestic violence group therapy. *Journal of Interpersonal Violence, 28*(5), 956–974. doi:10.1177/0886260512459381

Quasi-experimental methods: vignette

Edens, J.F., Epstein, M., Stiles, P.G., & Poythress, N.G. (2011). Voluntary consent in correctional settings: Do offenders feel coerced to participate in research? *Behavioral Sciences and the Law, 29,* 771–795. doi:10.1002/bsl.1014

Facet theory

Porter, L., & Alison, L. (2006). Behavioural coherence in group robbery: A circumplex model of offender and victim behaviour in group robbery. *Aggressive Behavior, 32,* 330–332. doi:10.1002/ab.20132

Salfati, C. G., & Bateman, A. L. (2005). Serial homicide: An investigation of behavioural consistency. *Journal of Investigative and Offender Profiling, 2,* 245–265. doi:10.1002/jip.27

Cross-sectional methods

Langevin, R., & Curnoe, S. (2014). Psychological profile of sex offenders using weapons in their crimes. *Journal of Sexual Aggression, 20,* 55–68. doi:10.1080/13552600.2013.769636

Lewis, T., Klettke, B., & Day, A. (2014). Sentencing in child sexual assault cases: Factors influencing judicial decision-making. *Journal of Sexual Aggression, 21,* 281–295. doi:10.1080/13552600.2013.804603

Rosenfeld, R., Rojek, J., & Decker, S. (2012). Age matters: Race differences in police searches of young and older male drivers. *Journal of Research in Crime and Delinquency, 49,* 31–55. doi:10.1177/0022427810397951

Longitudinal methods

Bowen, E., Heron, J., Waylen, A., Wolke, D., & The ALSPAC Study Team. (2005). Risk for domestic violence during and after pregnancy: Findings from a British longitudinal study. *British Journal of Obstetrics and Gynaecology, 112,* 1083–1089. doi:10.1111/j.1471-0528.2005.00653.x

Survey/questionnaire methods

Barkworth, J. M., & Murphy, K. (2014). Procedural justice policing and citizen compliance behaviour: The importance of emotion. *Psychology, Crime and Law.* Published online. doi: 10.1080/1068316X.2014.951649

Melinder, A., & Magnussen, S. (2014). Psychologists and psychiatrists serving as expert witnesses in court: What do they know about expert witness memory? *Psychology, Crime and Law.* Published online. doi:10.1080/1068316X.2014.915324

Szlachcic, R., Fox, S., Conway, C., Lord, A., & Christie, A. (2014). The relationship between schemas and offence supportive attitudes in mentally disordered sexual offenders. *Journal of Sexual Aggression*. Published online. doi:10.1080/13552600.2014.966166

Qualitative methods

Bourke, P., Ward, T., & Rose, C. (2012). Expertise and sexual offending: A preliminary empirical model. *Journal of Interpersonal Violence, 27* (12), 2391–2414. doi:10.1177/0886260511433513

Cromby, J., Brown, S.D., Gross, H., Locke, A., & Patterson, A.E. (2010). Constructing crime, enacting morality: Emotion, crime and anti-social behaviour in an inner-city community. *British Journal of Criminology, 50*, 873–895. doi:10.1093/bjc/azq029

Guo, J. (2012). "Anyone in my shoes will end up like me": Female inmates of responsibility for crime. *Discourse and Society, 23*, 34–46. doi:10.1177/0957926511424658

Single case methods: clinical

Bean, H., Softas-Nall, L., & Mahoney, M. (2011). Reflections on mandated reporting and challenges in the therapeutic relationship: A case study with systemic implications. *The Family Journal: Counselling and Therapy for Couples and Families, 19*, 286–290. doi:10.1177/1066480711407444

Nesca, M., & Dalby, J.T. (2010). Maternal neonaticide following traumatic childbirth: A case study. *International Journal of Offender Therapy and Comparative Criminology, 55*, 1166–1178. doi:10.1177/0306624X10376204

Single case methods: experimental

Campbell-Fuller, N., & Craig, L.A. (2009). The use of olfactory aversion and directed masturbation in modifying deviant sexual interest: A case study. *Journal of Sexual Aggression, 15*, 179–191. doi:10.1080/13552600902759556

Evaluation methods: RCTs

Cohen, J.A., Mannarino, A.P., & Knudsen, K. (2005). Treating sexually abused children: 1 year follow-up of a randomised controlled trial. *Child Abuse and Neglect, 29*, 135–145. doi:10.1016/j.chiabu.2004.12.005

Troquete, N.A.C., van den Brink, R.H.S., Beintema, H., Mulder, T., van Os, T.W.D.P., Schoevers, R.A., & Wiersma, D. (2013). Risk assessment and shared care planning in out-patient forensic psychiatry: Cluster randomised controlled trial. *The British Journal of Psychiatry, 202*, 365–371. doi:10.1192/bjp.bp.112.113043

Evaluation methods: quasi-experimental methods

Palmer, E., Hatcher, R., McGuire, J., Bilby, C., Ayres, T., & Hollin, C. (2011). Evaluation of the addressing substance-related offending (ASRO) program for substance-using offenders in the community: A reconviction analysis. *Substance Use and Misuse, 46*, 1072–1080. doi:10.3109/10826084.2011.559682

Zhang, S.X., Roberts, R.E.L., & McCollister, K.E. (2011). Therapeutic community in a California prison: Treatment outcomes after 5 years. *Crime and Delinquency, 57*, 82–101. doi:10.1177/0011128708327035

Evaluation methods: single-case methods

Burns, M., Bird, D., Leach, C., & Higgins, K. (2003). Anger management training: the effects of a structured programme on the self-reported anger experience of forensic inpatients with learning disability. *Journal of Psychiatric and Mental Health Nursing, 10*, 569–577. doi:10.1046/j.1365–2850.2003.00653.x

Evaluation methods: qualitative methods

Garrett, T., Oliver, C., Wilcox, D.T., & Middleton, D. (2003). Who cares? The views of sexual offenders about the group treatment they receive. *Sexual Abuse: A Journal of Research and Treatment, 15*, 323–338. doi:10.1177/107906320301500408

Levenson, J.S., & Prescott, D.S. (2009). Treatment experiences of civilly committed sex offenders: A consumer satisfaction survey. *Sexual Abuse: A Journal of Research and Treatment, 21*, 6–20. doi:10.1177/1079063208325205

Evaluation methods: cost–benefit analyses

Block, S., Foster, E.M., Pierce, M.W., Berkoff, M. C., & Runyan, D.K. (2013). Multiple forensic interviews during investigations of child sexual abuse: A cost-effectiveness analysis. *Applied Developmental Science, 17*, 174–183. doi:10.1080/10888691.2013.836033

Shanahan, M., & Donato, R. (2001). Counting the cost: Estimating the economic benefit of pedophile treatment programs. *Child Abuse and Neglect, 25*, 541–555. doi:10.1016/S0145–2134(01)00225–3

Evaluation methods: process evaluation

Cherner, R., Nandlal, J., Ecker, J., Aubry, T., & Pettey, D. (2013). Findings of a formative evaluation of a transitional housing program for forensic patients discharged into the community. *Journal of Offender Rehabilitation, 52*, 157–180. doi:10.1080/10509674.2012.754826

Stead, M., Eadie, D., McKell, J., Bauld, L., Parkes, T., Nicoll, A., Wilson, S., & Burgess, C. (2014). Process evaluation of Alcohol Brief Interventions in wider settings (Young People and Social Work) (2012/13 RE007). NHS Health Scotland. Retrieved from http://www.healthscotland.com/uploads/documents/23021-1.%20ABIs%20in%20Wider%20Settings%20report.pdf

Further reading

Barnard, M. (2012). Critical qualitative theory: Opening up the black box of criminal justice interventions. In E. Bowen & S. Brown (Eds.), *Perspectives on evaluating criminal justice and corrections* (Advances in Evaluation Series). Bingley, England: Emerald.

Bergin, T. (2013). Markets for suspicion: Assessing cost-benefit analysis in criminal justice. *Interdisciplines: Journal of History and Sociology, 4*. Retrieved from http://inter-disciplines.de/bghs/index.php/indi/article/view/97/78

Boruch, R.F., Cecil, J.S., Turner, H., Victor, T., & Hyatt, J. (2012). Resolving ethical issues in randomised controlled trials. In E. Bowen & S. Brown (Eds.), *Perspectives on evaluating criminal justice and corrections* (Advances in Evaluation Series). Bingley, England: Emerald.

Bowen, E., & Brown, S.J. (Eds). (2012). *Perspectives on evaluating criminal justice and corrections* (Advances in Evaluation Series). Bingley, England: Emerald.

Braun, V., & Clarke, V. (2013). *Successful qualitative research: A practical guide for beginners*. London, England: Sage.

Cohen, M.A. (2000). To treat or not to treat? A financial perspective. In C.R. Hollin (Ed.), *Handbook of offender assessment and treatment* (pp. 35–49). Chichester, England: John Wiley and Sons.

Engel, W., Jann, B., Lynn, P., Scherpenzzeel, A., & Sturgis, P. (2014). *Improving survey methods: Lessons from recent research* (European Association of Methodological Series). Abingdon, England: Routledge.

Gendreau, P., Goggin, C., & Smith. P. (1999). The forgotten issue in effective correctional treatment: Program implementation. *International Journal of Offender Therapy and Comparative Criminology, 43*, 180–187. doi:10.1177/0306624X9943200

Gillam, B. (2000). *Case study research methods* (Real World Research series). London, England: Continnuum.

Gillham, B. (2001). *Research interview* (Real World Research series). London, England: Continnuum.

Gillham, B. (2008). *Developing a questionnaire* (Real World Research series). London, England: Continnuum.

Groves, R.M., Fowler, F.J., Couper, M.P., Lepkowski, J.M., Singer, E., & Tourangeau, R. (2009). *Survey methodology*. Chichester, England: Wiley-Blackwell.

Harkins, L., & Beech, T. (2007). Measurement of the effectiveness of sex offender treatment. *Aggression and Violent Behavior, 12*, 36–44. doi:10.1016/j.avb.2006.03.002

Hough, M. (2010). Gold standard or fool's gold: The pursuit of certainty in experimental criminology. *Criminology Criminal Justice, 10*, 11–22. doi:10.1177/1748895809352597

Oppenheim, A. (1998). *Questionnaire design, interviewing and attitude measurement*. London, England: Continnuum.

Steckler, A., & Linnan, L. (Eds.). (2002). *Process evaluation for public health interventions and research*. Chichester, England: John Wiley and Sons.

References

Alexander, C.S., & Becker, H.J. (1978). The use of vignettes in survey research. *Public Opinion Quarterly, 42*, 93–104. doi:10.1086/268432

Anderson, I., & Lyons, A. (2005). The effects of victims' social support on attributions of blame in female and male rape. *Journal of Applied Social Psychology, 35*, 1400–1417. doi:10.1111/j.1559-1816.2005.tb02176.x

Asscher, J.J., Dekovi, M., van der Laan, P.H., Prins, P.J.M., & van Arum, S. (2007). Implementing randomised experiments in criminal justice settings: An evaluation of multi-systemic therapy in the Netherlands. *Journal of Experimental Criminology, 3*, 113–129. doi:10.1007/s11292-007-9028-y

Barter, C., & Reynold, E. (1999). The use of vignettes in qualitative research. *Social Research Update, 25*. Retrieved from http://sru.soc.surrey.ac.uk/SRU25.html

Borg, I. (2005). Facet theory. *Encyclopedia of statistics in behavioral science*. Chichester, England: Wiley.

Bornstein, B.H. (1999). The ecological validity of jury simulations: Is the jury still out? *Law and Human Behavior, 23*, 75–91. doi:10.1023/A:1022326807441

Braun, V., & Clark, V. (2013). *Successful qualitative research: A practical guide for beginners.* London, England: Sage.

Brown, J.M. (2011). Facet theory and multi-dimensional scaling methods. In K. Sheldon, J. Davies, & K. Howells (Eds.), *Research in practice for forensic professionals* (pp. 60–85). London, England: Sage.

Brown, J.M., & Barnett, J. (2000). Facet theory: An approach to research. In G. M. Breakwell, S. Hammond, & C. Fife-Shaw (Eds.), *Research methods in psychology* (2nd ed., pp. 105–118). London, England: Sage.

Brown, S. (2010). *Treating sex offenders: An introduction to sex offender treatment programmes.* Cullompton, England: Willan.

Bryant, A., & Charmaz, K. (Eds.). (2007). *The SAGE handbook of grounded theory.* London, England: Sage.

Burgess, A., Welner, M., & Willis, D.G. (2010). Educator sexual abuse: Two case reports. *Journal of Child Sexual Abuse: Research, Treatment, & Program Innovations for Victims, Survivors, & Offenders, 19,* 387–402. doi:10.1080/10538712.2010.495045

Campbell, S. (2003). The feasibility of conducting an RCT at HMP Grendon. London, England: Home Office Online Report. Retrieved from http://webarchive.nationalarchives. gov.uk/20060715141954/http://dspdprogramme.gov.uk/media/pdfs/Feasibility_HMP_ Grendon.pdf

Canter, D. V., & Heritage, R. (1990). A multivariate model of sexual offences behaviour: Developments in "offender profiling." *Journal of Forensic Psychiatry, 1,* 185–212. doi:10.1080/09585189008408469

Coolican, H. (2013). *Research methods and statistics in psychology* (5th ed.). Abingdon, Oxon: Routledge.

Farrington, D.P. (2003). Key results from the first 40 years of the Cambridge Study in Delinquent Development. In T. P. Thornberry & M. D. Krohn (Eds.), *Taking stock of delinquency: An overview of findings from contemporary longitudinal studies* (pp. 137–183). New York, NY: Kluwer/Plenum.

Fife-Shaw, C. (2012). Questionnaire design. In G. M. Breakwell, J. A. Smith, & D. B. Wright (Eds.), *Research methods in psychology* (4th ed., pp. 113–139). London, England: Sage.

Freeman, K.A. (2003). Single subject designs. In J. C. Thomas & M. Hershen (Eds.), *Understanding research in clinical and counselling psychology* (pp. 181–208). Mahwah, NJ: Lawrence Erlbaum.

Friendship, C., Beech, A., & Browne, A. (2002). Reconviction as an outcome measure in research: A methodological note. *British Journal of Criminology 42,* 442–444. doi:10.1093/bjc/42.2.442

Guttman, L. (1968). A general non-metric technique for finding the smallest co-ordinate space for a configuration of points. *Psychometrika, 33,* 469–506. Retrieved from http://link.springer.com/article/10.1007%2FBF02290164

Hammond, S., & Brown, J.M. (2005). Comparing three multivariate statistical procedures when profiling prolific residential burglaries. *Forensic Update, 80,* 9–16.

Hanson, R.K., & Nicholaichuk, T. (2000). A cautionary note regarding Nicholaichuk et al. (2000). *Sexual Abuse: A Journal of Research and Treatment, 12,* 289–293. doi:10.1177/107906320001200405

Hole, G. (2012). Experimental design. In G. M. Breakwell, J. A. Smith, & D. B. Wright (Eds.), *Research methods in psychology* (4th ed., pp. 39–74). London, England: Sage.

Hollin, C. R. (2008). Evaluating offending behaviour programmes: Does only randomization glister? *Criminology and Criminal Justice, 8*, 89–106. doi:10.1177/1748895807085871

Hollin, C.R. (2011). Strengths and weaknesses of randomised control trials. In K. Sheldon, J. Davies, & K. Howells (Eds.), *Research in practice for forensic professionals* (pp. 235–248). Abingdon, Oxon: Routledge.

Lad, S. (2013). A case report of treatment of offence related PTSD. *Journal of Forensic Psychiatry & Psychology, 24*, 788–794. doi:10.1080/14789949.2013.832352

Larzelere, R.E., Kuhn, B.R., & Johnson, B. (2004). The intervention selection bias: An underrecognized confound in intervention research. *Psychological Bulletin, 130*, 289–303. doi:10.1037/0033-2909.130.2.289

Lösel, F. (2008). Doing evaluation research in criminology: Balancing scientific and practical demands. In R. D. King & E. Wincup (Eds.), *Doing research on crime and justice* (2nd ed., pp. 141–170). Oxford, England: Oxford University Press.

Mann, R.E. (2009). Sex offender treatment: The case for manualisation. *Journal of Sexual Aggression, 15*, 121–131. doi:10.1080/13552600902907288

Marshall, W.L. (2009). Manualization: A blessing or a curse? *Journal of Sexual Aggression, 15*, 109–120. doi:10.1080/13552600902907320

Marshall, W.L., & Pithers, W.D. (1994). A reconsideration of treatment outcome with sex offenders. *Criminal Justice and Behavior, 21*, 10–24. doi:10.1177/0093854894021001003

Maxwell, J.A. (2012). *A realist approach for qualitative research*. London, England: Sage.

Quinsey, V.L., Harris, G.T., Rice, M.E., & Lalumière, M.L. (1993). Assessing the treatment efficacy in outcome studies of sex offenders. *Journal of Interpersonal Violence, 8*, 512–523. doi:10.1177/088626093008004006

Rosenfeld, B., Byars, K., & Galietta, M. (2011). Conducting psychotherapy outcome research in forensic settings. In B. Rosenfeld & S. D. Penrod (Eds.), *Research methods in forensic psychology* (pp. 309–324). Hoboken, NJ: Wiley.

Searle, J. (1995). *The construction of social reality*. London, England: Penguin.

Silverman, D. (2000). *Doing qualitative research: A practice handbook*. London, England: Sage.

Smith, J. A. (2004). Reflecting on the development of interpretative phenomenological analysis and its contribution to qualitative research in psychology. *Qualitative Research in Psychology, 1*, 39–54. doi:10.1191/1478088704qp004oa

Yan, R. K. (2013). *Case study research: Design and methods* (5th ed.). London, England: Sage.

Willig, C. (2013). *Introducing qualitative research in psychology* (3rd ed.). Maidenhead, England: McGraw-Hill.

Wilson, B. A. (2006). Single-case experimental designs. In M. Slade & C. E. Priebe (Eds.), *Choosing mental health research: Mental health research from theory to practice* (pp. 9–23). New York, NY: Routledge.

Chapter 4

Types of data

In this chapter, we will outline the different types of data that you can gather in a forensic psychology research project. This is one aspect of research design that can be overlooked when considering how to address a research question. However, the type of data that you gather has significant implications for the method of analysis that you are able to use. Some types of designs tend to lend themselves to the inclusion of a specific type of data (e.g., experimental, grounded theory), whereas other designs (e.g., cross-sectional, survey) can be used with a wide range of data types. A common oversight in research projects is that data are collected without prior thought as to exactly what type of data should be collected, the implications for data analyses, and whether these will allow the research question to be answered. Finding yourself with data that cannot be analysed as expected, data that does not address your research question, or worse, data that cannot be analysed at all, is clearly not great. Therefore, it is very important to think these details through carefully at your research proposal stage, hence our emphasis on the importance of considering the type of data that you *want* to gather. Once you have read this chapter, you should be able to:

- understand how to operationalise your variables;
- understand the differences between qualitative and quantitative data;
- understand different types of quantitative data and the implications on the analysis process; and
- apply this knowledge to your own research questions.

Variables

In order to establish the type of data that you will include in your study, you first need to determine the different variables that you will include in your research design. It is important that you are clear about these variables and can describe them and map them out clearly in your research proposal (a discussion on operationalisation appears later in the chapter). It is worth explaining this

64 Designing and planning

to your supervisor or a colleague when you are designing your study to ensure that you have designed a study with appropriate variables that will address your research question. The type of variables that you will include in your study will vary by research design, as summarised herein. In identifying your variables, you will need to consider exactly how you are going to operationalise your variables. For example, in a prison, you may want to examine the effectiveness of a treatment programme. This is a good starting point for framing your research question, but it does not help you to establish exactly how you are going to define 'effectiveness'. Effectiveness could be established in several ways, such as a demonstrated change in a psychometric scale or by examining reconviction levels of the offenders who completed the programme. The important point here is that you do need to establish exactly how you are going to define your variables within your study. It is a good idea to spend some time thinking about the different ways in which you can operationalise your variables and choosing the most appropriate definition for your project. This will vary according to a number of factors (e.g., ease of access to certain data), so you need to consider feasibility when defining your variables and the data that will be required to fulfil that definition.

Independent and dependent variables

In experimental (including single-case) and quasi-experimental designs you are testing the effect of one or more variables on one or more different variables. In experimental designs you will manipulate the variables (e.g., create vignettes that vary according to a limited number of experimental variables, or deliver, stop and re-deliver an intervention to employ an ABA single-case design), whilst in quasi-experimental designs you are likely to be taking advantage of natural differences (e.g., offenders who have received an intervention compared to those who have not) in variables to test the effects on other variables. In these designs, you will have at least one independent variable (IV) – the variables that you think cause the change to the other variables – and at least one dependent variable (DV) – the variables on which you think there is an effect. In the simplest design, you might test the effect a single IV has on a single DV, or you might have more than one IV and/or DV. If, for example, you were conducting an experimental mock case vignette study to examine the effect of the judge's instructions and confession evidence on whether participants (mock jurors) thought that the defendant was guilty or not guilty, then the IVs would be (a) the type of instruction given by the judge and (b) the presence or absence of a confession, and the DV would be selection of a guilty or not guilty 'verdict'. If you were conducting a quasi-experimental evaluation study assessing the impact of a treatment programme on recidivism, then your IV would be treatment condition (e.g., received treatment versus no treatment), and your DVs would be (a) sexual recidivism, (b) nonsexual violence recidivism and (c) nonviolent recidivism.

Common confusion

Don't be too ambitious. It is extremely difficult to understand the effects of more than three IVs, particularly when you are considering the interactions between these variables, so it is a good idea to restrict your study to no more than three IVs. The design of your study should address your research question; however, you might need to modify/simplify your research question if it would require the inclusion of more than three IVs. This does not mean that you have to include three IVs; designing your study to address the research question is most important. If this requires a single IV, then do not add additional IVs for the sake of it.

In these designs, it is very important that you think carefully through the numbers of levels (conditions) you have in each of your IVs and make sure that you design your study so that you include all the required conditions. It is not uncommon for people to design a study, collect their data and only realise at the analysis stage that they did not collect data for all the required levels of the IVs. It is not possible to conduct the analysis if data are missing for some conditions, so it is important to think this through carefully in your design stage and get this checked by a supervisor/colleague. This is particularly important when you have 'control' conditions, such as where there is an absence of information/interventions for one or more of your IVs. In order to determine the conditions you need for your study, it is a good idea to draw out all the combinations of your IVs and the associated levels. For example, if you were conducting an experimental study where you have three IVs (e.g., gender of the victim, gender of the perpetrator and relationship between the victim and perpetrator) with two levels (male or female) of the first two IVs and three levels (stranger, acquaintance and partner) in the relationships IV, then you would need the conditions shown in Table 4.1.

As you can see, this would mean that you would need twelve conditions. From this example, you should be able to see how the number of experimental conditions you require can increase substantially depending on the numbers of levels in each of your IVs and the number of IVs. This is another reason why you should be careful about the number of IVs you include in your study (as this also increases your requirements for sample size), and it also illustrates why you need to consider carefully the number of levels of IVs you include in your study.

Predictor and criterion variables

In cross-sectional and longitudinal designs, we do not manipulate variables and cannot make inferences about cause and effect, so it does not make sense to talk about independent and dependent variables. Therefore, we consider predictor

66 Designing and planning

Table 4.1 Example of conditions within an experimental design

Condition	Gender of victim	Gender of perpetrator	Relationship
1	Female	Female	Stranger
2	Female	Female	Acquaintance
3	Female	Female	Partner
4	Female	Male	Stranger
5	Female	Male	Acquaintance
6	Female	Male	Partner
7	Male	Female	Stranger
8	Male	Female	Acquaintance
9	Male	Female	Partner
10	Male	Male	Stranger
11	Male	Male	Acquaintance
12	Male	Male	Partner

variables and outcome or criterion variables. So, for example, your outcome variable might be reoffending and your predictor variables might be a number of variables that you expect to predict whether someone reoffends or not (e.g., age, type of offence, severity of offence, type of criminal sanction etc.). In theory, you can have as many predictor and outcome variables as you want, although the number of predictor variables will have an impact on the number of participants you will need. It can be complicated to write up a study with more than one outcome variable and so, particularly for student projects, it is probably easier to investigate only one outcome variable.

Common confusion

Although you should think of variables in terms of predictor and criterion (outcome) variables, partly to remind you not to overstate your findings in terms of making erroneous claims about cause and effect, the statistical package you use to analyse your data, might request that you select an 'independent' and a 'dependent' variable. In this instance, think of your predictor variables as IVs and your criterion variable as a DV.

Survey/questionnaire methods

In this type of study, you need to think carefully about your purpose. It could be that you are conducting the survey to establish whether a number of variables predict certain criterion variables (e.g., you might be interested to see whether characteristics such as age, level of education, previous victimisation etc. predict attitudes to crime and/or fear of crime). In this instance, you should be able to see that your study is similar to the cross-sectional study with predictor and criterion variables. It is important that you are clear about the purpose of your survey/questionnaire, as it is all too easy to collect data on a number of variables (e.g., participants' views on a wide range of topics) without considering what this tells you, other than the number of participants who thought one thing as opposed to another. If you collect data in a format where you can describe how many people indicated that they agreed with a statement or not, then it will be difficult to use this data to predict another variable, so you must think through the type of data that your survey will produce and how you would analyse that data (see the 'Levels of measurement' section later in the chapter).

Common difficulties

To avoid the problem of collecting data that you cannot analyse, it is a good idea to complete the study as 'dummy' participants and score/code the responses and/or enter them into whatever statistical package you will use. You can then try to run the analysis on the dummy data to see if the type of analysis you expect to conduct is possible.

Confounding variables

As outlined in the previous chapters, you should be aware of potential confounding variables; these are variables that are not IVs, DVs, predictor or criterion variables but which have an impact on the DVs or criterion variables. One way of taking account of these is to measure variables that you expect to have an influence on your DVs or criterion variables and include these in your analyses. As we have stressed many times already, it is important to consider these at the start of the study; it is unlikely that you will be able to collect data retrospectively, so you need to build the measurement of these variables into your design.

Qualitative methods

In qualitative designs, we do not think of variables in the same way; however, it is still very important to consider whether the data you wish to collect are in line with your research questions and ontological and epistemological positions at the design stage of the study. A common mistake is to assume that qualitative methods involve interviewing people, without any consideration given to the purpose of the study and the theoretical background on which qualitative methods are premised. The field of qualitative methodology is very diverse, and it is beyond the scope of this book to explore the theoretical underpinnings of the range of approaches (likewise we have not discussed the theoretical underpinnings of experimental research); however, we would advise you to develop an understanding of the theory of the method you are using (as well as the

68   Designing and planning

theories that underpin the topic area that you are investigating), as this will help ensure that you understand your results, can place these within the contexts of the strengths and weaknesses of the approach you have used, and do not over-interpret your findings.

As outlined in the previous chapter, there are many different perspectives that underpin qualitative designs. In addition to these, a fundamental distinction is between inductive or data-driven designs compared to theory-driven, deductive designs. If your study is driven by a specific set of questions or predictions, then deductive designs are more appropriate; however, if your research question is exploratory and you have no clear expectations about what you will find, then inductive designs are more appropriate.

As you might have realised, the designs outlined in the previous sections of this chapter are *hypothetico-deductive* – that is, the researcher conducts the research based on clear predictions (hypotheses) about the relationship between variables deduced from the literature (as we outlined in Chapter 3). This type of approach is rare in qualitative research, although one technique that can be used in this way is deductive content analysis. For example, you might want to test the extent to which offenders' talk about their offences fits with a typology/theory. You would develop a coding system based on the theory/typology and count the number of times offenders made statements in line with each category. Content analysis can also be used in an inductive way. If, for example, you had no clear expectations about the categories that you would find in offenders' talk (perhaps because you are looking at something previously not considered), then you would develop the codes/categories yourself by exploring the offenders' talk.

In this instance, the deductive versus inductive approach has the most impact on the analysis; however, the approach you use (bearing in mind the perspectives also outlined in the previous chapter) will also have an influence on how you collect data. A structured interview with specific questions that elicit a limited range of responses may be suitable for a deductive study but is unlikely to be suitable for an inductive one. In inductive designs, you are more likely to want to ask participants open, broad questions, allowing them to guide the information that is provided. It is important, therefore, that you are clear in the design phase of your study what approach is most appropriate for your research question and which design and method are most appropriate.

Activity

Find two empirical papers in which studies are outlined using the following designs (you can use the examples listed at the end of Chapter 3): (a) experimental, (b) quasi-experimental, (c) cross-sectional, (d) survey and (e) qualitative. Read the introduction and methods sections of the papers.

- For papers in which designs a and b were employed, identify the IVs and DVs.
- For papers in which designs c and d were used, identify the criterion and predictor variables.
- For papers in which design e was used, identify the ontological and epistemological position and the method of data collection.

Levels of measurement

Once you have determined the types of variables that you will include in your study, you next need to establish what level of measurement is required for each variable. The level of measurement has important implications for the type of analysis that you are able to conduct, so, as we have said before and will stress again, it is important to think this through carefully at the design stage. If you are not sure of the level of measurement and/or implications for data analysis, check with your supervisor or a colleague before you proceed to the data collection stage. Variables can take the form of four different levels of measurement: nominal, ordinal, interval and ratio, which are explained in more detail next.

Nominal/categorical data

It is very likely that you will be familiar with this type of data, as common examples include: male/female, yes/no, guilty/not guilty. Examples such as these are known as *binary variables*. *Nominal variables*, however, can have three or more responses (e.g., yes/no/don't know) (Field, 2013). These variables represent categories that are distinct, in that individuals should belong to one category or another (e.g., male or female). It is important to note that if you are creating categorical responses (perhaps in a survey), your categories do not overlap – individuals should be able to be located within one category of your variable only.

Common difficulties

Be careful not to impose categories on your data. For example, if you ask participants to select their age from a predetermined set of groups, this restricts the level of detail that you have about people's ages and the analysis you can conduct (thus reducing your level of data). If you ask people to state their exact age, then you can group/categorise this data at a later stage, and also benefit from the detail. If you feel that people would rather select a category than state their exact age, then this might be a good reason to choose this approach; however, think this through very carefully and only do this if the analysis that would be appropriate for categorical data is appropriate to address your research question(s).

Common confusion

When you collect nominal/categorical data, you might need to assign categories a number code in order to enter the data in a statistical package (e.g., SPSS) and conduct data analyses. It is important to always remember that these numbers are codes – they do not represent a numerical value. Statistical packages do not know the difference between a number that you enter as a code for a category or a number with a true numerical value; you will be able to run an analysis on the codes you entered as if they were numbers. You therefore need to remember that this is not valid; if you assign a code of 1 to 'yes', 2 to 'no' and 3 to 'don't know', 'don't know' is not three times as much as 'yes'. It is not uncommon for people to calculate the mean for gender, for example, based on the '1's they entered for male and '2's for female (or ethnicity based on the number codes they assigned to the different groups), so you must take care to avoid this.

Ordinal data

This level of data still represents categorical data; however, it is at a level of sophistication above nominal data, in that the categories should have an order (Field, 2013). Low, medium and high risk are an examples of ordinal data, in that high risk denotes meaning relative to low or medium risk (i.e., a greater level of risk in comparison to the other categories). Questions where respondents are asked to indicate answers on a scale from '1 – strongly disagree' to '5 – strongly agree' (Likert scale) produce ordinal data. As can be seen, different responses represent more or less of something (Fife-Shaw, 2012), as compared to nominal data, which do not give the same level of comparison between categories. For example, if two participants were asked a questionnaire item on a scale of 1–5 and one participant indicated a 4 (an agree response) and the second participant indicated a 5 (a strongly agree response), the second participant is more positive to the item than the first participant.

Within forensic psychology research, you will commonly find that ordinal-level data is frequently treated as if it is interval-level data within the analyses that are carried out within the study. This goes against the assumptions of many statistical tests (see Chapter 12), but it is frequent practice within many types of studies (e.g., surveys/questionnaires). The main points here are (a) that your previous searching of the literature should establish whether this is commonly used within the research area that you want to examine and (b) that you are clear with regard to the reasons why you are going to treat ordinal-level data as interval-level data.

> ### Common confusion
>
> Do not fall into the trap of believing that ordinal-level data actually represent numbers. Field (2013) outlined a good example of rating contestants on *X-Factor* on a scale of 1–10, where one judge gives a contestant a score of 4, whereas the second judge gives the contestant a score of 8. You cannot state that the second judge is twice as positive about the contestant as the first judge because this is a rating scale of ordinal-level data. The rating scale does not represent actual number, merely points on a ten-point scale.

Interval data

Interval data may look very similar to the type of ordinal-level data that we discussed in the previous section; however, the important difference for interval data is that the different points on the scale must actually represent the same level of difference between each of the points (e.g., the difference between rating something as either 1 or 2 must be the same as rating something as either 3 or 4). An example of this would be that if two participants scored either 70 or 80 on a task, the difference between these two participants would be the same as the difference between two participants who scored 100 and 110 on the same task.

Ratio data

Ratio data is not frequently seen within forensic psychology research; however, it is important to recognise this level of data. Ratio-level data has an actual zero value (Fife-Shaw, 2012). At this level of data, the differences between participants' scores actually represent numerical differences in the values. An example of ratio-level data would be if you had a project where you were measuring the reaction times of participants to a stimulus. In this type of task, it is possible that a participant could have a reaction time of 0 (however humanly unlikely). Also, you would be able to state that a participant who had a reaction time of 200 ms was twice as fast as a participant who has a reaction time of 400 ms.

Text-based data

Levels of measurement do not apply to text-based data, but it is included here to remind you that you need to consider a similar issue when you are developing schedules (for interviews, focus groups etc.) to collect text-based data. As outlined in the previous section on survey/questionnaire methods, the type of text-based data you collect should be grounded in your epistemology, inductive versus deductive approach and so on. Therefore, in the same way that you must consider the design of your data collection methods to ensure that you have an appropriate level of measurement for your research question/intended analysis, you should consider whether the design of your methods/questions will elicit the type of desired text response for your study.

Common difficulties

It is not uncommon for people to say that they want to conduct an inductive, exploratory study, but then to develop an interview schedule that has a long set of specific questions that limit the responses the participants can provide, or that 'lead' them through an event/experience in a particular way. If you want to explore people's perceptions or experiences of an event from an inductive approach, then your questions, especially at the start of an interview (focus group etc.) should ask people to tell you about their attitudes/experiences in an open, unguided way, allowing the participants to determine the way in which the information should be structured and so on. Later in the interview, you might want to ask some more specific questions about what you have been told, perhaps to clarify something, or so that you can understand the participants' perspectives. In forensic psychology, you should be familiar with the impact that even subtle differences in questions/context/tone of the interviewer can have on the information elicited as a result of research in relation to eye-witness testimony. It is important to consider this information, as well as knowledge about question formation, when designing your study.

Activity

Using the papers that you used to complete the previous activity:

- identify the level of measurement of each of the variables included in the study for the quantitative studies and
- identify the way in which the data were collected in the qualitative studies to assess whether the data were appropriate for the study design.

Evaluation data

It is worthwhile at this point to highlight the particular debates that are present regarding evaluation data. There are a significant number of points of contention regarding the appropriate form that components such as follow-up time periods and outcome measures should take; therefore, these are examined in more depth herein.

Outcome measures

Within the evaluation literature, there is considerable discussion regarding the merits of different outcome measures. One of the most common outcome measures within forensic psychology is recidivism (i.e., whether an offender reoffends). This measure is frequently used in experimental and quasi-experimental design evaluation studies (and is often used in cross-sectional and longitudinal designs). It is obvious why a measure of recidivism is an important outcome measure to consider when evaluating interventions aimed at reducing or eliminating reoffending; however, it is important not to overlook the limitations and challenges associated with using this as a measure of effectiveness. These limitations and challenges include: determining successful outcome, how to measure recidivism most effectively, considering what is an appropriate follow-up time period and considering the impact of low base rates (Brown, 2010).

'Determining successful outcome' refers to the decision about what reflects a good outcome for an intervention. Although you can find many evaluation studies of interventions, it is rare that this is clearly determined in the report/paper. Idealistically, some would argue that only 100% effectiveness (i.e., no further offending engaged in by any of the 'treated' offenders) should be considered as a successful outcome (e.g., Zonana, 1997). This is somewhat unrealistic, and therefore many researchers now consider more viable ways to determine success (e.g., a reduction in offending behavior). The problem with using 'reduction' rather than 'eradication' of reoffending is that it attracts criticism because reduction should be easy to achieve, and as such, all evaluations would demonstrate successful outcomes. A balance is needed, therefore, between the demands of 100% effectiveness and determining that any level of change denotes 'success'. As noted by Marshall (1992), even small measures of change in offending behaviour can have a considerable impact in the reduction of the number of victims of crime and the saving of public monies.

In effect, this issue tends to be side-stepped in evaluation studies, with most researchers testing to see if there is a statistically significant difference between the outcome measures of treated versus comparison/control groups. This potentially has a number of problems. It is perhaps easier to demonstrate statistically significant change in people who have the most 'severe' difficulties, so for example, it might be easier to show that a programme has been more effective with high-risk offenders than low-risk offenders, even though the high-risk offenders at the end of a programme might still be a higher risk than offenders who completed a programme that did not demonstrate statistically significant differences in recidivism. The level of postintervention recidivism in the nonsignificant intervention might also be considerably lower than that of the statistically significant intervention. Therefore, it is important that statistical

74 Designing and planning

significance is not considered in isolation. Measures of clinical change (see Bowen [2012] in the 'Further reading' section) that take into account the level of offenders' positions in relation to nonoffending populations postintervention might be more appropriate in evaluation studies.

The second issue in this area that needs to be considered is the measurement of recidivism. Although at face value measuring recidivism seem relatively easy to achieve (e.g., simply determining whether an offender has committed a crime or not), the complexities of actually establishing this need to be thought through. There is much debate within the literature regarding the reliability of official measures of crime. For example, estimations regarding prevalence of sexual offences suggest that there are very low levels of reporting to the police for these offences (Ministry of Justice, 2013), and in the UK there is no offence of 'domestic violence'. The simple truth is that although offenders may commit crimes following an intervention, these crimes may not feature in the official statistics/records. Therefore, there are numerous strengths and weaknesses to measures of official statistics. For example, arrest data may reflect a more accurate measure of offending behaviour, but without a conviction it is not possible to be certain that the offender actually committed the crime. You may choose to use conviction data, however only a very small number of crimes committed result in a conviction, so the measure (although more reliable in certainty that the offender committed the crime) is unlikely to reflect the true level of offending. These challenges are not easy to overcome, and this has led some researchers to use alternative measures of offending behaviour (e.g., self-report). In these types of studies, offenders are asked to report the level of offending that they have engaged in. Although this overcomes the limitations of official measures of crime, it introduces new challenges with questions regarding the likely truthfulness of any responses and the ethics of collecting data about crimes that have not been reported and/or investigated. The key message at this point is that it is not easy to measure recidivism in a way that is perfect, any of the current approaches have limitations, and you need to recognise these in the approach that you choose (and when reporting/writing up findings from your project).

The third issue to consider within this area is the time period between the completion of the intervention and when you will reexamine the levels of offending. This issue also reflects some of the challenges highlighted previously in relation to official measures of crime. Should an offender be arrested for an offence and charged, it is likely to take a significant period of time (dependent upon the type of crime) before the person is tried and sentenced (if found guilty for that offence). Therefore, any follow-up period needs to reflect this; shorter follow-up periods are likely to show lower levels of recidivism than longer follow-up periods. This issue means that studies that have a one-year follow-up time period are considered too short to be able to accurately determine effectiveness (Brown, 2010). This is a particular issue that is going to be important for projects that need to be completed in a short period of time (e.g., postgraduate dissertations). If follow-up data has not already been gathered for a programme, it may be difficult, if not impossible, to gather this data within the scope of a short-term project.

Much of the research in the UK in this area has determined that the most effective follow-up time period is two years. Friendship, Beech, and Browne (2002) argued this on the basis that this allows sufficient time for arrest and potential conviction to be completed, and that offenders are most likely to reoffend within this time period. This does not mean that longer follow-up periods should be ignored, as some studies have used follow-up periods of over ten years or more. The feasibility of this length of follow-up time must be considered, as it is frequently beyond the scope of a typical researcher to have follow-up periods of this length. Furthermore, the longer the follow-up period, the longer the time between the intervention and the outcome; this is time within which a wide range of other factors will have had an influence and it is likely that the impact of the intervention will be reduced. Furthermore, the intervention may have changed during this time period or even ended, and it is questionable how helpful it is to service providers to know that the provision ten years ago was or was not effective when they want to know how well the current provision is working.

The final issue to consider in this area is that recidivism rates for serious offences (e.g., murder and sexual offences) tend to be relatively low. These low base rates of recidivism mean that it can be challenging to establish effectiveness of a programme given that the lack of reoffending could be due to the programme, or it could be due to the low rate of reoffending. This issue can be addressed by having large sample sizes; however, feasibility becomes an issue should this approach be adopted where it may be impossible to increase the sample size to sufficient levels due to cost and time required. There are many other issues to consider if using this type of outcome measure (e.g., the type of reoffending that should be measured), so if you wish to include this measure in your study, you should research the issues carefully (e.g., see the 'Further reading' section).

Treatment change measures of effectiveness

Alternative measures include the use of personal or clinical characteristics to demonstrate change within a treated group, which are tested prior to the intervention (pretesting) and after it (posttesting). In this approach the researcher will need to examine the purpose of the intervention and the model of change (unfortunately, it is not uncommon to find interventions where there is no clear model or theory about how the intervention is expected to produce the desired change) to identify characteristics that would be associated with positive change following the completion of the programme. For example, within the sexual offending treatment programme literature, indicators of effectiveness that have been used include measures of cognitive distortion, empathy,

76 Designing and planning

self-esteem, intimacy, social competence and attitudes towards women and children, to name just a few. This method can lack validity, however, as changes in responses may be due to practice effects; this method is more robust if a control/comparison group (particularly if individuals are matched from each group) can be tested on the same measures and over the same time periods (although it can be challenging to find a suitable group). Moreover, changes in the measures may not be linked to outcome – there are only a small number of studies in which both within-treatment change and outcome have been measured, which shows that there is a complex relationship between treatment change on such measures and outcome (see Beggs [2012] in the 'Further reading' section for more information about this issue).

A difficulty with this method is that a researcher has to determine which constructs to measure, and also, given the wide variety of possible constructs, which to ignore. This issue becomes further confused by the range of measures that are available to measure the constructs that have previously been employed and whether these measures are appropriate for use within offending populations. The fact remains that determining effectiveness within an evaluation is not easy and that there is no perfect methodology that is available to researchers (as we would be using it already). Therefore, as a researcher, it is instead important to recognise the limitations of any approach that you adopt and to be fully informed of how the decisions that you make in terms of the type of data that you gather can impact on the conclusions that you can draw from the analysis.

Summary and final checklist

As we emphasise throughout this book, rigorous preplanning should identify any potential issues and, therefore, any subsequent impact can be minimised as much as possible. In considering the types of data that you want to use/collect in your study, the following checklist is important to bear in mind:

1   Remember to identify and operationalise the variables that you are going to use within your study. This is important whether your study is a qualitative or quantitative design. It is very useful to keep notes on the decisions that you make at this point and particularly how you are going to define your variables. This will keep you on track with your study and clear about the data that you need to collect.

2   Consider any potential confound variables or limitations regarding the way in which you operationalise your variables. In relation to confound variables, you need to consider how you are going to measure or reduce the impact of such variables. In relation to the limitations of how you define your variables, it is important to recognise that there may be no 'perfect' way to measure your DV, but recognising any potential limitations will be important when you come to drawing conclusions about your findings and potentially writing up your project.

3   Think about the level of data that is needed for the analysis that you want to carry out on your data. It may be useful to read this chapter in conjunction with Chapter 12 on data analysis to ensure that you fully understand how the type of data you collect impacts on the type of analysis that you can carry out on your data.

Further reading

Clinical change

Bowen, E. (2012). Within-treatment change: Identifying the individual in group change. In E. Bowen & S. Brown (Eds). *Perspectives on evaluating criminal justice and corrections* (Advances in Evaluation Series). Emerald.

Treatment change

Beggs, S.M. (2010). Within-treatment outcome among sexual offenders: A review. *Aggression and Violent Behavior, 15*, 369–379. doi:10.1016/j.avb.2010.06.005

Recidivism/outcome measure

Friendship, C., Beech, A.R., & Browne, K.D. (2002). Reconviction as an outcome measure in research: A methodological note. *British Journal of Criminology, 42*, 442–444. doi:10.1093/bjc/42.2.442

Friendship, C., & Thornton, D. (2001). Sexual reconviction for sexual offenders discharged from prison in England and Wales. Implications for evaluating treatment. *British Journal of Criminology, 41*, 285–292. doi:10.1093/bjc/41.2.285

Friendship, C., Thornton, D., Erikson, M., & Beech, A. (2001). Reconviction: A critique and comparison of two main data sources in England and Wales. *Legal and Criminological Psychology, 6*, 121–129. doi:10.1348/135532501168235

Theories of experiments/science

Fife-Shaw, C. (2012). Introduction to quantitative research. In G. M. Breakwell, J. A. Smith, & D. B. Wright (Eds.), *Research methods in psychology* (4th ed., pp. 17–38). London, England: Sage.

Robson, C. (2011). *Real world research* (3rd ed.). Chichester, England: Wiley. (Chapter 2)

Theories of qualitative methods

Braun, V., & Clark, V. (2013). *Successful qualitative research: A practical guide for beginners*. London, England: Sage. (Chapter 1 and 2)

Willig, C. (2013). *Introducing qualitative research in psychology*. Maidenhead, Berkshire: McGraw-Hill Education. (Chapter 2)

References

Brown, S. (2010). *Treating sex offenders: An introduction to sex offender treatment programmes*. Cullompton, England: Willan.

Field, A. (2013). *Discovering statistics using IBM SPSS statistics* (4th ed.). London, England: Sage.

Fife-Shaw, C. (2012). Questionnaire design. In G. M. Breakwell, J. A. Smith, & D. B. Wright (Eds.), *Research methods in psychology* (4th ed., pp. 113–139). London, England: Sage.

Friendship, C., Beech, A. R., & Browne, K. D. (2002). Reconviction as an outcome measure in research: A methodological note. *British Journal of Criminology, 42,* 442–444. doi:10.1093/bjc/42.2.442

Marshall, W. L. (1992). The social value of treatment for sexual offenders. *The Canadian Journal of Human Sexuality, 1,* 109–114.

Ministry of Justice. (2013). An overview of sexual offending in England and Wales. Retrieved from http://www.justice.gov.uk/statistics/criminal-justice/sexual-offending-statistics

Zonana, H. (1997). The civil commitment of sex offenders. *Science, 278,* 1248–1249. doi:10.1126/science.278.5341.1248

Chapter 5

From research question
to research design

In this chapter, we will be reviewing the learning from the previous chapters. The purpose of this is to introduce you to the case studies that we are going to be using for the rest of the book to give you practical examples of how you can move from a general research idea to a fully developed project. We will be developing five potential ideas into research designs, detailing the range of methodologies that could be employed for each case study, and selecting an approach that would be appropriate. This will also hopefully remind you that there are a significant number of decisions that you need to make before you start contacting participants or gathering data. As we have emphasised throughout, any time that is spent at this point of the research project will be worthwhile in designing out potential issues and considering the challenges ahead. Please still keep in mind that research can take many variations, so the design that we select is not the only design that would be appropriate; these examples are included in the book to give you some ideas of the processes involved, not to recommend a specific approach to particular research questions. Once you have read this chapter, you should be able to:

- assess the suitability of a range of methodologies for specific research questions;
- determine the types of data that can be gathered to address research questions;
- identify key issues to consider when designing your own research project; and
- apply this knowledge to your own research question.

Case study one

There has recently been a lot of media attention given to the issue of intimate partner violence (IPV), particularly in relation to service providers who deal with victims of this type of crime. A local service provider with 200 employees has contacted you because they want to be sure that they are providing the best service response that they can to victims of IPV. The service provider is not clear about what aspects of service they want you to evaluate, but they have specified that they want to know how their employees respond to victims of IPV. The service provider is willing to be guided by you about the specific factors to examine; they do not routinely gather any service user satisfaction data, nor do they systematically identify a wide range of victim characteristics within their records. Furthermore, due to the sensitive nature of the service and the potential for harm, the service provider does not want you to contact current service users (victims) or previous or future victims that have used or will use the service. Finally, although the service provider understands that you may need access to its employees, they do not want to commit the time or resources required for lengthy data collection procedures because the organisation has limited resources and is overstretched.

Following the initial discussion with the service provider, you conduct a literature search which reveals that victim sexuality is a factor that has been shown to impact on the responses given by service providers to IPV victims. The approach that most researchers have taken has been qualitative (e.g., Simpson & Helfrich, 2007); however, in this instance this may not be an option because the service provider does not want to commit time and/or resources to lengthy data collection procedures. There are a small number of experimental studies in which victim sexuality has been examined using a vignette design (e.g., Basow & Thompson, 2012), and you decide that this would be an appropriate approach to adopt in your study. From the literature search, you also determine that the type of abuse (e.g., physical or nonphysical abuse) also has an impact on responses to IPV victims, with physical abuse responded to more seriously than nonphysical abuse. This is despite research demonstrating that the impact of nonphysical abuse can be just as severe as physical abuse (Mechanic, Weaver, & Resick, 2008).

You continue to search the literature to examine what other variables have been used in previous studies. One key point to remember here is that you should not attempt to integrate all the variables that have been investigated previously. There are a range of other factors that you could explore, including victim and/or perpetrator gender and ethnicity. Deciding on what factors to examine can be challenging, as there is often a wish to examine everything; however, overcomplicated designs place undue pressure on the study (e.g., due to larger sample sizes being required and/or difficulties in interpreting findings when there are many variables). Given the constraints (size of the organisation, limited resources/time for data collection, predominantly female IPV victims), you decide to focus only upon the two previously identified factors of victim sexuality and type of abuse suffered.

Designing a research question

In designing an appropriate research question from the information that the service provider has identified, it is clear that the focus of this research will need to be on the service provider's employees, as the emphasis has been placed on the response that they provide to IPV victims. Furthermore, as you have learned from the search of the literature, two victim-related factors are particularly important: victim sexuality and the type of abuse (or a combination of these two factors). You also understand that much of the research in this area is based upon attribution theory (Heider, 1958). This leads you to design a research question phrased as follows: What is the impact of victim sexuality and type of abuse (physical or nonphysical) on service providers' responses to IPV victims?

Choosing a research design

First, you could consider whether you want to use a qualitative design. A qualitative approach may be useful in this regard because it will enable you to gather detailed rich information from the employees. However, the service provider does not want to commit time and resources to lengthy data collection procedures, and you think that this will mean interviews/focus groups will not be feasible. You therefore need to identify a data collection method that requires minimal time from each participant. Because you need to examine the impact of two victim-related factors on employees' responses, a general attitudes questionnaire is difficult to design that will assess this effectively (you could ask participants to complete the same questions for a number of different types of victims, but this will involve large numbers of similar questions, which will take time to complete and could induce fatigue/practice effects) and it will not enable you to understand how the service providers' responses may vary. Therefore, you consider that a vignette design would be appropriate.

As you will remember from Chapter 3, a vignette-based study involves the use of a short description or scenario, after which participants are asked to respond to some questions regarding the scenario. The research question fits this experimental design nicely, as there are two variables that will be your IVs (victim sexuality and type of abuse). You now need to consider whether you are going to use a between- or within-groups design. This is where you can be guided by the previously published literature in this area. Although within-groups designs (where participants respond to all the vignettes) are used within forensic psychology for vignette-based studies, it is far more common for a between-groups design to be used (where participants read one of a number of possible vignettes and the responses of participants reading the same vignettes are compared).

Types of data and research materials

As this is a study with two independent variables with each variable having two levels (i.e., 1: physical; 2: nonphysical), this leads you to a 2 (victim sexuality) × 2 (type of abuse) experimental vignette design. This means that you have four conditions to your design and therefore will need to develop four scenarios: (1) a female heterosexual victim who suffers physical abuse, (2) a female lesbian victim who suffers physical abuse, (3) a female heterosexual victim who suffers emotional abuse and (4) a female lesbian victim who suffers emotional abuse. This will enable you to compare the responses to heterosexual and lesbian victims, as well as responses to victims of physical and emotional abuse. A strength of this design means that you will also be able to examine the impact of any interaction between these two variables.

Now you need to find and gain permission to use a previously used vignette, or write your own. The former can be a simpler option in that the vignette should have been tested for reliability, or you can determine from the studies in which the vignette was used whether there are any problems (e.g., floor or ceiling effects), which in theory should be less likely because the study has been published. However, caution still needs to be used here before accepting the quality of a vignette, and you must examine it and the study carefully to determine if it will be suitable. Check the language in the vignette, as a vignette used in one country/culture may not be suitable in a different country/culture; if you change the wording of a vignette, then you will need to pilot it.

Research advice

Should you identify a vignette that would be suitable, it is considered appropriate and polite to ask the authors who developed the vignette for permission to use it in your study. (Journal articles normally contain the email address of one author. It is worth checking online to determine whether the author is still at the institution listed on the article; if the author has moved institutions, you should be able to find the new institution/contact details via the web.) Most authors are very supportive of this process and will be very willing to grant you permission to use the materials. If you need to make any adaptations to the vignette, you should also highlight these for the author, and you should outline the study so the author is fully aware of how the vignette will be used. It is also polite to send a copy of your report or a summary of your findings when you have completed the study.

You may not be able to find a suitable vignette to use. This does not mean that you should entirely disregard the previously published vignettes. Instead, you should use the information provided within the materials sections of journal articles to give you guidance as to how you should develop your own vignette. Also, think about parallel areas of research. In the case of perception of victims, there is a substantial literature regarding rape victim blaming from which you may be able to adapt materials. It is a good idea to discuss the vignette with the service provider, who should be able to give you a typical scenario that you can try to encapsulate in the vignette. Also, if you find a vignette from the literature, it would also be a good idea to check this with the service provider to ensure that it is appropriate. You should then write a vignette and pilot the vignette with participants who are similar to the participants you intend to use for the study, to ensure that there are no problems (see Chapter 11 on collecting data for how to carry out this process).

You also need to decide how you will measure responses to the vignettes. Given that the service provider has only provided general guidance in this area, it is up to you to identify the types of DVs and data that you want to gather. Again, your literature search can guide you in this area, and you may be able to use similar DVs/questions found in previous studies. Responses that you may want to gather include: blaming attitudes, attributions of responsibility, perceived severity of the abuse, and perceived trauma suffered by the victim. This is not an exhaustive list, but it should give you an idea of the possibilities that are available. Remember that this research is being requested by the service provider, so you should discuss the use of any potential questions with them so that you can assist them in making decisions to gather responses that are most relevant to the service that they provide.

Make sure that you operationalise your variables carefully and consider the level of measurement of the data you will collect – you could ask questions that will produce nominal/categorical, ordinal, or interval level data. The latter provides more options for data analysis, although there are ways in which you can combine data types (e.g., in mock juror studies, participants can be asked whether the person in the vignette is guilty or not guilty and then to indicate their level of confidence in this assessment; these two questions are then combined to produce a 'score' which is then analysed). There are a range of ways in which the DVs can be formulated; the key issue here is to think these through carefully, so that you are clear what data will be produced, how you will use them and what analyses you will conduct.

Case study two

You are interested in the sentencing of offenders, particularly regarding the different ways in which community and prison sentences are used within the court system. You are also interested in the theoretical perspectives relating to the purposes of sentencing; however, you are not sure what you want to examine in this area. You know that there is a theoretical underpinning of the purposes of sentencing and that there are generally considered to be five: retribution, incapacitation, deterrence, rehabilitation and restoration (McGuire, 2008).

Searching the literature

At the moment this idea is very broad, so you need to narrow down your area of interest. You carry out literature searches and identify that there is a significant body of literature in which the impact that contact with the criminal justice system has on the well-being of a victim of crime is considered. For example, Kaukinen and DeMaris (2009) found that reporting assaults to the police seemed to exacerbate the impact of sexual assault on victims, increasing the levels of depression they reported. Other studies have focussed on involvement with court trial processes and the impact of procedures such as giving evidence (Smith & Skinner, 2012). However, you are interested in examining the theories of sentencing, so you combine your interest in this aspect of sentencing with the current research that has examined the impact of contact with the criminal justice system on the well-being of victims.

Designing a research question

At this point you have identified an area in which you wish to research, but you need to develop this idea into a research question. The first thing that you need to consider is that you have focussed upon victim well-being, but what do you mean by this? Do you want to examine physical well-being or psychological well-being? Given that this is likely to be a project that is based in forensic psychology, it would be most appropriate for you to decide to focus upon psychological well-being, but it may be worthwhile to consider whether you want to include an aspect of physical well-being as well. As always, searching the literature will be useful to identify how you can develop and add to the current knowledge base.

From your examination of the purposes of sentencing, you know that there are five theoretical aspects of sentencing that you could examine; however, you need to consider how you are going to assess sentencing outcomes and how these connect with the purposes of sentencing. Following your review, you decide to focus upon three sentences: community sentences, prison sentences and acquittal. In fitting this with the purposes of sentencing, you use the current literature to argue that community sentences overlap with the sentencing purposes of both restoration and retribution, whereas prison sentences fits in with retributive and incapacitation purposes. Acquittal does not relate to sentencing, but you think it is important to include it because it relates to a potential for a lack of perceived justice by the victim of a crime. This process has led you to design the following research question: What is the impact on the psychological well-being of victims of crime where the perpetrators are sentenced to either prison or a community sentence, or are acquitted?

Choosing a research design

You now know that you want to examine three different sentencing outcomes – community sentences, prison sentences and acquittal – on psychological well-being of victims. However, you also know that you want the research to be victim focussed in that the research question relates to victim well-being. This research question could direct you down two particular designs:

(1) a qualitative design in which you explore victim well-being to examine the differing impacts of sentencing outcomes, or (2) a quantitative design in which you test certain hypotheses related to sentencing and victim well-being. However, it is worthwhile to consider using designs that have the least impact upon the sample of victims. Using a qualitative design will require victims to relive certain aspects of their victimisation, and you need to consider whether this is appropriate when a quantitative design may answer your research question more simply and easily and with potentially less impact on the victim. Furthermore, if you decide that you want to be able to test how these three sentencing outcomes may predict victim well-being, this will further lead you towards choosing a quantitative design. A quantitative design will enable you to test a predictive model, which implies a cross-sectional regression type design, where you test how the sentencing outcomes link to psychological well-being across three groups of victims (i.e., a group of victims where the perpetrators were imprisoned, a group where the perpetrators received community sentences, and a group where the perpetrators were acquitted).

Types of data and research materials

You now need to consider what data you are going to collect. For this research question, you may be able to find a dataset in which a large number of victims have been assessed, in which case you could design your study using a preexisting dataset. Assuming that there is no appropriate dataset for you to use, you will need to consider how you are going to measure victim well-being and how you are going to collect your data. Again, searching the literature will help here. Note that there will be a range of studies in which well-being has been assessed, many of which will not have a forensic focus; these can be as useful as forensic studies in determining the measures that would be most appropriate. In examining the literature, you need to identify the range of measures that have been used. When contemplating these, you should consider aspects such as reliability and validity; suitability for the proposed population; and practicality of the measure (e.g., if a scale is very long, then it is unlikely to be feasible in some research projects). All of these issues need to be carefully considered when choosing an appropriate scale to measure victim well-being. For example, Laxminarayan (2013) used a measure of secondary victimisation to assess well-being following involvement with the criminal justice system that was originally developed by Orth (2002). There are benefits to using a scale like this because it is only five items, and it will therefore have less of an impact on the victims completing the scale. Other studies have focussed on much more general aspects of psychological well-being. For example, Green and Diaz (2008) assessed the impact of crime victimisation using the Impact of Events Scale (Zilberg, Weiss, & Horowitz, 1982) as an operationalisation of posttraumatic stress following crime victimization. You can consider using measures such as these as there are numerous scales that will enable you to measure well-being

86 Designing and planning

via depressive symptomology, posttraumatic symptomology, or suicide ideation. What you want to measure will depend upon how you have operationalised your DV of psychological well-being. Because you want to focus on well-being rather than other clinical symptoms, you choose to use the Mental, Physical and Spiritual Well-Being Scale (Vella-Brodrick & Allen, 1995). This is a thirty-item scale, but this will provide you with three aspects of overall well-being (i.e., mental, physical and spiritual subscales). This provides you with a much more detailed view of well-being than other scales would have provided.

Case study three

In this particular study, you are working as a programme facilitator on an intervention that has been delivered to a large number of offenders. The intervention is based upon a theoretical model of change that interests you. However, you want to be sure that the programme is having an impact on the offenders that are completing it; otherwise, this leads to questions as to why time and resources are being spent on this intervention. You want to understand what differs between offenders who complete the programmes and those who do not. The programme has not been evaluated previously.

Searching the literature

Remember that searching the literature is an important starting point for identifying a rationale for carrying out the study. Since this programme has not been evaluated before, you are unlikely to find literature that specifically relates to this programme; however, studies in which similar programmes have been evaluated will be useful, as will the general evaluation literature to identify methodologies and designs that have been used previously. The literature review highlights some issues that you need to consider, such as how to match offenders in a matched-pairs design and compare programme completers with other comparison groups (e.g., Palmer, Hatcher, McGuire, Bilby, Ayres, & Hollin, 2011). Furthermore, it reveals that one of the most commonly used outcome measures in programme effectiveness studies is reconviction data collected after a follow-up period subsequent to the completion of the programme. You use this information to design your evaluation study.

Designing a research question

In designing a research question, you know that you want to examine 'effectiveness' in relation to the intervention. This leads you to construct a research question that would be phrased something like: Do offenders who complete the intervention programme demonstrate treatment change, or have better post-treatment outcome, than a comparison group? This is quite a vague research question, and you will need to update it when you think about your design and determine the comparison group.

Choosing a research design

As with all research questions, there are many ways in which you could address this question. You consider a qualitative approach, such as conducting interviews or focus groups with treated offenders to gain insight into what elements of the programme they think are effective. In this instance, however, you do not have an opportunity to speak to the offenders, but you do have access to data that has been collected by the treatment providers; therefore, a quantitative approach is more appropriate. Since the programme has been completed and you are not able to allocate offenders to treatment or not, a quasi-experimental design is also selected.

Types of data and research materials

First you should consider your IV. This might seem obvious (i.e., those who completed the treatment versus those who did not); however, there are a number of other groups and ways in which this can be operationalised that you need to consider. Is it the case, for example, that the offenders who 'completed' the programme attended each and every session? Do you want to compare those who attended all sessions with those who missed some? How many sessions can people miss and still be deemed to have completed the programme? These are issues that you will need to think carefully about (unfortunately these issues are rarely clearly defined in evaluation study reports), and you must consider how you will deal with the issue of drop-outs (see the following 'Common difficulties' box and the 'Further reading' section).

Common difficulties

It is very common that some participants will drop out of treatment or an intervention. There are a range of reasons for this that will vary depending on the context and type of intervention. Drop-out rates can be quite high; for example, Hall (1995), in his meta-analysis, observed that one-third of offenders dropped out of sex offender treatment in the programmes for which this information was reported. In some instances individuals are excluded from an intervention; commonly such individuals are categorised as drop-outs and rarely are these individuals categorised separately or given a range of titles (excluded/failed etc.). It is rare for drop-outs to be included in evaluation studies and reports, despite the fact that non-completion of a programme/intervention should be identified as a difficulty and might suggest that steps are needed to increase the engagement and/or motivation of individuals who start the intervention. Some argue that to evaluate a programme you should consider only those that complete the intervention (as it is the intervention that is being assessed and you can only do this by examining those that complete it); however, others argue that this inflates programme effectiveness. Furthermore, drop-outs generally have higher rates of recidivism than those who do not take part in treatment, though this is probably due to characteristics that make them (a) more likely to drop-out and (b) more likely to reoffend, and a programme with high drop-out rates could be argued to be problematic. Excluding drop-outs from the treated group, when it is not possible to exclude offenders with similar characteristics from the nontreatment group, biases the study in favour of treatment and violates the principles of RCTs. A practical difficulty is that once someone has dropped out of a programme (or has been excluded), it is difficult to obtain 'posttreatment' measures for that person; this is likely to be a more significant problem for a design reliant on pre-/posttesting than one reliant on official rates of recidivism (offences/arrests etc.). Where possible (e.g., when recidivism is used as an outcome variable), it has become more common for researchers to include a drop-out group as well as a treatment and no treatment group; however, this does not take account of the fact the nontreatment group will not have been adjusted for the people who would have been likely to drop out of treatment had they started it. These types of adjustments can be made using propensity scoring (see the 'Further reading' section) if data on a wide range of variables are available for reasonably large samples of offenders and you are able to perform propensity score analyses.

Now you need to determine your DVs, which can take a number of forms. You could be interested in whether the programme is effective in stopping reoffending (i.e., gather binary-level data: reoffended or did not reoffend) after a certain time period following completion of the intervention. If you do not want to use a specified follow-up period, you could measure variables such as length of time until the offender committed another crime. However, you may want to think carefully about using measures like this because there may be confounding factors that could impact on this length of time, which means it may not be a reliable measure. You could also gather data at the nominal level about the type of offence for which the recidivists were convicted (e.g., sexual offences, nonsexual violent offence, or nonviolent offence). Finally, the data could be at the ratio level in that you count the number of offences for which the offender has been reconvicted. This would be ratio-level data because the variable has a true 0 (in that the offender may not have been reconvicted) and the numbers represent true numerical values.

These types of data collection focus on data that you could gather after the completion of the programme. However, you may decide that to evaluate the programme, you want to gather data at two time points: before programme completion and after programme completion. In this case, the types of data that you could gather begin to broaden out depending upon what you want to learn from the participants. For example, if you wanted to examine attitude change, you could administer an attitude questionnaire or scale before and then after completion of the study. This would give you ordinal-level data (which could be analysed as interval data). You could also carry out risk assessments (provided they were not based on static variables) before and after completion of the study, which could also be used as measures of change following completion of the programme. You could also use a measure of well-being or a measure of some aspect of psychological functioning (e.g., problem solving skills) that the intervention was targeting for change. The choice of DV should be focussed on the model of change of the intervention; for example, if one aspect of the programme is to change cognitions around offending, then measuring cognitions pre- and posttreatment would be appropriate. As ever, the choice of appropriate measures should be guided by the literature. Try to always choose well-validated and reliable measures.

Case study four

In this particular case study you are interested in how jurors evaluate evidence, but there is a large body of literature already available about how jurors perceive different types of evidence. You want to make a novel contribution to the literature in this area. Rather than just being interested in general attitudes about a particular type of evidence, you are interested in understanding how jurors use the information presented in their decision making about the case, particularly their deliberations, as well as the impact on the eventual verdict. Examining these types of issues will ensure that your findings will have practical implications in relation to juror decision making.

Searching the literature

Remember that the aim is always to be as innovative and as novel as possible in your research project. The literature regarding juror decision making when presented with different types of evidence is very broad. For example, the literature regarding how jurors perceive eyewitness testimony (and variations of this) is particularly well developed. Therefore, you search the literature to examine what types of evidence have been less focussed upon within the literature. This leads you to identify that there has been some debate about jurors' understanding of DNA evidence due to the complexities of some of the scientific and probability issues involved in the presentation of this evidence. This leads you to question how jurors perceive this type of evidence and use it in their deliberations about a case.

You note that most studies investigating mock jurors use a vignette design and focus on the decisions made about the case (e.g., guilty or not guilty), which does not provide any details of jurors perceptions of the information or how they use it in decision making. Therefore, you consider that a more innovative approach, using a qualitative methodology, would be more informative. You are also able to determine that students are frequently used as participants within mock juror studies, but you want your study to be more comparable to real jurors by using a sample from the general population. In addition, since you want to know how juries (rather than individual jurors) use the information, you will need to research groups of individuals.

Designing a research question

It is clear that you want to examine how DNA evidence may be perceived by jurors. In designing a research question, you know that you want to examine how jurors use the information in their decision making as well as the impact this has on the verdicts. This leads you to construct a research question that would be phrased something like: How do mock jurors use DNA evidence in their decision making, and how does this impact the verdict?

Choosing a research design

The research area of juror decision making predominantly uses quantitative methods, usually those with a vignette-type design. However, you can find no published studies that have examined juror deliberations in relation to DNA evidence. Since you are interested in how DNA evidence is used in the decision-making process, not just the final determination of guilt or innocence, you decide that a qualitative approach is most appropriate. With your own project, always remember that you will need to consider the underpinning epistemology that will guide how you frame your own research. For this particular project, it is appropriate to adopt a critical realist approach as this is suitable to the research question, in which jurors' understanding of DNA evidence is seen as a construction based on their own perspectives and standpoints (e.g., see Maxwell, 2012).

Types of data and research materials

Within the qualitative study, you wish to explore how jurors perceive DNA evidence within a court trial. In this type of study, the type of data that you could gather could be quite varied. For example, you could interview individual participants as mock jurors after presenting them with case materials to examine how the individuals perceived the evidence. Another way that you can gather data is to ask the participants to attend a focus group to discuss as a group how the DNA evidence is perceived. Finally, if you wanted to add more ecological validity to your study, you could ask the mock jurors to engage in a mock jury deliberation. As highlighted previously, you are interested in the decision-making process, so you decide that a design that includes a group deliberation will be the most appropriate for your research question. This means that you would present case materials to a mock jury and then ask them to deliberate as to whether they consider the defendant to be guilty or not guilty. It is this process that will be of the most interest to you in qualitatively analysing the main themes that guide their decision making.

Case study five

In this case study there is an intervention that is being run by a local service provider. You want to know whether this intervention will have the desired effect on the small groups of participants who are about to start attending the intervention. The programme has only just been started, so no previous evaluations have been carried out. The challenge with this particular project is that you know that only a very small number of participants have been chosen to complete the programme, which means that the larger-scale evaluation method that was used in case study three is not appropriate. The intervention is an anger management training programme that is run in the community, and individuals can self-refer if they identify as having a problem with using violence.

Searching the literature

As ever, you need to start by searching the literature. In this case, you will need to identify methods that have been used to evaluate programmes that have only very small samples. In this instance, you will need to search different types of literature (i.e., literature relevant to anger management, literature relevant to measures that would be relevant to assess the programme, literature relevant to the most appropriate design to use).

In relation to the design, you identify that small samples often lead people to consider qualitative methods in exploring effectiveness with participants; however, you are concerned whether this approach will enable you to measure the impact of the programme on the participants. Your search also reveals that you could examine this quantitatively, using the ABA approach to assess the effectiveness of the intervention. This means that you would need to gather data from your individuals prior to treatment, during treatment and after treatment. As you will know from reading case study three, one of the most common methods of assessing programme effectiveness is to use is reconviction data; however, other approaches use changes in psychometric measures as a proxy for effectiveness. You use this information to design your evaluation study.

92 Designing and planning

Designing a research question

In designing a research question, you know that 'effectiveness' is what you want to establish in relation to the anger management programme. This leads you to construct a research question that would be phrased something like: Do participants who completed an anger management programme demonstrate change over the course of treatment? This broad research question allows you to develop your ideas from this point to examine exactly what you mean by 'effectiveness' and what specific changes you expect to see in the individuals who complete the programme.

Choosing a research design

Your search of the literature has demonstrated that you could approach this question using qualitative methods; however, you want to establish whether there is actually an impact of the programme in terms of effectiveness, not just participants' perceptions/experiences of what they consider to be effective. You could use a comparison group approach here, but the small sample size means that a within-group design is much more appropriate. Also, you are able to gather data prior to the programme beginning, so this guides you to choose to use a small sample methodology such as the ABA approach.

Types of data and research materials

Remember that it is important to operationalise your variables. You first need to establish how you want to operationalise 'effectiveness'. Your reading of the previous literature has led you to consider using reconviction data as a DV, but the service provider would like to know quickly whether the programme is having an impact so that they can make appropriate changes if needed; it is a new approach and they believe that some modification might be required. This means that examining reconviction data is not suitable and that a within-treatment approach is most appropriate, using psychometric measures. Because the programme is focussed on addressing/managing anger issues, your literature search should have led you to consider exactly how you are going to measure anger reduction. You could do this in a number of ways, such as self-reported level of anger incidents, or you could use a scale that assesses levels of anger. For example, Burns, Bird, Leach and Higgins (2003) used the Novaco Anger Scale (Novaco, 1991) and also the Spielberger State-Trait Anger Expression Inventory (Spielberger, 1991). The scale that you decide to use should always be guided by your reading of the literature, and remember that you should always try to identify those scales that are the most rigorous and psychometrically sound. As you have chosen an ABA type design for your study, this leads you to assessing change at three time points across the programme: before,

From research question to research design   93

at the mid-point and upon completion of the programme. Remember that you will need to be very clear on how you are going to analyse this data; many of the more usual statistical tests require far larger sample sizes than will be used within this study, so you need to particularly research the analysis methods that are appropriate for small sample studies.

Activity

Having read this and the previous chapters of this book and completed all the activities up to this point, you should now be in a position to design your own study. Use the checklist below to design and outline your study, and discuss this with your supervisor and/or a colleague to ensure that your design is appropriate (e.g., ensure that the study will actually answer the research question that you wish to address, that you have operationalised your variables and that your methods for collecting text-based data are appropriate, and consider how you will analyse the data that you will produce). In the next chapter, practicality and feasibility issues will be considered, which might mean you need to revise some of the decisions at this stage, but it is helpful to have a plan of what you would ideally like to do at this stage so you can consider the feasibility/practicality issues that are most relevant to your study.

Summary and final checklist

In this chapter, we have summarised the initial design phases of conducting a research study, from developing the original idea, to refining this via a literature search into a research question, through to operationalising variables and methods of collecting text-based data. In the next phase of designing your project, a number of practicality and feasibility issues need to be considered; however, before continuing to the next stage, you should be able to identify each of the following for your study:

1   Your research topic area, focus and aim.
2   Your research question(s) (following a search of the literature on the evidence-base in relation to this topic/area).
3   A design that is appropriate for your research question/situation/context (following a search of the literature on the evidence base in relation to this topic/area, and reading in relation to methodological designs, and, where appropriate, reading in relation to measures/scales/vignettes used in previous studies).
4   Based on the previous items and the literature review your variables:

Designing and planning

- IV(s) and DV(s) for experimental and quasi-experimental studies, or
- criterion and predictor variables for cross-sectional and longitudinal studies, or
- the data collection approach, guided by ontological and epistemological considerations for qualitative studies.

Further reading

Brown, S.J. (2012). Propensity score analysis. In E. Bowen & S.J. Brown (Eds.), *Perspectives on evaluating criminal justice and corrections*. (Advances in Evaluation Science Series.) Bingley, England: Emerald.

McConaghy, N. (1999). Methodological issues concerning evaluation of treatment for sexual offenders: Randomization, treatment dropouts, untreated controls, and within-treatment studies. *Sexual Abuse: A Journal of Research and Treatment, 11*, 183–193. doi:10.1177/107906329901100302

References

Basow, S.A., & Thompson, J. (2012). Service providers' reactions to intimate partner violence as a function of victim sexual orientation and type of abuse. *Journal of Interpersonal Violence, 27*, 1225–1241. doi:10.1177/0886260511425241

Burns, M., Bird, D., Leach, C., & Higgins, K. (2003). Anger management training: the effects of a structured programme on the self-reported anger experience of forensic inpatients with learning disability. *Journal of Psychiatric and Mental Health Nursing, 10*, 569–577. doi:10.1046/j.1365–2850.2003.00653.x

Green, D.L., & Diaz, N. (2008). Gender differences in coping with victimization. *Brief Treatment and Crisis Intervention, 8*, 195–203. doi:10.1093/brief-treatment/mhn004

Hall, G.C.N. (1995). Sexual offender recidivism revisited: A meta-analysis of recent treatment studies. *Journal of Consulting and Clinical Psychology, 63* (5), 802–809. doi:10.1037/0022-006X.63.5.802

Heider, F. (1958). *The psychology of interpersonal relations*. New York: Wiley.

Kaukinen, C., & DeMaris, A. (2009). Sexual assault and current mental health: The role of help-seeking and police response. *Violence Against Women, 15*, 1331–1357. doi:10.1177/1077801209346713

Laxminarayan, M. (2013). The effect of retributive and restorative sentencing on psychological effects of criminal proceedings. *Journal of Interpersonal Violence, 28*, 938–955. doi:10.1177/0886260512459385

Maxwell, J.A. (2012). *A realist approach for qualitative research*. London, England: Sage

McGuire, J. (2008). What's the point of sentencing? In G. Davies, C. Hollin, & R. Bull (Eds.), *Forensic psychology* (pp. 265–292). Chichester, England: Wiley.

Mechanic, M.B., Weaver, T.L., & Resick, P.A. (2008). Risk factors for physical injury among help-seeking battered women: An exploration of multiple abuse dimensions. *Violence Against Women, 14*, 1148–1165. doi:10.1177/1077801208323792

Novaco, R.W. (1991). *The Novaco Anger Scale 9* (September 1991 version). Irvine: University of California.

Orth, U. (2002). Secondary victimization of crime victims by criminal proceedings. *Social Justice Research, 15*, 313–325. doi:10.1023/A:1021210323461

Palmer, E. J., Hatcher, R. M., McGuire, J., Bilby, C.A.L., Ayres, T. C., & Hollin, C. R. (2011). Evaluation of the Addressing Substance-Related Offending (ASRO) program for substance-using offenders in the community. *Substance Use and Misuse, 46*, 1072–1080. doi: 10.3109/10826084.2011.559682

Simpson, E.K., & Helfrich, C.A. (2007). Lesbian survivors of intimate partner violence: Provider perspectives on barriers to accessing services. *Journal of Gay & Lesbian Social Services: Issues in Practice, Policy & Research, 18*, 39–59. doi:10.1300/J041v18n02_03

Smith, O., & Skinner, T. (2012). Observing court responses to victims of rape and sexual assault. *Feminist Criminology, 7*, 298–326. doi:10.1177/1557085112437875

Spielberger, C. D. (1991). *Manual for the State-Trait Anger Expression Inventor: Revised research edition*. Odessa, FL: Psychological Assessment Resources.

Vella-Brodrick, D.A., & Allen, F.C. (1995). Development of psychometric validation of the Mental, Physical, Spiritual Well-Being Scale. *Psychological Reports, 77*, 659–674. doi:10.2466/pr0.1995.77.2.65

Zilberg, N.J., Weiss, D.S., & Horowitz, M.J. (1982). Impact of event scale: A cross-validation study and some empirical evidence supporting a conceptual model of stress response syndrome. *Journal of Consulting and Clinical Psychology, 50*, 407–414. doi:10.1037/0022-006X.50.3.407

Chapter 6

Practicality and feasibility issues in research

In this chapter, we will outline some of the key practicality and feasibility issues that you need to consider before starting your research. We have already touched on some of these issues in previous chapters. For example, in case study one, the limited resources that the service provider is willing to commit to the study and the lack of data held by the organisation are practicality/feasibility issues that have an impact on the potential research project. In the 'Evaluation' section of Chapter 3, we discussed a range of issues that determine the type of design that can be used to assess an intervention. Such issues are present in all research studies. In forensic psychology, Davies, Sheldon, and Howells (2011) identified a range of difficulties that researchers can face, whereby issues can be at either the meta level (e.g., security restricts access to participants) or at the local level (e.g., study findings may challenge an intervention being delivered). All researchers need to be aware of potential issues and build in contingency plans to deal with these. It is important to understand that it is still likely that something may go wrong or not as you had planned during your study, and you should reflect on how you will deal with such situations prior to the start of the study.

Feasibility is something that can be easily overlooked by inexperienced researchers, but some of the issues outlined herein, if not considered carefully, can cause substantial delays to research or even stop it from being completed. Obviously this is not something that you want to occur in your own research; therefore, please use this chapter to ensure that, in addition to the learning that you have completed from the previous chapters, you now also consider practicality and feasibility issues. This builds on Chapter 5, in which problem solving was used in relation to specific case studies. Once you have read this chapter, you should be able to:

- identify a range of feasibility and practicality issues that can impact on your study;
- understand the importance of access to participants;
- understand the importance of determining an appropriate sample size;
- reflect upon the length of time that research can take to complete; and
- build contingency plans into your research.

Practicality and feasibility issues

When you develop an idea for a research study, your thinking can be based around answering a particular question or developing an understanding about a particular issue. For example, in case study two, the aim is to understand the impact of different types of sentencing on victims, and in case study four, the aim is to understand how jurors perceive and use DNA testimony in trial deliberations. As we outlined in Chapter 5, your proposal can be developed using your thinking and the literature to develop a research question. In this sort of study, it is possible to design an 'ideal' study to address your research question, with little consideration at this stage to practicality and feasibility issues. So once you have developed the initial idea, you need to construct the design by considering exactly who you would like the participants to be and how you will conduct the study, which will be grounded in feasibility and practicality constraints. In other circumstances (e.g., as in case studies one, three and five), the idea for the study may develop from particular circumstances or opportunities in which the practicality/feasibility issues are more likely to be apparent from the start and might be constrained by the organisations and circumstances with which you are working. For example, if individuals have already been assigned to receiving an intervention, this is a practicality issue that is going to impact on your design. In case study five, only a very small number of people complete the intervention, which has already influenced our thinking about this project.

In reality, feasibility and practicality issues are enmeshed in designing a project, and it is unlikely that you would design something without any consideration to these issues. Because there are a number of issues that inexperienced researchers often overlook, we will discuss some of the most common issues in order to illustrate the need to carefully think things through in your design stage. Every study will have a unique combination of constraints, and although we will provide some examples here, you will need to identify those that will influence your study. Remember to do this within the design phase of your study.

Activity

Read through the case studies outlined in Chapter 5 and list the feasibility and practicality issues that were included in each example.

Time

Perhaps because it is so obvious, this is one of the constraints that is most frequently overlooked or not fully considered. Most projects have a time limit; for example, if you are completing research as part of an academic course, there is a

98 Designing and planning

deadline when you must submit your research report or dissertation. Whilst this is an obvious deadline, inexperienced researchers often overestimate what can be one in the time available (e.g., they do not give enough time to the planning stage or they underestimate the amount of time that is needed to conduct interviews, transcribe and qualitatively analyse data).

The time that you have for your project therefore needs to be reflected in the design you select. Although you may wish to conduct follow-up data collections at six months and one year, for most students this is unlikely to be achievable unless you are using data that has already been collected. This needs to be balanced with the fact that designs that can be conducted within the time frame might be less methodologically rigorous. The best way to assess whether your project is feasible within the allotted amount of time is to discuss it with your supervisor, an experienced researcher and/or your line manager if your research is being conducted in your forensic workplace. You also need to carefully think through all aspects of your study; for example, if you are asking participants to complete and return a paper-based study or questionnaire, you need to factor in the time it takes to send out the questionnaire as well as the time for them to be returned, in addition to the time required to input the data into a statistics package and conduct the analyses. Similar issues are apparent in qualitative research, where it takes time to interview participants, transcribe recordings and analyse data. The simple point is that you need to consider how long your research will take to complete and plan accordingly (see Chapter 8). This book will give you a clearer overview of the stages involved in a research project and the issues to consider, which should enable you to develop a realistic timetable.

Activity

Determine the time that you will have available for your study in terms of (a) the length of time in terms of weeks/months and (b) the amount of time you can devote to your research throughout the duration of the project. List any periods when you will not be able to conduct research and other deadlines you will have. This information is important to use in designing your study and will also be required in the completion of your research proposal (see Chapter 8).

Access to participants and data

Although we have touched on some of the constraints around access to participants (e.g., in the 'Evaluation' section of Chapter 3 and in some of the discussions about the case studies in Chapter 5), we have focussed most upon developing a well-reasoned design for your study. A crucial factor in the successful completion of any study, however, is gaining access to appropriate participants and/or data. This is a particularly important issue in forensic psychology because many of the populations (e.g., offenders, police officers and victims/survivors) and data of interest (e.g., details of offences, reconviction rates) are difficult to access.

Many forensic psychology students have unrealistic hopes and expectations about conducting research with offender populations. The simple truth is that unless you work within an environment/organisation with offenders, or you have very well-placed contacts within such an organisation (or your supervisor/line manager does), you are very unlikely to be permitted access to a population of offenders. Even if you or your supervisor/line manager has such contacts, time constraints (particularly in relation to ethical approval, see Chapters 7 and 9) may mean that such a project is not feasible; however, there may be existing data sets that you can access, as discussed in Chapter 3. This means that research with offenders will not be possible for undergraduate students (and we would encourage such students to consider projects that do not require access to offender populations), and it can be very challenging for master's-level students (we would encourage such students to have a discussion with your supervisor to see whether access can be facilitated in any way).

Even if you work within contexts where you have access to offender populations or have excellent contacts, this still does not guarantee that you will be given access to the offenders (e.g., at the time of writing, undergraduate and master's students working in probation and/or the new Community Rehabilitation Companies are not permitted to conduct research studies in this context; see Chapter 9). Many organisations and secure environments are inundated with requests for research access/support, and such requests require time and staff resources. No matter how supportive an organisation is, it is simply not possible to support everyone's research study. Therefore, priority might be given to particular types of projects (e.g., in line with the challenges and research questions of the organisation) or individuals (e.g., doctoral students over undergraduate and master's students).

If you do have access to offender populations (perhaps your organisation is funding your studies and expects you to complete a study in your work environment), it is important that you follow the processes outlined in the earlier chapters in this book. Any research you do must be grounded in the literature, have a clear purpose and be well-designed. It is not appropriate to say that you are going to interview offenders simply because you have access to them. Why are you going to interview them? What research issues are you going to address? What is the research question? How does this build on previous research? Often the people who have the most difficulty designing a research study are those who have access to a particular group of people (offenders, victims/survivors, forensic staff) because their focus in on the group of people that they wish to include in the study as opposed to the research questions that they should address.

100 Designing and planning

Similar issues occur with other forensic psychology-related samples, such as police forces. The perceived importance of engagement with academic research varies considerably from police force to police force and also varies according to the police force priorities. So, for example, if that particular police force is focussing upon improving their response to domestic violence cases, a research proposal in relation to domestic violence (e.g., case study one) may be perceived very positively. A different police force, however, may not have this issue as a key priority at this time and therefore may not be interested in the research. Furthermore, the access that your project requires may also impact on its likelihood of being granted access. For example, in our experience, police forces can often be more amenable to sharing some types of crime data compared to providing access to police officers being interviewed. Please do not take this to mean that police forces happily hand out crime data, just that it can be easier to achieve this compared to other means of access that your project may require. Obviously this does not mean that you should tailor all of your research questions to use crime data. As we have discussed in previous chapters, the type of data that you require will always be guided by your research questions.

There are also issues that you should consider in relation to accessing participants. It might be that you have access to victims/survivors, for example, but you should consider the appropriateness of your research and ethics in terms of the potential harm and distress that taking part in your research might cause (see Chapter 7). You should also consider the potential impact of your results. For example, many students wish to assess staff attitudes to particular groups of offenders. First, this type of research is questionable on the grounds of how useful it is – if you find out that a group of staff hold positive attitudes to a group of offenders, what does that mean for the organisation or for developing our forensic psychology understanding? Second, as well as potentially seeing the limited gains from such research, organisations may be concerned about the potential impact of the results of your study – what if you find that the staff have negative attitudes to a group of offenders? It is important, therefore, that you consider fully why you wish to access particular groups of participants. Clearly your research or your course is a priority to you, but you should make efforts to ensure that your research has a purpose and that it is ethical to ask participants to take part in it (i.e., that your research has a theoretical, literature-based purpose and/or that the results will be useful to an organisation).

In accessing participants, even groups that consist of the general population can be challenging to access. For example, there are restrictions (both legal and ethical) that prevent researchers from accessing jury populations. Under English law, it is illegal to "obtain, disclose or solicit any particular of statements made, opinions expressed, arguments advanced or votes cast by members of a jury in the course of their deliberations" (Section 8 of the Contempt of Court Act, 1981). Similar laws are in place in the US, although on occasion researchers do gain access to jurors after the trial. Therefore, if you wish to understand juror decision making, you should reconcile with yourself that you will not be able

Practicality and feasibility issues in research   101

to access real jurors, though you could consider mock jury research (as in case study two).

When conducting research with the general population, it is important to consider the practicalities. We have had many conversations with students who say that they will ask members of the public to take part in their study, and we ask the students how they will contact each participant and where and when they will do so. It then becomes clear that students have not considered these issues. In theory, the general population is a readily accessible group of participants, but in reality, and from a practicality point of view, it is relatively challenging. If you just think about how you will ask people to take part in your study, you will begin to see what we mean. Asking your friends and family – who might know what you are interested in, might feel obliged to take part in your research, are likely to share similar characteristics/background to you etc. – is unlikely to produce a representative sample that will produce reliable and valid results and should generally be avoided. If you want a sample that is representative of the general population, then you need to ensure that you do not select from specific groups, and this is actually quite challenging. How are you going to approach people to ask them to take part in your study? Shopping centres and other locations (e.g., offices) are private organisations, and you will need gatekeeper permission to conduct research in such settings (see Chapter 9). Conducting your research on the internet might be an option, but remember that although more and more people frequently access the internet, some groups are not best represented by such an approach. Not only is it unlikely that you will be able to get a sample that is fully representative of the general population, but you also need to consider carefully the practicalities of how you will ask potential participants to take part in your study.

Although we have stressed this issue so far in relation to the general public, this applies equally to other groups, and it is most often overlooked. For example, how exactly will you initially contact offenders or staff and ask them to take part in your study? How would you contact victims/survivors? If you wish to compare different groups of participants, then you will need to carefully consider how you will access each group, as some groups may be more difficult to access than others. You will need to develop a clear strategy as to how exactly you will gain access to your participants and ask them to take part in your study.

Psychology students are one of the easiest samples to access if you are carrying out a project within a university. However, there are also challenges in asking this group to take part in your study. Psychology undergraduates tend to be largely comprised of female students aged between 18 and 21 years. First, this is a particular problem if gender differences are an important part of your research question. It can be very difficult to gain sufficient numbers of male participants, so you need to carefully consider how you are going to achieve this. Second, the limited age range of the samples means that generalisability can be questionable, which introduces limitations to the research findings that your study will demonstrate. Therefore, you need to balance your decision

102 Designing and planning

making in terms of the ease of access to participants compared to limitations of the findings. This may not always be an issue; for example, when researching a new topic area, a student population can often offer a baseline upon which to develop the research. If you do not know whether A relates to B, then using a student population can answer that question fairly easily. You can then build upon this with research with either general or forensic-based populations. The point that you need to remember is that although using undergraduates seems easy and attractive, you need to have a rationale as to why you are using that population.

You should also consider ethics and sensitivities in relation to asking people to take part in your study; hopefully you can see that asking students in class to put their hands up if they would like to be interviewed about their experiences of being sexual assault victims is not an appropriate method of identifying participants and requesting their help with your study. Although the issues in this example are fairly obvious, you need to discuss with colleagues and your supervisor/line manager the most appropriate ways to advertise your study and ask people to take part to ensure that you do not cause distress and harm (see also Chapter 7).

It is also important to take account of any disabilities/difficulties that potential participants may face. How will you design your study so that people with differing education levels can take part equally well? Will it be possible for people with disabilities and/or difficulties to take part? How will you be inclusive of all appropriate groups and ensure that you are not inadvertently excluding groups or disadvantaging them? The point that we are trying to make is that you need to factor in both time and resources to ensure that you have considered and negotiated access to your participants and/or identified the data that you will use in your study. Neglecting this aspect of your study can often be the downfall (or at least the delay) of even the best theoretically designed studies.

Activity

1 Identify the samples that will be most appropriate for the case studies outlined in Chapter 5.
2 Determine the sample(s) that will be appropriate for your own study, and consider how and where you will approach potential participants and ask them to take part in your study.

Calculating a required sample size

Sample size is an important consideration, and you should justify your proposed sample size in your proposal and ethics applications (see Chapter 9).

Practicality and feasibility issues in research   103

In quantitative designs, calculating a sample size is particularly important in establishing that you have enough power in your statistical analyses; in qualitative designs it is important that you are able to justify your sample size, with the most appropriate sample sizes varying by the type of qualitative approach and the type of analysis used. Generally, researchers tend to believe that the larger a sample is, the better the research. To some extent this is broadly true. The larger a sample size is, the more likely it is to be representative of the relevant population (Haslam & McGarty, 2014) or representative of the data on the participants/issues being examined. However, this does not mean that you should collect data with a larger and larger sample until you run out of time. Given that that you will be asking participants to give up some of their time to take part in your study (and given the associated risks of participating in research, see Chapter 7), it is more important that you recruit a *sufficient* number of participants.

Quantitative studies and power analysis

During your undergraduate studies, you will have considered type one and type two errors (see the accompanying box). If you do not have a sufficient number of participants within your sample, you increase the likelihood of making a type two error. What this means in practice is that your statistical analyses might not have the *power* to detect any significant effects because your sample size is too small. The *power* or *sensitivity* of a statistical test is the probability that the test correctly rejects the null hypothesis when it is false. It can also be thought of as the probability of correctly accepting the hypothesis when it is true. Carlucci and Wright (2012) define *power* as the ability to detect differences between groups. The power of a test equals $1 - \beta$ (where β is the probability of a type two error, see the 'Type one and type two errors' box).

Type one and type two errors

Type one error: This is where you conclude that the IV had a significant effect upon the DV. In essence, you reject the null hypothesis, when in fact the null hypothesis is true (i.e., you conclude a relationship/effect exists when in fact it does not). The rate of the type one error is called the *size* of the test and is denoted by α. It usually equals the significance level of a test. In a simple null hypothesis, α is the probability of a type one error.

Type two error: This is where you conclude that the IV did not have a significant effect upon the DV. In essence, you fail to reject the null hypothesis, when you should have done so (i.e., you conclude that there is no effect/relationship when one does in fact exist). The rate of the type two error is denoted by β.

104 Designing and planning

It is clearly important that you design a study that is able to identify any effects that are actually present; hence, it is important to consider sample size and power when designing your research project. Many organisations will expect you to have considered this in the design of your project and to include this in research proposals and ethics applications. If you consider this early on, you can consider whether a study is feasible given the potential number of participants that are available to take part in your study. So, when approaching an organisation, it is helpful to know how many participants you require for your study to have sufficient power; this allows the organisation to consider whether they have the resources/participants available to help you.

It is possible to calculate the power of your analysis once you have collected your data and conducted your analyses (this is relatively easy with most statistical packages). You can use this to assess the reliability and validity of your findings (and potentially include this in your discussion, see Chapter 15). More importantly, in terms of designing your study, when you know the number of variables you will include, the type of variables, the type of data and the number of levels, you can calculate the sample size that you will need to try to ensure that your analysis has sufficient power. There are many ways that you can do this. Field (2013) outlines a number of different packages, but one that we would recommend is G*Power (Faul, Erdfelder, Lang, & Buchner, 2007). This is a free downloadable programme that you can easily find using an internet search engine. It allows you to compute the required sample size a priori (prior to data collection) and/or to compute your power post-hoc (after completing analyses). This programme will allow you to calculate sample sizes for most of the statistical tests/designs that you are likely to use (e.g., ANOVA, t-tests, chi-square, correlation). It is also fairly easy to use and has a comprehensive user manual.

If you include power analysis in the design phase of your study, you can adjust your study to try to ensure that you have sufficient power. For example, your initial ideas and reading of the literature might suggest that you should examine ten predictor variables, or three IVs; yet when you do an a priori power calculation, this reveals that you will need a larger sample size than is feasible. You could then calculate the sample size needed for smaller numbers of predictor variables, IVs or DVs (or even using a different design; e.g., a repeated measure design generally requires fewer participants). If this sample size is more achievable and you can reasonably justify selecting the most appropriate variables to include in your study, or using the different design, then this would be a better approach to take. Ultimately, it is best, where possible, to conduct analyses that are likely to have sufficient power.

Qualitative studies

Power is not an appropriate concept for qualitative designs. This might lead you to conclude that it is easier to determine the appropriate sample size to use in a qualitative study; however, this issue can be more difficult to determine, can be surrounded in debate, and might be difficult to establish at the start of a study. For example, you may be trying to understand perceptions of a particular issue, and it might only be by conducting interviews with participants that you gain a full understanding of the range of perceptions and therefore the number of people to whom you will need to talk in order to fully identify this range. The differences between individuals might not be revealed until you talk to people from different cultures and backgrounds, which might mean that you realise that you need to speak to a wider range of people than originally anticipated. On the other hand, you may find that perceptions are very similar and that you do not need to ask as many people as you had anticipated.

For these reasons, in many qualitative approaches the concept of *saturation* is more important than the sample size. *Saturation* is most commonly described as the point when data collection ceases to provide new or relevant data. This can be a difficult concept to understand, and there are some differences of opinion about this concept, so you should read carefully about saturation and the approach that you wish to use if you wish to conduct qualitative research (see the 'Further reading' section of Chapter 3). As you should be able to see, it is not possible to determine at the start of the study when saturation will be achieved.

Reading about the analysis that you intend to conduct should reveal some guidance about appropriate sample sizes. For example, in a review of IPA studies, Brocki and Wearden (2006) found that samples ranged between one and thirty participants; however, Smith (2004) argued that there was a consensus emerging towards smaller sample sizes. As qualitative designs have become more frequently used in forensic psychology, greater consideration has been given to appropriate sample sizes; for instance, Dworkin (2012) considered this issue in order to provide guidance for authors submitting papers to the *Archives of Sexual Behavior* journal. This is a useful short paper to read in order to more fully understand the range of issues that you should consider. It might become more common in the future for journals and organisations to provide such guidance, in which case you should also locate and read this. You might be surprised to see that Dworkin recommended a sample size of twenty-five to thirty participants for grounded theory based on in-depth interviews. This might not be feasible for your study, and you will find that views on these issues vary greatly. The key point is that you should think about your sample size and issues such as saturation in the design of your study. Moreover, you should justify the approach that you will take to recruiting participants and how you will determine your initial and/or final sample size, saturation and so forth in your research proposal and ethics applications.

Operationalising your variables

So far, we have considered the selection of variables in a relatively broad way – the type of IVs you will use (e.g., ethnicity) and the type of data that will be produced (e.g., categorical). However, as you design your study more

106 Designing and planning

carefully and consider practicality and feasibility issues, you will need to operationalise all your variables. Your consideration of the sample size and saturation in qualitative designs might lead you to define the area that you wish to examine more narrowly; for example, rather than examining perceptions and experiences of restorative justice, you may wish to examine a specific group of offenders' perceptions, perhaps young offenders who committed property crimes, assuming you have access to such a group. Similarly, you might have considered that you would include ethnicity as a variable; however, when you discuss your study with a potential gatekeeper, it is highlighted that the ethnicity within that organisation is relatively homogenous. Therefore, you will need to consider another organisation, if this is a key variable in relation to your research question, or consider removing this variable or recoding it as a control variable. Then you will need to consider exactly how you will record this data, for example, asking each person to state his/her ethnicity or to choose from a set of categories; if the latter, you will need to determine the categories to include.

If you have determined that you will conduct a pre- and posttreatment evaluation, then you will need to decide exactly what variables you will measure and what tests you will use; some of these decisions might be influenced by practicality issues, such as the availability of tests (e.g., are you able to use them, can you get access to the tests and scoring instructions, will you have to buy them and who will cover the costs of this) and the time it will take for an individual to complete all the tests. In addition to selecting a battery of tests that can be completed in the time that you have available with the participants, you should also consider what is feasible for an individual to complete in one testing session. Even if you have access to participants for a long time, consider the potential for participants to get tired and/or bored. It is a good idea to try to complete all the tests yourself to see how long they take, but bear in mind that participants are likely to take longer than you because they are not familiar with them.

Space does not allow us to discuss all the potential issues that you should consider. Essentially, as there is an inevitable interaction between practicality and feasibility issues and how you design your study, you need to make decisions early on about how you are going to carry out and complete your study. If you ignore these issues, you risk designing a study that looks brilliant on paper but is impossible for you to conduct in reality. So you need to allow time to carefully think these things through and seek relevant information from the literature to ensure that your proposed study is doable.

Activity

Return to your practicality and feasibility issues that you listed in the first activity in this chapter from the case studies in Chapter 5. Re-read the case studies and add to the list of feasibility and practicality issues that will influence the design of each study by considering the following:

Is there a time limit to the study?

Are there constraints on who the participants will be and how many participants will be available to take part?

Are there limits on how participants can be allocated to different conditions or elements of the study?

Where will the study should be conducted? Are there limits on this?

How would you ask participants to take part in the study? What are the challenges associated with this?

How would you ensure that all appropriate participants can take part if they wish to? That is, how will you take account of education levels, learning difficulties, physical and other disabilities/difficulties?

Contingency plans

Without wishing to be overly negative about the research process, most researchers can give you examples of research projects where something went wrong or did not go according to plan. In fact, it is rare to find a project in which absolutely everything went as planned. Most problems are minor and can be dealt with (e.g., data collection at a particular time needs to be cancelled but is able to be rescheduled); however, some problems are so significant that the project can either not be completed or it needs to be significantly revised. Some of the significant difficulties that we know of include: access to participants suddenly being revoked, lab equipment breaking or being stolen and gatekeeper organisations closing down. Although we have stressed the importance of planning to avoid as many problems as possible, some problems can and do arise that are entirely unexpected, however carefully you plan.

You should be able to evaluate the likelihood of these issues occurring in your project, and you may want to build contingency plans into a project. For example, if the design of your project means that you need to compare groups and you know one group might be more difficult to access than others, it may be a good idea to design the study with three comparison groups. This will mean that if you are not able to get access to one group, you can complete the study with the other two. You can also have a contingency plan for a completely different project – a 'plan B' that you can pick up relatively quickly should 'plan A' not be possible. The plan B project should be something that can be achieved quickly in relation to ethical approval and access to participants (e.g., a study using existing data, or a student population if you are in a university environment). Crucially, you will need to consider how long plan B will take to complete and determine the date that you will need to make a decision to switch to plan B if plan A is problematic. Given that you are likely to have limited time for plan A, it will not be a good use of your time to plan your back-up project in huge detail, but you should have an outline plan of what you will do should you need to change to another project quickly (e.g., if plan

108   Designing and planning

A does not receive ethical approval). Without making you paranoid that you need to have a plan in place for every possible contingency, it is good project management to have at least considered what you would do if certain important aspects of your research project encountered problems. This is particularly important if your project needs to be delivered in a certain time frame, such as a dissertation. Project management is covered in more depth in Chapter 8, where this is discussed in relation to the research proposal. We strongly recommend that you think about contingencies for key aspects of your project when project planning.

Issues that can arise in the research process

1.   I have been denied access to my proposed participants.

This can be a problem that ends some research projects; however this does not necessarily mean that you need to throw away your ideas completely. The impact on your project will depend on the stage you are at when you are denied access. If you discuss your study with potential gatekeepers in the design stage and it is clear that you will not get permission, then you can change your project. Many inexperienced researchers do not approach potential gatekeepers (you should discuss doing this with your supervisor/line manager and seek his/her approval) until they are at the stage of seeking ethical approval. If you find out at this stage that you cannot gain access, then this is more problematic because you have less time for your study; therefore, you should consult gatekeepers in the early stages of your project design.

In some instances gatekeeper approval is withdrawn. If this happens to you, you should consider refocusing your research. For example, if you intended to examine three groups but can only access two, then you can complete the study with two groups. If you are left with one group, it may be possible to compare people on the basis of a characteristic of the group (gender, age or ethnicity). Or perhaps you can conduct the study with a different group (e.g., on the general population instead of on staff, or on students instead of on the general population). Although these options might not be ideal, if you have limited time and a requirement to complete a study (e.g., for your course), then this is likely to the best that you can achieve.

2.   I have not been given ethical approval for my study.

The important reaction to this response is to understand why you have not been given ethical approval. Most ethics systems provide comments that will explain why approval has not been given and often what you

---

Practicality and feasibility issues in research 109

will need to alter in your project to achieve approval. If this is a simple matter of making a minor adjustment to your project, you should do this; without ethics approval, you cannot carry out your study (see Chapter 9). However, if you are making changes to your project, big or small, you should just take a small amount of time to consider whether this has an impact on any other part of your project. For example, if you need to change the scale that you are using, how will this impact the amount of time it takes for participants to complete the study? Do you need to seek any additional permission to use the new scale? If the feedback indicates that you will not be given ethical approval for the project, even if you make changes, then you will need to revise your study (e.g., revert to your plan B study). You should have enough time left to do this, but you will need to bear in mind the limited time when planning your plan B study.

3. I am experiencing data collection issues.

These are discussed in more detail in Chapter 11. It is a good idea to read Section 2 of the book so you can consider all aspects of conducting a study in your design phase, consider any contingency plans that you can build into your study, and reflect on how you would deal with any problems issues should they arise.

Activity

- For each of the five case studies, think of some possible contingency plans that could be built into the design of the study. What type of study would you consider as a plan B for each case?
- Consider the contingency plans that you can design into your own study and spend some time considering a plan B.

Case studies

If you have completed all the activities in this chapter, you should have considered the practicality and feasibility issues that are likely to influence the case studies. Each of the case studies is briefly discussed below in relation to some key issues; the issues outlined below are not intended to be exhaustive, but rather to give you an overview of the key aspects to consider. For each case study, an example will be provided of the specifics of the study (e.g., research questions, variables, sample size) so you can see the type of information that would be

110 Designing and planning

appropriate for these case studies and can use this information through the remainder of the book.

Case study one

The service provider has acknowledged that you will need access to their employees; however, it is very likely that the mechanics of this access may not have been considered. You will need to balance your needs (e.g., in gathering data as quickly and efficiently as possible) with those of the service provider. Careful negotiation should help in this situation, and it is important to remember that often a researcher has to fit around the needs of an organisation that is granting access to participants. You decide, therefore, that using an online survey is most appropriate, as it will enable relatively easy data collection and the service provider manager has indicated that you will be able to send participation requests by email.

Case study one research details

Design: Between–groups experimental vignette.

Hypotheses: A lesbian victim will be less likely to be viewed as a victim of IPV than a heterosexual victim. Nonphysical abuse will be less likely to be viewed as IPV than physical abuse. There will be an interaction between these variables, such that nonphysical abuse experienced by a lesbian victim will be less likely to be viewed as IPV than nonphysical abuse experienced by a heterosexual victim.

Variables: Two IVs, each with two levels: (1) physical or nonphysical IPV and (2) female heterosexual or lesbian victim. Four dependent variables: four questions assessing the degree of agreement that the scenario is IPV, taken (with permission) from a previous study. Each will be scored on a ten-point Likert scale. Although strictly speaking these are ordinal variables, you will treat these as interval data in your analysis.

Anticipated analysis: MANOVA (2×2 between groups with four DVs).

Materials: Vignette used with permission from a previous study and adapted in line with the IVs. Study conducted online.

Participants: Service provider's employees who are asked to participate by email.

Sample size: G*power indicates that 128 participants are required (with 0.80 power, medium effect size).

Case study two

The crucial feature of this study will be gaining access to victims/survivors where a perpetrator has been convicted for the crime. It is also important

Practicality and feasibility issues in research   111

that there is variability in the sentences received by offenders so that you can compare the responses across groups of victims. You need to consider carefully how you will contact this group because of the potential distress to victims. You contact a number of local/regional organisations who feel it is an important issue to consider and who agree to ask victims to take part in the study in their normal contact with victims. You feel that asking participants to take part in this way is appropriately supportive and ethical. Since sample size is an important consideration, you need to be aware before approaching the organisations how many participants you need overall, so that you can assess the viability of the study.

Case study two research details

Design: Regression design.

Hypothesis: The type of sentence received by a perpetrator will have an impact on the psychological well-being of the perpetrator's victims.

Variables: Outcome variables coded on the sentence the perpetrator received. (Victims will be asked to specify the sentence in a questionnaire.) Each sentence will be coded on the following dichotomous variables: retribution (yes or no), incapacitation (yes or no), deterrence (yes or no), rehabilitation (yes or no) and restoration (yes or no). Outcome variables: score on the General Health Questionnaire and five questions from a previous study designed to assess the impact of the crime and criminal proceeding on the participants. Covariates of demographic (gender, age, ethnicity) and crime type (nonviolence, violence, sexual violence) will be included.

Anticipated analysis: Hierarchical regression.

Materials: Victim support charities will ask participants they speak to if they would like to take part in the study. Questionnaires will be sent by mail to participants who express an interest in taking part, and they will be returned by mail.

Participants: Victims initially contacted by victim support charities.

Sample size: G*power indicates that 92 participants are required (with 0.80 power, 0.15 effect size).

Case study three

In an evaluation of an intervention, you will either need to use data that has been collected by the service provider or collect the data yourself. There are many challenges, advantages and disadvantages to both methods. If data has been collected, then this clearly saves time and can make ethical approval a quicker process (you will need to be sure that permission has been obtained by the service provider for data to be used for research purposes, see Chapters 7 and 9);

112 Designing and planning

however, you are reliant on the quality of the data collected by others and its potential usefulness for evaluation purposes. Collecting data yourself means that you have more control over what is collected, but this takes time, and depending on what design you will use, you will need to be able to collect data pre- and postintervention and/or after a posttreatment follow-up period. The practicality issues of what data are available and the time that you have to collect data will be crucial in determining what design you can use and the feasibility of the evaluation. In this case study we will assume (see participant section in the 'Case study three research details' box) that the service provider has data on a large number of offenders, including conviction data two years posttreatment.

Case study three research details

Design: Quasi-experimental design using statistical analysis to control for differences between the groups. Data already collected for the intervention to be utilised.

Research question: Do offenders who complete a court-mandated intervention programme demonstrate lower recidivism rates than treatment drop-outs and/or a comparison group of similar offenders who were not mandated to attend the intervention?

Variables: IV treatment group with three levels: (1) those who were court-mandated to attend treatment and completed it; (2) those who were court-mandated to attend treatment and dropped out; (3) those who were convicted but not mandated to attend treatment., i.e., non-treatment comparison group. DV: recidivism at two years posttreatment. Control variables: age at time of sentence, sentence length, number of previous convictions.

Anticipated analysis: ANOVAs, logistic regression (to compare groups on recidivism), Cox regression (survival analysis).

Materials: Not applicable as data were already collected.

Participants: Offenders managed by a service provider who has recorded the data you will be using. All offenders are asked to agree the use of their data for research purposes during a wider 'terms of conditions' contract signed during the first meeting with the service provider.

Sample size: G*power indicates that for the ANOVA 159 participants are required (with 0.80 power, medium effect size).

Case study four

The key aspects of conducting this type of study will be: (a) developing materials that summarise a case and the DNA information about which you can ask mock jurors to reach a verdict and (b) finding participants and making the arrangements so the group can view/read the materials at the same time

Practicality and feasibility issues in research 113

and deliberate about the case. To make the study as ecologically valid as possible, you would need to develop detailed mock case information and realistic DNA information and use a sample of participants that are representative of real jurors. You should not underestimate how challenging this will be, and you might need to make some compromises to ensure that your study is feasible. Reading previous mock jury studies will give you some ideas about the ways in which you can present 'cases' to 'jurors', and you might identify some materials that you can adapt. If you need to develop your own materials, then basing them on a real case is likely to be more realistic than developing a fictitious mock case, unless you have a great deal of experience of the courtroom. Finding groups of people who are reasonably representative of real jurors who can give up their time to take part in a study such as this can be challenging; note that this study will require a substantial amount of time from all participants because they will need to gather as a group, listen to or read the case materials, and then deliberate as a group and reach a decision as a group. So you will need to be creative in thinking of ways in which this can be achieved and be very well organised to make all the arrangements.

Case study four research details

Design: Qualitative, critical realist.

Research question: How do mock jurors understand DNA evidence and use it in their deliberations to reach a verdict?

Data: Mock jurors' group discussions/deliberations.

Anticipated analysis: Thematic analysis.

Materials: Case materials adapted from previous mock jury studies using a case that has been well publicised, which you will present to participants in a written format. Presentation of DNA evidence that you will present to mock jurors that is written with the help of a lecturer/expert on the topic. Note that you will also need good recording equipment or a location with such equipment.

Participants: With permission and support from a large court service, real jurors who attend jury service but who are not needed or for whom cases are completed quickly.

Sample size: Four groups of between nine and twelve jurors. Because this is quite a unique study, there is little information about ideal sample sizes. This would produce four discussions (perhaps four hours or more of discussion) a sample of between 36 and 48 participants. At the start of the study, it is difficult to say how many jury discussions would be required to reach saturation, but because you can only conduct one discussion per week (in line with juror availability) and jurors might not be available each week, the suggested number is partly determined by feasibility in terms of time available.

114 Designing and planning

Case study five

This study is dependent on the time that you have available to complete the study and the number of individuals who complete the programme (and are willing to take part in the evaluation) within this time, bearing in mind that testing will be needed prior to the start of the intervention and after it has been completed. You would need to discuss with the service provider how and when testing will be conducted. During treatment, you will need to take account of the fact that the testing will be required in addition to the time taken to deliver the intervention. During the pre- and posttreatment stages, you will need to consider how best to test individuals, since they might have less interest in taking part during these stages. Care will also be needed to select measures that are appropriate; as outlined previously, these need to be related to the intervention and the model of change (i.e., the theory behind how the intervention will have an impact on individuals – what is expected to change) and the availability of reliable and valid measures. You should try to ensure that the measures used have been validated on a sample that is similar to the sample used in the study.

Case study five research details

Design: ABA small N experimental design

Research question: Do participants who completed an anger management programme demonstrate change in anger, anxiety and problem solving over the course of treatment?

Variables: IV stage of treatment with weekly measure taken (a) before treatment, (b) during treatment and (c) after treatment. Three DVs measured by a battery of psychometric scales to include a measure for (1) state anger, (2) state anxiety and (3) problem solving.

Anticipated analysis: Time series analysis.

Materials: Psychometric scales selected due to the availability of reliable and valid data in the relevant population.

Participants: Three participants selected as they start the treatment in the period of time available for your study, including the time for pre- and posttreatment testing.

Sample size: Not applicable since this is a small N (single-case) design.

Summary and checklist

A number of practicality issues have been considered in this chapter that will influence the feasibility of your study. It is likely that there will need to be some compromises or trade-offs in terms of the design that would be most ideal to address your research question and what is possible to achieve with the time, resources, participants and data that you have available. You should always have practicality and feasibility issues in mind when you design a research project. Having read the chapters and completed the activities up to this point in relation to your own project, you should be able to be clear and specific about the following details of your study:

1   Your research question and, where appropriate, your research hypotheses.
2   Your design.
3   Your variables and/or the type of data that you will collect or use.
4   Your intended participants or data and a justifiable sample size (for qualitative designs) or required sample size for statistical power (for quantitative designs).
5   The method with which you intend to approach participants and/or collect data.
6   The materials you will need for your study and, where appropriate, how you will develop them and/or obtain permission to use them.
7   Any equipment you will need (e.g., psychometric tests or recording equipment).
8   The intended method(s) of data analysis.

Further reading

Davies, J., Sheldon, K., & Howells, K. (2011). Conducting research in forensic settings: Philosophical and practical issues. In K. Sheldon, J. Davies, & K. Howells (Eds.), *Research in practice for forensic professionals* (pp. 3–15). Abingdon, England: Routledge.

Dworkin, S.L. (2012). Sample size policy for qualitative studies using in-depth interviews. *Archives of Sexual Behavior, 41,* 1319–1320. doi:10.1007/s10508-012-0016-6

Field, A. (2013). *Discovering statistics using IBM SPSS statistics* (4th ed.). London, England: Sage.

G*Power can be downloaded here: http://www.gpower.hhu.de/en.html (Please note that the above link may change, but that if you use an internet search engine, you should be able to access it).

References

Brocki, J.M., & Wearden, A.J. (2006). A critical evaluation of the use of interpretative phenomenological analysis (IPA) in health psychology. *Psychology and Health, 21,* 87–108. doi:10.1080/14768320500230185

Carlucci, M.E., & Wright, D.B. (2012). Inferential statistics. In G.M. Breakwell, J.A. Smith, & D.B. Wright (Eds.), *Research methods in psychology* (4th ed., pp. 191–209). Chichester, England: Sage.

Contempt of Court Act (1981). Retrieved from http://www.legislation.gov.uk/ukpga/1981/49/section/8

Davies, J., Sheldon, K., & Howells, K. (2011). Conducting research in forensic settings: Philosophical and practical issues. In K. Sheldon, J. Davies, & K. Howells (Eds.), *Research in practice for forensic professionals* (pp. 3–15). Abingdon, England: Routledge.

Dworkin, S.L. (2012). Sample size policy for qualitative studies using in-depth interviews. *Archives of Sexual Behavior, 41*, 1319–1320. doi:10.1007/s10508-012-0016-6

Faul, F., Erdfelder, E., Lang, A.-G., & Buchner, A. (2007). G*Power 3: A flexible statistical power analysis program for the social, behavioral, and biomedical sciences. *Behavior Research Methods, 39*, 175–191.

Field, A. (2013). *Discovering statistics using IBM SPSS statistics* (4th ed.). London, England: Sage.

Haslam, S.A., & McGarty, C. (2014). *Research methods and statistics in psychology* (2nd ed). Chichester, England: Sage.

Smith, J.A. (2004). Reflecting on the development of interpretative phenomenological analysis and its contribution to qualitative research in psychology. *Qualitative Research in Psychology, 1*, 39–54. doi:10.1191/1478088704qp004oa

Chapter 7

Ethics in forensic psychology research

In this chapter, we will outline some of the key ethical issues that are relevant to designing research studies. Although ethical issues are a key consideration in many relevant topics areas, ethical issues in forensic psychology have been somewhat neglected (Ward & Willis, 2013). Much of the focus of this discussion tends to relate to client-focussed aspects of psychology practice (e.g., Francis, 2009) and does not identify some of the issues that are more relevant to research-related practice. For example, the American Psychological Society (APS) has 'Speciality Guidelines for Forensic Psychology', but these guidelines reflect client-based decision making rather than research-focussed ethical issues. This is not to say that these guidelines are not of any value, as you may face issues that relate to the client groups that you use for research (e.g., offenders). However, these important issues are not the only factors that need to be considered. For example, given the challenging nature of many of the topics in forensic psychology, a researcher also needs to be aware of issues regarding protection of his or her own mental and physical safety, as well as considering how to access support, if needed. This is an issue that is not always so relevant for other areas of psychology, and so we will consider it in this chapter. Once you have read this chapter, you should be able to:

- understand general ethical principles and how they relate to research contexts (e.g., confidentiality and informed consent);
- appreciate that many forensic psychology related participants (e.g., offenders and victims/survivors) are vulnerable;
- recognise the effect of holding dual roles (e.g., researcher and practitioner) within forensic environments and the impact this may have on your research and practice; and
- realise the importance of safeguarding your safety and the safety of other researchers.

Ethical values

There are considered to be four general ethical principles that relate to both research and professional practice: respect, competency, integrity and responsibility (Haslam & McGarty, 2014). You will find these referred to in the individual ethics principles for your relevant country (e.g., British Psychological Society [BPS], American Psychological Association [APA]).

1 *Respect:* Psychologists should respect all people, regardless of individual, role and cultural differences (e.g., age, ethnicity). Two particular issues that relate to research activity – informed consent and confidentiality – are of obvious importance in maintaining the respect principle. Within this principle, it is usually stressed that vulnerable individuals should be particularly protected in relation to their dignity and rights.
2 *Competency:* Psychologists should be well trained and should maintain their levels of knowledge. This also means that individuals should also recognise the limits of their competency and not operate beyond these limits. Operating beyond the limits of competency increases the likelihood of risk of harm to clients or research participants.
3 *Integrity:* Psychologists should always be open and honest in their interactions with individuals. In a research context, integrity is important in interacting with research participants; psychologists need to be truthful about the risks and benefits of taking part in research. Integrity can also involve withholding information (e.g., to maintain anonymity or confidentiality of research participants).
4 *Responsibility:* Psychologists have a responsibility to both their clients and the general public (e.g., avoidance of harm). In research, this involves avoiding harming participants by examining all potential risks that may be involved in research participation, maintaining confidentiality and so on. Within this principle are also the responsibilities to: (a) conduct well-designed studies that contribute to our understanding of forensic psychology; (b) use financial compensation where appropriate for research participants; and (c) avoid compromising participants (e.g., by inducing them to take additional risks because of the loss of the financial payment).

These values relate to forensic psychological practice in general. In addition, there are ethical values that are more specifically associated with carrying out research. For example, the BPS's (2010) 'Code of Human Research Ethics' aligns with, and adds to, the aforementioned values. Their four values are as follows:

1 *Respect:* This is the same as the principle outlined previously, but is particularly focussed on both providing informed consent to participants and respecting participants' wishes in terms of choosing to not be involved in a research project. This includes enabling participants to withdraw from research and allowing them to change their minds about participation (e.g., by providing opportunities to withdraw from a study during and after the data collection/participation or providing a 'cooling-off' period).

2   *Scientific value:* Research must be well designed, robust and well implemented to ensure that the results are valid and reliable. Within this value, the importance of considering the risks and benefits associated with taking part in the research is emphasised.
3   *Social responsibility:* This situates psychological research within the context of the society in which it exists. Researchers must acknowledge these social structures and understand the impact that their research may have, so that any potential disruption and harm is minimised.
4   *Maximising benefit and minimising harm:* This aligns with the broader respect principle outlined previously. In essence, the importance of this value is that research should provide maximum benefits (e.g., to society, research users and participants) and minimise the potential for harm.

It is important to note that there are many psychological societies (as well as those for related disciplines, such as criminology) around the world, each with their own codes of conduct and guidelines with which you should familiarise yourself. You may also be bound by similar related guidelines and practice codes (e.g., those of the Health and Care Professionals Council [HCPC] for practitioner psychologists in the UK) that you should note and practice within. We have listed the details of the most common sources that you are likely to need in the 'Further reading' section, but bear in mind that these change frequently (so search for the most up-to-date codes/guidance) and that there may be others you need to consider. You should also abide by the policies and guidelines of your university/college and the organisations for which you work and within which you are conducting research.

Remember that it is your responsibility to become familiar with these guidelines prior to carrying out or completing any research projects and to operate within them. However, as Ward and Willis (2013) emphasised, it is also important not to be ethically blind – that is, to restrict your ethical concerns to those that are outlined within official guidelines. Ward and Syersen (2009) argued that these guidelines tend to focus upon expected or standard concerns that arise as part of the research process. They do not teach researchers to be aware of the potential for other issues to arise that may be outside of these expected concerns or the experience of the researcher. Although we have emphasised throughout the book the importance of prior planning and thinking through your research project, you also need to be prepared for the unexpected to happen and continually reflect on your research (and practice). It is likely that you will have a research supervisor, line manager, or colleague with whom you should discuss any concerns. To minimise the potential for difficulties and ethical problems in designing your research, you should spend time considering the ethics of your project and the processes that you will employ (as well as the issues already covered in this book) to ensure that your research is conducted in line with relevant codes of conduct and guidance, as outlined in more detail herein.

Informed consent

If you are using data that have already been gathered, it is important to establish whether consent for the use of the data for research purposes has been gained. Institutions are frequently aware of this requirement, and one strategy that may be used is to gain consent for potential ongoing or future research use when the data are initially gathered. This is frequently the case with data gathered within prisons and other large national organisations. In this way, use of the archival data is possible and there is no requirement for additional informed consent from the original participants (Zapf, Green, & Rosenfeld, 2011). It is important that you do not assume that consent for data to be used in research (particularly by researchers who are external to the organisation) has been obtained; you must check this and ensure that the appropriate consent has been provided. This is something that you need to establish early on, as you would not be able to use data when consent has not been established.

Case study three

It is important that we consider whether consent has been given for the use of the participants' data. Imagine that you have been told that the prison can provide pre- and posttest psychometric data to use in the evaluation. Discuss with staff how consent was obtained for the data to be used in a research study and, if necessary, ask to see a copy of the form or information that offenders were asked to sign or agree to.

There is some debate regarding the ability of participants within the forensic psychology field (e.g., offenders) to truly volunteer and/or consent to participation in research projects. Later in this chapter we further discuss definitions of participants as vulnerable individuals and whether offenders fall within this definition. Overholser (1987) argued that informed consent should contain three components: competence, knowledge and volition.

- *Competence* relates to the ability of a participant to give informed consent (and considers whether the participant is legally competent to give consent).
- *Knowledge* refers to the information that has been given to the participant regarding the research project. This needs to be both full and complete, so that a participant can make a fully informed decision. It can be difficult to identify all the potential benefits and risks that taking part in a project can involve (particularly when considering the entire 'life' of a project – many people fail to consider the potential impact of the publication of the findings, for example) and it is important to fully consider these and provide

potential participants with all the relevant information that they need in order to make a fully informed decision.

- *Volition* refers to nature of the consent to take part in the project. A participant should freely volunteer or agree to take part in the research project, and the participant's rights to (a) not take part in the study or (b) withdraw from the study at any point, including after data collection, must be respected.

All three components must be achieved to ensure that informed consent is provided. Therefore, it is important to consider how each of these three components will be achieved in your own project.

Activity

Consider and list all the potential risks that an offender may face when completing a research study and discuss these with a supervisor/colleague. Note that some will be fairly easy to identify; for example, the offender may disclose details of an offence or individual at risk. But do not forget to consider issues, such as being identified as a particular type of offender to other offenders or nonoffenders, or the potential impact of the study findings/publication on an offender. What would be the implications for an offender who completed a programme that was found to be ineffective, or to actually have negative effects? When you have considered the risks, also consider and list the potential benefits to the offender in taking part in the study. Identify strategies that can be used by researchers to minimise each of the risks, and identify strategies that can be used to maximise each of the benefits. Finally, think about how these risks and benefits should be communicated to potential participants.

Confidentiality

Confidentiality falls within the ethical principle of respect, which the BPS defines as having a particular regard for people's right to privacy. Research that is carried out with the general population usually holds confidentiality in the highest regard, and the BPS emphasises the right that participants have to not be identifiable in any published research. This is because we often ask participants questions that are personal (e.g., sexual orientation) or that relate to their personal attitudes (e.g., measuring homophobic beliefs). Therefore, it is essential that participants trust the researcher to keep such information confidential, particularly where this has the potential to identify them. It is important to note that individuals and organisations can be identified in a number of ways, so it is important to bear in mind that just removing the names of people/organisations might not be enough to ensure confidentiality. You might say, for example, that you collected data from a high security prison in England, and then later when discussing problems with data collection explain that the prison was recategorised during the data collection period. These two pieces of information together may identify the prison (i.e., if there was only one high security prison that was recategorised), so you need to think carefully about the information you present. It is also easy to overlook how individuals can be identified. For example, you may interview staff in a small organisation about a new policy and describe them as employees and managers and also mention their genders and ethnicities. You may then describe that the female nonwhite managers held different views from the rest of the managers and describe these views. Without realising it, you might have revealed the views of one or two people in the organisation who would be recognisable to those working in the organisation and possibly also others outside it. This is also an issue with qualitative data; when you include extracts of interviews in a report, you need to be careful that the extracts you include will not reveal the speaker's identity. (You should also consider whether a warning that confidentiality cannot be ensured, because of this problem, needs to be included in the information you provide to participants.)

When working in forensic contexts, the limits of confidentiality also have to be carefully considered, balancing the rights of research participants with the psychologists' values of protecting the public. For example, it is not ethical to ignore information that suggests specific individuals are at risk of harm. As the BPS notes (as do other ethical guidelines), participants have to be aware of the limits of confidentiality, and there are specific situations (e.g., when information is provided that suggests individuals are at risk) in which you will need to breach confidentiality so that steps can be taken to minimise these risks. In some countries and jurisdictions, there are mandatory reporting requirements that will also need to be considered.

Cowburn (2010) discussed this issue in more detail in relation to research that involves sexual offenders, who during the course of the research may disclose previously unreported criminal offences or future planned offending. These are issues that do not just apply to sex offenders (bear in mind that these issues might also apply to individuals who are not offenders). Overholser (1987) suggested some methods that can be used to protect the confidentiality of offenders, including: instructing participants to only discuss previous crimes in general terms, with no specific details of the crime, and using questionnaires with participant numbers rather than identifiable information. However, these methods have their limitations. The best possible way of dealing with this is that all participants are clearly informed about confidentiality and that the limits of confidentiality are clearly outlined. Cowburn (2010) argued that the result of this can be a stifling or silencing of research participants, and you may not get the full picture of their offending behaviour. This is a compromise that has to be made when carrying out research with participants in forensic settings; it is more important that ethical practices and principles (both your own and your governing body) are upheld. You need to prepare for this in three ways: (1) think carefully about the data you need for your study and how you will collect it, so that you can minimise the likelihood that such issues will be discussed/disclosed; (2) inform potential participants clearly about the limits to confidentiality; and (3) plan what action would be taken if such information was disclosed, which should also be clearly communicated to potential participants.

Case study five

Although the design of this study will involve the use of psychometric tests, there is still the possibility that in interacting with participants they will disclose to you aspects of their past behaviours that resulted from anger. Because the individuals have self-referred based on recognition of their problems with anger, they may be motivated to address the problem and keen to explain to you why they are completing the intervention. They may not have been sanctioned by the criminal justice system (CJS), and some of the behaviours they describe could constitute criminal offences (e.g., general violence, child abuse, intimate partner violence). Therefore, it is important in this case study that the limits of confidentiality are clearly outlined to participants so that they are aware of the impact of any potential disclosure and of the steps you will take should such information be disclosed. You need to bear in mind that these issues need to be explained in a way that people without psychological, ethical and CJS experience can easily understand.

Common confusion

Researchers often think that they should collect a great deal of information and then they can decide what to use and analyse later in the project. This is not an ethical approach for a number of reasons. For example, it is a waste of participants' time to provide data that you will not actually use, and it is also dishonest (unless you clearly explain you will collect a lot more data than you need, which is likely to make potential participants rightly question your approach). It also suggests that your research project has not been well thought out or appropriately designed. Therefore, you should carefully plan your project and only collect the data that you actually need to answer your research question(s).

124 Designing and planning

Common difficulties

Most forensic psychology researchers/students are aware of the need to store data securely. Remember that you should store consent forms in a secure location that is separate from the data, to avoid identification of the data. Many people forget to consider how long the data and consent forms should be kept and stored and how the data will be securely destroyed. You should not keep data longer than necessary, and you should ensure that data is not left in storage beyond the date it is needed. You may have different types of data, for which different lengths of storage may be appropriate; for example, data that reveals participants' identities (interview recordings, raw data) are likely to be copied in some way for analysis (e.g., transcribed or entered into statistical software). This data should be de-identified since it will be needed longer than the original sources. Once you are satisfied that the original sources are no longer required (make sure you have checked the accuracy of transcriptions, data analysis etc.) they can be destroyed. It is good practice to label data with a date by which you will destroy the data, as a reminder. You must employ good data management procedures so that data are (a) securely stored and (b) destroyed when appropriate. You should inform participants how data will be stored, how long it will be retained, and when it will be destroyed.

Debriefing and withdrawal

Debriefing participants and providing information to enable them to withdraw from the study are issues that can be neglected; however, both are important components of behaving ethically as a researcher. *Debriefing* refers to the phase after the participant has completed the study. As a responsible and ethical researcher, it is appropriate to then provide further explanation regarding the aims and purpose of the study. Here you should also include sources of information for participants to find out more information about the topic (bearing in mind the sources of information people can use – offenders in prison, for example, generally cannot access the internet) and also sources of support for participants. You should also explain how participants can contact you (the researcher) and find out about the results of the study.

Case study one

The debriefing process is important in every study. When dealing with topics that are considered sensitive, however, thoroughly debriefing participants becomes even more essential. You will remember that case study one involves asking participants to read a vignette that involves an incident of IPV. Although the sample will be service providers who are likely to come into daily contact with IPV victims, it is still important to consider the impact that the study may have on participants, particularly because it is possible that some of the participants will be IPV survivors. Therefore, when you are debriefing participants, you should provide the participants with information and guidance on accessing further support should this be required. This can be as simple as directing participants to organisations that can assist with trauma (e.g., the organisation might have a counselling service and you can provide the details of how to access it, or you can refer them to external sources of support, such as appropriate charities and helplines such as the Samaritans). If you are referring participants to a service within the organisation and anticipate that the service might be used by a number of the participants, then you should discuss this with the organisation during the planning stage to ensure that you provide the best support possible for your participants. Remember that, as the researcher, you should not take on the role of counselling the participants yourself (see the later section that discusses vulnerable participants).

Activity

For case studies one, two, four and five, identify (a) an appropriate source of information for participants to find out more about the topic of the study and (b) at least two appropriate resources that participants can be directed to for support.

As part of the respect principle, it is important that there are clear routes to participants being able to withdraw their data (see Chapter 9 to learn how to do this). Although most researchers are aware that participants can withdraw from the study at any point, many do not consider how this might actually happen and do not provide an easy means for participants to do this. In some studies it is relatively easy for participants to cease participation (e.g., stop completing a scale or questionnaire), but in other designs participants might feel less able to withdraw (e.g., if they are in an experiment in a lab or are completing a group task). You need to think about this and include measures that enable people to withdraw if they wish to do so (e.g., ask people if they are happy to continue between trials in an experiment or between questions in group discussions). Remember that you should respect individuals' wishes to withdraw;

researchers are often concerned about gathering data from a sufficient number of participants, and it is easy to get so caught up in this (particularly when close to deadlines) that you may unwittingly put subtle pressure on participants (e.g., in a general chat you say you are so glad they have agreed to take part, as you need XX more participants and only have a few days left to collect data). It is important to be mindful of this and to look out for cues that participants may not want to continue (e.g., there is a change in demeanour, they look uncomfortable); you should check with participants to ensure they are okay and wish to continue with the study.

The other aspect that is often overlooked is participants' rights to a cooling-off period, in which they can change their mind about participating in the study and ask for their data to be withdrawn. Providing an opportunity for participants to do this is not always straightforward (e.g., when data are anonymous, collected online) and you need to think carefully about the best approach to providing this opportunity to participants. In some situations, it might not be possible for participants to withdraw after the data has been collected; if this is the case, this should be made clear in the information provided at the informed consent stage. You should, however, try to provide this opportunity. A method can usually be identified with a bit of careful thought/consideration. The method for contacting you to request withdrawal from the study should be clearly outlined in the debrief information.

Giving participants details of research findings

Research participants should be given the results of the study or the opportunity to obtain the results. This is often overlooked, especially if the participants are offenders. As discussed in more detail in Section 3 of this book, you should think about what you present/make available. Sending participants a copy of your dissertation/research paper is not likely to be appropriate, because it will be long and in a format that many people will struggle to understand. The dissemination process is an important stage of the research process, and you should carefully consider how you will let the relevant stakeholders know about the outcome of your study and what formats will be most appropriate for each group of stakeholders (see Section 3). You should plan how you will do this at the start of the project, and the details of how you will inform participants about the results should be included in the debrief. Remember, by the time of the dissemination stage, participants may no longer be at the organisations/locations where you collected the data (e.g., they have moved institutions/organisations, been released from prison etc.); where possible, you should provide people with the opportunity to contact you for a copy/summary of the results. You should also give details of when you expect the results to be available. Remember to think through where you might be at this stage and what contact details are appropriate (e.g., your university contact details might not be appropriate if you will not have access to them once you have completed the course/left the university).

Online research methods

The use of online research methodologies has increased considerably over the past ten years. These methods are not limited to online surveys; experiments and vignette studies can be conducted online, and you can also consider gathering data from online resources such as news sites, discussion forums, blogs and so on. Web-based research offers a number of benefits to a researcher, such as the ease of collecting data and accessing geographically diverse participants. Remember that this is unlikely to be an appropriate method for accessing some groups (e.g., prisoners, offenders in the community with conditions that limit internet use). However, these methods are particularly useful in relation to recruiting participants from the general population or for engaging with participants from specific populations that you would otherwise struggle to access. Some of the other benefits of this approach are:

- Reducing the likelihood of demand characteristics. Because of the 'distance' between the participants and researcher, the participants are less likely to be influenced by the presence of the researcher.
- Ease of withdrawal from completing the study. Participants who are physically present while research is being conducted may feel more obligated to stay.
- Encouraging participation in the research. Online methods allow participants to take part in the study at a time that is most suitable for them, which may encourage participation (Daftary-Kapur & Greathouse, 2011).

Given the explosion in the use of internet research methods, there are now guidelines issued by most psychological associations that relate specifically to their use. The BPS (2013) has issued additional guidelines that enable researchers to interpret the original Code of Human Research Ethics (BPS, 2010) in relation to internet-mediated research (see 'Further reading' for the link to this document). In line with the original four principles previously outlined in relation to research with human participants, these guidelines highlight additional issues that need to be considered in internet-facilitated research. For example, in relation to the respect principle and acknowledging the importance of participants' rights to privacy, carrying out research using the internet makes it much more difficult to define the public or private spaces. Posts on a discussion forum or comments page may be considered public; however, the individuals who made the posts/comments may view their contributions as private and not wish for them to be included in research projects. The BPS (2013) guidelines acknowledge this difficulty and suggest that most people who post on such forums have no real expectation of privacy, and such data can therefore be legitimately used for research purposes. However, the researcher should not neglect the privacy of the individual and should carefully ensure that no identifiable information is included in the data gathered for analysis.

Ensuring that valid consent is given to take part in a study is another important aspect of the respect principle. Traditional methods of data collection usually involve a written consent signed by the participants, which is not possible in internet data collection. The BPS (2013) guidelines suggest using tick boxes or radio buttons to ensure that participants can make a clear indication of consent. Some online survey providers allow you to require a response to a question (such as one indicating either consent or nonconsent to take part in the study) before participants are able to progress to the remainder of the survey. Since this ensures that participants give consideration to consent, this approach should be used where possible.

Another area that can be difficult to manage in online studies is the debriefing. Although it might be relatively straightforward to display this information at the end of the study, this information might not be accessible at a later time. When designing online studies, you should familiarise yourself with the methods/resources you will use so that you understand what the participation experience will be like: what participants will see, in what format, when and so forth. Then you can consider how to make the relevant information available; for example, you could design a study web or Facebook page with the debrief information (which you could also use to provide a summary of the results), or you could provide the opportunity for information to be sent by email. Because online approaches to research are still relatively new, and web-based resources are constantly developing, you will need to use a bit more thought and initiative in designing your study and research materials, which means that you need to spend time thinking these things through at the planning/designing stage.

Forensic psychology participants as vulnerable populations

Particular care has to be taken with many forensic psychology samples because they constitute vulnerable individuals. The BPS (2010) outlines specific examples of groups of people who should be considered vulnerable. These include:

- children aged under 16 years;
- individuals with cognitive and/or communication difficulties;

- individuals who are patients in care;
- individuals who are in custody or on probation; and
- individuals who engage in illegal activities such as drug use.

It is likely that individuals that you wish to include in your research will belong to these groups. The BPS (2010) also discusses the use of undergraduate students as research participants because they are considered to be vulnerable. They note the importance of considering the unequal relationships or power imbalances that can occur when asking undergraduate students to participate in research, and they note that additional care must be taken to ensure that informed consent and understanding are achieved. In identifying any individual as vulnerable, it means that as a researcher, you need to maximise every opportunity to ensure that ethical principles are adhered to and that the participants understand every aspect of the research project (e.g., in terms of informed consent, withdrawal).

There can be particular challenges in gaining informed consent for some samples. Widom and Landry (2011) identified children under the age of 16 who have been subjected to abuse as a particularly challenging sample from whom to gain clear informed consent. Because the child is under 16 years, the normal procedure would be to gain consent from the parent or guardian; however, in cases where child abuse has been uncovered, the parent or guardian may be the perpetrator. This may raise a conflict in providing consent on the basis of what is in the best interests of the child (given that the parent/ guardian has been shown to not act in the best interests of the child). Many ethical guidelines provide direction in these situations. For example, the BPS (2010) identified that there may be special situations where the findings of such individuals should not be suppressed and that a rationale for not achieving parental consent can be approved by an appropriate research ethics committee. Similar issues arise with children who have been removed from the care of their parents/guardians. In these situations, it is very important to understand who is legally responsible for the child and to ensure that consideration is paid to the wishes or preferences of the children. These circumstances are fairly unusual and are not likely to be an issue with most research projects. However, this emphasises the importance of being aware of general ethical guidelines and specific guidelines that relate to research participation. Ignorance is not an adequate defence in dealing with these situations, so ensure that the planning for your project allows appropriate time to consider the implications of the use of certain participants.

Consent from children

Do not assume that because a parent/guardian has provided consent for a child to be involved in a study that the child has given his/her consent. If you wish to conduct research with child participants, then you need to consider the issue of informed consent carefully at a number of levels: (a) you will most likely need consent and support from an organisation (e.g., school, youth organisation); (b) you will need the consent of guardians/parents; and (c) you will need to obtain consent from the children. The way in which you present information to each of these groups will need to be different, so that it is appropriate and understandable to each group. In relation to parents, you will need to review appropriate guidelines/policies to determine whether opt-out consent (e.g., parents are informed that the study will take place in the school and they can contact you if they do not want for their children to be involved) or opt-in consent (people are informed about the study and asked to indicate if they would like to be included) is required. For practical reasons, opt-out consent can be easier to manage and is likely to result in a larger pool of potential child participants, but for a number of reasons this may not be sufficient or appropriate (e.g., parents might not receive the information, especially if children are asked to give it to their parents; they may prefer not to have to write a letter; or they may struggle to read/write). These issues are further complicated if you wish to conduct research with children who are away from their parents (e.g., in a young offenders' facility). If you wish to include children in your research, you should consider these issues carefully and discuss them with people who have experience conducting research with children and with the organisations (schools etc.) providing access to the children.

An issue that should also be carefully considered as part of defining participants as vulnerable is that some research projects might cause stress or distress to participants. There are situations where this is a reasonable part of the project (e.g., if the project is assessing responses to a particular stressor). However, as a researcher, you need to ensure that you minimise any stress or distress experienced during the study and ensure that this stress/distress does not continue beyond the data-gathering environment (Haslam & McGarty, 2014). Given the topics that we tend to research within forensic psychology, the potential for stress or distress cannot be ignored. There are obvious examples where you need to carefully consider the impact of your research on participants (e.g., in asking victims of crimes to recount their experiences). In other projects, the potential for distress may seem less apparent (e.g., in asking participants to read vignettes of mock crimes). In addition, offenders can often be overlooked as vulnerable participants who may experience stress or distress as a result of taking part in a project.

Ethics in forensic psychology research   131

> ## Case study two
>
> You will remember that this case involves recruiting victims of crime to identify the impact of different sentencing outcomes. Being a victim of a crime is a clearly distressing event, so you need to consider the impact of participation particularly carefully when recruiting this type of participant. This is particularly important given the potential for secondary victimisation (Campbell et al., 1999), which can occur inadvertently when questions are phrased insensitively. Secondary victimisation can result in victim self-blaming, which has been shown to have a considerable impact on a victim's well-being (Ullman, 1996); therefore, it is important that you consider the impact of the ways in which you phrase questions and that you also be careful in the ways in which you design your study and all the materials you give to participants.

Cowburn (2010) considered the potential for sexual offenders to become distressed (e.g., when discussing childhood experiences), an issue that may also apply to many other groups of offenders. The challenge in this situation is that there may be an impulse to offer advice that may constitute therapy. You must remember the purpose of why you are discussing this topic with the participants – to acquire data to address a research question, not to provide advice. This does not mean that you cannot source avenues of support for the participants; as previously mentioned, this is appropriate. However, you should not personally engage in providing a therapeutic response. This ensures your objectivity in the gathering of data for your research project. Cowburn (2010) suggested that it can be useful to identify to research participants (when dealing with challenging topics that may cause distress) that data gathering procedures should not be considered therapeutic but also outline where support can be found.

Balancing the practitioner and researcher roles

There are many examples of how people who work in the forensic psychology arena many occupy dual roles within their workplaces. This section is going to consider the issues associated with being a researcher and also a practitioner within the same environment. An example of a dual role would be a trainee forensic psychologist working in a prison who also wishes to complete research for his or her postgraduate degree. Broadly speaking, you should try to avoid dual relationships in undertaking research, but where this is unavoidable, proceed cautiously and with advice (Ward, 2013). For example, Munthe, Radovic, and Anckarsater (2010) discussed the ability of offenders to give informed consent (in the context of mentally disordered offenders, but the principles are the

132 Designing and planning

same for all offenders). They identified that because offenders' freedoms are restricted (e.g., physically), their abilities to give informed consent to participate in a research study are similarly limited. They give an example of where consent may not be freely given when there is conflict between the roles that the researcher is undertaking, for example, as an offender programme facilitator but also as a researcher carrying out research on the same group of offenders. In this situation, where a researcher's primary role is as an offender programme facilitator, carrying out research on the group of offenders can raise conflicts. Offenders may feel pressured (subtly or explicitly) to consent to take part in the research because they believe that this will translate to a positive perception of them within the offender programme setting (Ward & Willis, 2013). Similar issues will apply if you assess offenders and then ask them to take part in a study, if you are working with them on a one-to-one basis, or other similar situations.

Case study three

The issue of dual roles could arise in case study three because the researcher is working as a programme facilitator. This is simple to solve in this particular case study, as no original data is going to be gathered because the programme has already been completed. However, it is important for the researcher to ensure that he or she is conducting the research impartially. When working on interventions (or any task), it is not surprising that you believe that the intervention is important/effective. In addition, it is 'human' to be subject to a number of biases that mean you are more likely to note data that confirm your views and ignore data that disconfirm them (i.e., confirmation bias, which [among other cognitive biases] you should be familiar with from your undergraduate psychology studies). Without realising it, you might spend more time conducting analysis trying to find support that the intervention is effective and ignoring data that demonstrate the opposite or no effect. Lösel and Schmucker (2005), for example, found large treatment effects in evaluation studies of sex offender programmes where the researchers were affiliated with them, which they hypothesised was due to greater monitoring of the programme. Measures should be taken, therefore, to avoid such biases as much as possible.

Case study five

In case studies and small sample studies, it is quite common for the researcher to have a dual role e.g., he or she is delivering the treatment/intervention or works in a small team of staff who work with the participants/patients/offenders). In this instance, and if data is collected for an intervention evaluation for which you have a role in delivering the intervention, it is important that you consider carefully how participants are approached and asked to take part in the study (e.g., during a group treatment session would not be appropriate) and who does this (e.g., asking a colleague who is not part of the treatment team to explain the study and seek research consent might be appropriate). Informing participants about the rights to refuse participation, stressing that this will have no consequence to the offender in terms of the programme and broader sentence/progress, and explaining your different roles are important ideas that must be presented clearly. The manner in which this information is presented and the response to offenders' potential reluctance or lack of enthusiasm are also important to consider. Remember, individuals can feel pressured to participate/conform as a result of very subtle cues (remember and/or recap the conformity research you will have covered in your undergraduate coursework); therefore, you should give careful thought to the manner in which this information is presented and communicated to potential participants.

The obvious solution to this issue is communication, and ensuring that you are clear when explaining the study and the participants' potential involvement (Munthe, Radovic, & Anckarsater, 2010). However, Ward and Willis (2013) argued that it may never be possible, when dual relationships exists, for offenders to fully consider the risks and benefits associated with taking part in a project. To address this issue as much as possible, you should take additional care to explain the study and ensure that the offender is clear on the difference between: (a) his/her role as a research participant and (b) his/her role as an intervention group member (or whatever the other role is). It is important to ensure that you are clear regarding consent (i.e., that you fully comply with the respect principle that underpins many ethical guidelines within psychology, such as BPS or APA).

Protecting the researcher

An important aspect of the research process that researchers often neglect is their own protection during the process. This is understandable, given that much of our focus is outwards, working hard to ensure that we protect our participants and anyone else involved in the research process. For example, you will remember from the previous ethical values section that the key value of respect relates to the dignity and value with which we treat our research participants. It is important that we do not neglect this aspect of *any* research project. One of the most important issues to address within this discussion is the strong recommendation that researchers avoid researching topics that are too personally relevant (e.g., relating to one's own previous victimisation). It is understandable that individuals may wish to explore or attempt to explain an issue that is important to them; however, the risks (e.g., to well-being) that are present within such a situation might be too high for this to be appropriate. An example of this would be a researcher who is a survivor of rape wishing to examine the role of victim blaming in rape. Given the likelihood of discussion and consideration of scenarios/situations that are similar to the researcher's victimisation, it is clear that this is very likely to have a significant impact on the mental well-being of the researcher. Similarly, researchers who undertake research in the area of child sexual abuse may find that their personal lives (e.g., as parents) are affected by the completion of the research. Therefore, due to the associated risks, we strongly recommend that researchers avoid undertaking research in topics that are too personally relevant and that they also consider the potential impact of the research on all aspects of their own personal lives.

Particular methodologies can also be associated with either higher or lower risks of harm to the researcher. Quantitative methods of gathering data often offer the most 'distance' between the researcher and the participants because responses are reduced to numbers that may be more easily analysed without any emotional or physical impact. However, do not assume that using this approach is entirely risk free; you need to consider any potential impact that the data collection process, reading research on the topic, and thinking about the implications of your findings will have on your emotional and physical welfare. Qualitative methodologies (e.g., where you ask participants to discuss their experiences or read accounts/comments) can be challenging, and you should consider the impact on yourself and the impact that your distress might have on the participants. It is important that you consider whether the research is appropriate for you to complete, and also to consider strategies to promote your health and well-being throughout the research. You should identify sources of support, such as your supervisor, line manager, or a colleague, and/or access to resources such as counselling.

It is also important to consider your safety in carrying out your research; for example, will you be collecting data in a safe environment? The issues that you need to consider will be different depending on where you intend to collect data (e.g., in a secure establishment with community-based offenders, in survivors' homes etc.). It is becoming more common for organisations to request that researchers and/or a supervisor/line manager conduct a risk assessment as part of the design/approval process, whereby these issues are considered and strategies to minimise identified risks are developed. If this is not required, you should consider these issues carefully and discuss them with your supervisor or line manager.

Integrating ethics into your research

Overholser (1987) stated that a risk–benefit analysis should be part of the processes for planning the methodology of all research projects. This analysis

Ethics in forensic psychology research 135

should calculate the probability, severity and expected duration of potential risks within the project. This is an important part of the planning process, as you may identify that there is a potential for a high level of emotional harm within your project. This may make you automatically consider that you should not carry out this research using the proposed methodology. However, the calculation of the probability and the duration of this high level of emotional harm may reveal that there is a very small likelihood of this harm occurring and that it would be very short in duration. Overall, this may mean that the project can go ahead as long as contingencies are put in place to deal with any possible eventualities. This requires time that you need to build into the planning stage of your project, but it will save you time in the long run, as any potential issues neglected at this point are likely to be raised by an ethics approval committee.

Activity

You should now be in a position to consider the ethics of your own study. Use the following checklist to consider the issues relevant to your study, and consider the strategies that you will use to ensure that you conduct your research in an appropriate ethical manner. Discuss this with your supervisor/line manager and/or colleague to reflect on these considerations and ensure that you have identified relevant issues and developed appropriate strategies and approaches. Ensure that you make a note of these issues, as you will need this information in your proposal (Chapter 8) and when applying for ethical approval for your study (see Chapter 9).

Summary and checklist

In this chapter, we have reviewed the general ethical principles and considerations that you need to think about prior to carrying out any research. We have placed this chapter before the research proposal section to emphasise to you the importance of considering ethics and ethical principles when designing your own study. These issues are revisited in Chapter 9 from the point of view of writing information explaining your study to potential participants, writing consent forms and debriefing information, and applying for ethical approval. However, before proceeding to the research proposal stage, make sure that you consider and determine the following issues:

1   Is the research topic is suitable and safe for you to complete? How will you ensure the safety and well-being of your participants and yourself during the project?

136 Designing and planning

2 Do you have a dual role that should be considered and taken into account?
3 How will you ensure that you and your study follow the general psychology ethical principles?
4 How will you ensure that you and your study follow the research principles of informed consent, confidentiality, debriefing and withdrawal?
5 What measures will you employ to account for vulnerable participants?
6 Remember to discuss these issues with a suitable supervisor/manager and to make a note of all of these considerations, the strategies developed and decisions made.

Further reading

American Psychological Association. Responsible conduct of research. Retrieved from http://www.apa.org/research/responsible/index.aspx

Association for the Treatment of Abusers (ATSA). Research. Retrieved from http://www.atsa.com/research-0

Australian Psychological Society. Ethics. Retrieved from https://www.psychology.org.au/about/ethics/

British Psychological Society. (2010). Code of human research ethics. Retrieved from http://www.bps.org.uk/sites/default/files/documents/code_of_human_research_ethics.pdf

British Psychological Society. (2013). Ethics guidelines for internet-mediated research. Retrieved from http://www.bps.org.uk/system/files/Public%20files/inf206-guidelines-for-internet-mediated-research.pdf

Canadian Psychological Association. (2014). Canadian code of ethics for psychologists. Retrieved from http://www.cpa.ca/aboutcpa/committees/ethics/codeofethics

Canadian Psychological Association. CPA resources relevant to ethical issues. Retrieved from http://www.cpa.ca/aboutcpa/committees/ethics/resources

European Federation of Psychologists' Associations. (2005). Meta-code of ethics. Retrieved from http://ethics.efpa.eu/meta-code/

Health and Care Professions Council (HCPC). Standards of proficiency: Practitioner psychologists. Retrieved from http://www.hcpc-uk.org.uk/assets/documents/10002963SOP_Practitioner_psychologists.pdf

New Zealand Psychologists Board. Best practice documents and guidelines. Retrieved from http://www.psychologistsboard.org.nz/best-practice-documents-and-guidelines2

The Psychological Society of Ireland (PSI). Code of professional ethics. Retrieved from http://www.psychologicalsociety.ie/find-a-psychologist/code-of-ethics.html

Please note that these links may change, but if you search for the document or the organisation you will be able to find the most up-to-date versions.

References

British Psychological Society (BPS). (2010). *Code of human research ethics*. Retrieved from http://www.bps.org.uk/sites/default/files/documents/code_of_human_research_ethics.pdf

British Psychological Society (BPS). (2013). *Ethical guidelines for internet-mediated research*. Retrieved from http://www.bps.org.uk/publications/policy-and-guidelines/research-guidelines-policy-documents/research-guidelines-poli

Campbell, R., Sefl, T., Barnes, H.E., Ahrens, C.E., Wasco, S.M., & Zaragoza-Diesfield, Y. (1999). Community services for rape survivors: Enhancing psychological well-being or increasing trauma. *Journal of Consulting and Clinical Psychology, 67*, 847–858. doi:10.1037/0022-006X.67.6.847

Cowburn, M. (2010). Principles, virtues, and care: Ethical dilemmas in research with male sex offenders. *Psychology, Crime, and Law, 16*, 65–74. doi:10.1080/10683160802621974

Daftary-Kapur, T., & Greathouse, S. (2011). Forensic psychological research and the internet. In K. Sheldon, J. Davies, & K. Howells (Eds.), *Research in practice for forensic professionals* (pp. 63–77). Abingdon, England: Routledge.

Francis, R.D. (2009). *Ethics for psychologists* (2nd ed.). Chichester, Sussex: Wiley.

Haslam, S.A., & McGarty, C. (2014). *Research methods and statistics in psychology* (2nd ed). Chichester, England: Sage.

Lösel, F., & Schmucker, M. (2005). The effectiveness of treatment for sexual offenders: A comprehensive meta-analysis. *Journal of Experimental Criminology, 1*, 117–146. doi:10.1007/s11292-004-6466-7

Munthe, C., Radovic, S., & Anckarsater, H. (2010). Ethical issues in forensic psychiatric research on mentally disordered offenders. *Bioethics, 24*, 35–44. doi:10.1111/j.1467-8519.2009.01773.x

Overholser, J.C. (1987). Ethical issues in prison research: A risk/benefit analysis. *Behavioural Sciences and the Law, 5*, 187–202. doi:10.1002/bsl.2370050210

Ullman, S.E. (1996). Social reactions, coping strategies, and self-blame attributions in adjustment to sexual assault. *Psychology of Women Quarterly, 20*, 505–526. doi:10.1111/j.1471-6402.1996.tb00319.x

Ward, T. (2013). Addressing the dual relationship problem in forensic and correctional practice. *Aggression and Violent Behavior, 18*, 92–100. doi:10.1016/j.avb.2012.10.006

Ward, T., & Syersen, K. (2009). Vulnerability agency and human dignity: An ethical framework for forensic practice. *Aggression and Violent Behavior, 14*, 94–105. doi:10.1016/j.avb.2008.12.002

Ward, T., & Willis, G. (2013). Ethical problems arising in forensic and correctional research. In K. Sheldon, J. Davies, & K. Howells (Eds.), *Research in practice for forensic professionals* (pp. 16–33). Abingdon, England: Routledge.

Widom, C.S., & Landry, E.C. (2011). Research on child abuse and neglect. In B. Rosenfeld & S.D. Penrod (Ed.), *Research methods in forensic psychology* (pp. 487–506). Hoboken, NJ: Wiley.

Zapf, P., Green, D., & Rosenfeld, B. (2011). Competency to stand trial and criminal responsibility research. In B. Rosenfeld & S.D. Penrod (Ed.), *Research methods in forensic psychology* (pp. 156–173). Hoboken, NJ: Wiley.

Chapter 8

Research proposal

In this chapter, we will outline the information that is required in a clear research proposal and the methods that you can use to plan your research project. Even if you are not required to write a proposal, you will find it helpful to write one in order to clarify your ideas. It will be useful to refer to this throughout the project to ensure you remain on track. This chapter builds on the information provided in earlier chapters and is based on the assumption that in writing a proposal, you have searched the literature, designed a study, considered the types of data you will be collecting and identified any ethical and feasibility issues, such that you now have a clear idea about a study that you want to conduct and that you can communicate it in a concise, clear research proposal. An example proposal based on case study one is provided in this chapter.

Once you have read this chapter, you should be able to:

- list the key sections required in a research proposal;
- outline a research idea in a proposal;
- plan your project;
- identify a Gantt chart and prepare one for a project; and
- assess risks to the successful completion of your project and implement strategies to reduce and mitigate them.

Research proposal

A research proposal should clearly and concisely describe a research project. It should set the project in the context of existing theory, research and practice; specify the research question(s) and, where appropriate, specific hypotheses; propose the design and method that will be used; identify the variables/data that will be collected and the tools/schedules that will be used to collect data; suggest where the data will be collected and, if appropriate, whom the participants will be; and state the analysis that will be conducted. Research proposals can vary in the sections that are included (you may be required to submit a proposal in line with a specific template), so you might need to be flexible in where you include information. If a specific format is not requested, the following will provide a good outline for your study:

Research proposal   139

- Project title
- Summary of research (and, where appropriate, practice) background/context
- Rationale for your study and the aims, research question(s) and (where appropriate) hypotheses
- Proposed design and methodology, including (where appropriate) the types of variables and how these will be measured/assessed
- Proposed data sample/participants and research location(s)
- Proposed analysis
- Proposed timetable
- References

Research proposals do not need to be long. You might only need a short paragraph in some sections; however, the length and level of detail of the proposal will depend on the type of research you are conducting and the purpose of the proposal. A research proposal submitted to apply for a PhD studentship, for example, is likely to be more detailed than a proposal that you submit to your course team in order for a suitable supervisor to be assigned. It is important, therefore, for you to use the information that is provided/available to you (e.g., via web-based resources) and follow the appropriate instructions/advice (e.g., if you are applying to several universities for PhD funding, you might need to modify your proposals for each university so they meet each university's guidelines).

Project title

This should be a working title for your research study that clearly summarises the purpose of your study. For example, a title for case study two could be: "What is the impact on the psychological well-being of victims of crime where the perpetrators are sentenced to either prison or a community sentences, or are acquitted?" This title does not have to be the final title that you use; however, it is good practice to have this established early on.

Research context/background

This section should provide a summary of the research background that sets your research in context. In some instances, depending on the purpose of your study, you might also need to indicate the practice context; for example, if you are proposing to evaluate a new intervention, then you might need to briefly explain the background of the intervention development and introduce the new intervention. This section does not need to be a full literature review, but you should summarise the current evidence base and identify/outline key studies that are important for the way in which you are proposing to conduct your study. The theoretical framework of your study should be clear in this section (e.g., see case study one, which is based on attribution theory [Heider, 1958]). It is also useful in this section to identify where your research is novel and

140 Designing and planning

innovative – that is, how you are contributing to the current knowledge base in your topic area. This is important if your proposal is going to be reviewed (and potentially approved) by others; this assists them in understanding that your research is important and is going to increase understanding of a particular topic.

Rationale, aims, research questions and hypotheses

This section should build on the previous section; that is, the rationale for your study should be based on the research/practice contexts that you have summarised. You should then list the aim(s) of your study, which should be consistent with your rationale, and the specific research question(s). If you are using an experimental or quasi-experimental design, then you should list your research hypotheses. Remember that your project needs to be feasible; the purpose here is not to demonstrate that you can write lots of aims/research questions, but rather the purpose is to clearly and concisely list the appropriate, feasible aim(s) and research question(s). (It is perfectly acceptable to have a single aim and/or question.)

In the past, you might have been asked to specify your research hypotheses and null hypotheses (largely so people could assess that you understood these concepts); however, in a research proposal (and in your report/research paper), you only need to write your research hypotheses (i.e., you do not need to write out null hypotheses).

Design and methodology

This section is likely to be short: remember to be precise and clear. You should start by stating your design (e.g., an experimental study) and your specific approach/perspective in qualitative designs (e.g., inductive, critical realist); then, outline your variables (IVs, DVs and control variables, or predictor, criterion and control variables), including the levels or types of data you will collect in qualitative designs. Where appropriate, you should outline the measures/tools that you will use to collect your data, providing appropriate references for psychometric tests/measures. In this section, you should also specify any measures you will take to account for potential confound variables (e.g., that you counterbalance the order in which participants complete tasks or randomly allocate participants to conditions).

Data sample/participants and research locations

In this section you should outline your data source, bearing in mind that this could be an existing database, archival data, text material or data that you will collect from participants. You should be clear and precise about how you will select the sample from the data, or the sample of participants. If you wish to examine text-based data (e.g., newspaper coverage of crime stories), it will most likely not be possible to include every source, so you need to think about and specify how you will systematically select the data that you will examine. If you are collecting data from participants, you should be clear about the type of sample that you will seek (e.g., voluntary, random, opportunity), remembering that in a random sample, every person in the population should have an equal chance of being included in the sample (it is probably unlikely that you will include a truly random sample in your study). Here it would be a good idea to summarise key ethical processes (e.g., that participants will be invited to take part, given a participant information sheet, and asked to sign a consent form; or that you are using an open-access data source containing anonymised data). If you are collecting data from participants, it should be clear in this section where you will collect the data (this could be a physical location or an online environment).

Proposed analysis

In this section, you should outline the analysis that you expect to complete on the data. If you will be using qualitative analysis, then you should outline the type of analysis that you will use; for example, if you are planning to use thematic analysis, you might want to indicate that you will follow the steps outlined by Braun and Clarke (2006), or that you will use the steps outlined by Smith, Jarman, and Osborn (1999) if using IPA. You do not need to discuss this in great detail, but it should be clear that you have thought through the analysis that you will conduct and that you are aware of an appropriate approach to use.

If you are using quantitative analyses, then you should state what these will be and identify why these are appropriate to your hypotheses/data. At this stage, you will not have been able to screen data to ensure that you are able to carry out certain types of analyses (e.g., parametric tests, see Chapter 11 on collecting data), so you should state the parametric analyses that you expect to use but state that you will use nonparametric equivalents if the data do not meet parametric assumptions. If you expect that your data will not be normally distributed, or meet other parametric assumptions, then outline the nonparametric tests that you will use. Again, you do not need to go into detail about each and every test that you will use.

Common confusion

It is important that you use the analyses that are most appropriate for your research questions/data. You do not get extra marks for conducting parametric tests; in fact, if you use parametric tests when these are not appropriate, this will be questioned. Similarly, the aim is not to conduct every type of analysis that you can think of; rather, you should conduct the analyses that are appropriate to address the research question(s) and, where appropriate, the hypotheses that you have outlined.

142 Designing and planning

Timetable

A brief summary of your timetable should be provided in this section. You could do this by listing the key phases of the study (remember to allow time for ethical approval) and when you will complete them (as per the timetable in the example proposal shown later), or you could include a Gantt chart (see Figure 8.1) or some other outline of your timetable. As long as it is clear to the reader when the key phases of your research will take place, the format is not important, unless one is specified by the organisation for which you are writing the proposal. Remember, some elements can overlap; for example, you can be conducting/writing your literature review during the same time period that you apply for ethical approval, recruit participants and collect data.

References

This section should include the full references for all the sources you have included in previous sections. It is important that you format the references in the style appropriate for the organisation/application that you are completing.

Example proposal

The following proposal is for case study one. Note that due to the space requirements of this book, this is a very brief/concise proposal to illustrate the information required in each section. A brief outline such as this might be appropriate for your own purposes, but you might need more detail if, for example, you are submitting a PhD proposal or the proposal is the method of outlining your study for an ethical application.

Title

What is the impact of victim sexuality and type of abuse (physical or nonphysical) on service providers' responses to IPV victims?

Research background/context

The literature that examines how service providers perceive victims of IPV is relatively limited. Although there is some published research, this has largely been limited to using qualitative methodologies (e.g., Simpson & Helfrich, 2007). Furthermore, those studies that have used experimental methods have focussed on IPV behaviours that relate to physical abuse, despite the awareness that IPV can take multiple forms, including psychological abuse (Pico-Alfonso et al., 2006). Some studies have examined the impact of victim characteristics in relation to victim perception in IPV scenarios (e.g., victim sexuality) (Seelau & Seelau, 2005). For example, Brown and Groscup (2009) manipulated the gender of the victim and perpetrator in their study. The findings of this study demonstrated that participants judged the IPV in the same-sex relationship scenario to be less serious and that the participants were less likely to recommend that the victim leave the relationship. However, no differences were found in judgements of victim injury, levels of victim and perpetrator blame, or how abusive the IPV behaviour was judged to be. Similarly, Poorman, Seelau, and Seelau (2003) found that participants perceived allegations made by same-sex victims to be less believable than those made by heterosexual victims; however, they did not examine attitudes such as blame or responsibility. Furthermore, much of the literature that has examined IPV victim perception has been limited in its use of student based samples (e.g., Sylaska & Walters, 2014), and it is currently unclear how generalisable these findings may be to service providers' attitudes.

Rationale, aims and research questions

The above literature review has identified that there are clear gaps in the literature in providing us with a clear understanding of the impact of victim sexuality and type of abuse on service providers' responses to IPV victims. This project seeks to address these limitations by examining the following research questions:

1   How does victim sexuality impact on service providers' responses to IPV victims in attributions of (a) victim blame, (b) victim responsibility and (c) perceived severity of the abuse?
2   How does type of IPV abuse impact on service providers' responses to IPV victims in attributions of (a) victim blame, (b) victim responsibility and (c) and perceived severity of the abuse?

Design and methodology

This study will use a 2 × 2 between-participants design. As such, two IVs will be manipulated within this study via a vignette presented to participants. The first is victim sexuality, which will have two levels: a heterosexual female victim vs. a lesbian female victim. The second IV is type of abuse depicted within the scenario, which will also have two levels: physical abuse vs. emotional abuse. There will be three dependent variables measured within the study: (1) victim blame, (2) victim responsibility and (3) perceived severity of the abuse. Participants will be directed to an online survey where they will be provided with the participant information regarding the study and a consent statement. Participants will have to indicate consent before they are allowed to progress through to the survey. On the first page, there will be a short demographic survey in which data are gathered regarding gender, age and ethnicity. Participants will then be presented with one of four possible conditions within a scenario: (1) a female heterosexual victim who suffers physical abuse; (2) a female lesbian victim who suffers physical abuse; (3) a female heterosexual victim who suffers emotional abuse; and (4) a female lesbian victim who suffers emotional abuse. After reading the scenario, participants will then be asked to respond to three short scales that will measure the three dependent variables. As no fully developed victim and perpetrator blame or perceived severity scales could be identified in previous studies of victim perception in IPV cases, the literature on rape blaming will be utilised and the Strömwall, Alfredsson, and Landstrom's (2013) victim and perpetrator blaming scale will be used. Each of the blame scales has four items, and participants respond on a 0–10 rating scale, with higher scores indicating a higher level of blame being attributed to either the victim or the perpetrator. Previous reliability assessments have shown excellent levels of internal consistency of $\alpha = .91$ for the victim blame scale and $\alpha = .92$ for the perpetrator blame scale. To assess perceived severity of the assault, Davies and McCartney's (2003) perceived severity scale (two items) will be used in this study. As with the blame scales, this measure has also been reported to have excellent levels of internal consistency ($\alpha = .91$). None of the scale items need to be adapted as they refer to the scenario generally, so no further piloting of the scale items is required. The vignette from Basow and Thompson's (2012) study will be used within this study. Permission from all authors has been sought prior to use within this project.

Data/participants

Participants will be recruited from the service provider via a gatekeeper. Permission has already been granted by the organisation to recruit participants. A G*Power analysis has been carried out to assess what sample size is required for the project. This analysis has showed that the sample size needs to be a minimum of 128 participants.

Proposed analysis

Data screening prior to statistical analysis will be carried out. Testing to ensure that the data meet parametric assumptions will also be completed, as will any additional tests required by the individual inferential tests used. Assuming that the data meet parametric assumptions, a Pearson correlation will be carried out for the three dependent variables: victim blame, perpetrator blame and perceived severity. Based on previous theory/findings, these three variables should be correlated. This means that one MANOVA analysis is appropriate for the data to account for the shared variance in the dependent variables. If no relationship is found between the dependent variables, then three separate ANOVAs will be carried out. Irrespective of the analysis, the tests carried out will be informed by the design of the study such that a 2 (victim sexuality) × 2 (type of abuse) between-participants analysis will be completed (either MANOVA or ANOVA).

Timetable*

Week	July				August			
	1	2	3	4	1	2	3	4
Draft ethics and fieldwork materials	■							
Draft ethics application(s)		■						
Submit final ethics to Research Ethics Committee			■					
Build online questionnaire				■				
Launch questionnaire and collect data (following successful ethics application)					■			
Data analysis							■	
Final report writing								■

References

Basow, S. A., & Thompson, J. (2012). Service providers' reactions to intimate partner violence as a function of victim sexual orientation and type of abuse. *Journal of Interpersonal Violence, 27*, 1225–1241. doi:10.1177/0886260511425241

Brown, M.J., & Groscup, J. (2009). Perceptions of same-sex domestic violence among crisis center staff. *Journal of Family Violence, 24*, 87–93. doi:10.1007/s10896-008-9212-5

Davies, M., & McCartney, S. (2003). Effects of gender and sexuality on judgements of victim blame and rape myth acceptance in a depicted male rape. *Journal of Community & Applied Social Psychology, 13*, 391–398. doi:10.1002/casp.741

Pico-Alfonso, M.A., Garcia-Linares, I., Celda-Navarro, N., Blasco-Ros, C., Echeburua, E., & Martinez, M. (2006). The impact of physical, psychological, and sexual intimate male partner violence on women's mental health: Depressive symptoms, posttraumatic stress disorder, state anxiety, and suicide. *Journal of Women's Health, 15*, 599–611.

Poorman, P.B., Seelau, E.P., & Seelau, S.M. (2003). Perceptions of domestic abuse in same-sex relationships and implications for criminal justice and mental health responses. *Violence and Victims, 18*, 659–669. doi:10.1891/vivi.2003.18.6.659

146 Designing and planning

Seelau, S.M., & Seelau, E.P. (2005). Gender-role stereotypes and perceptions of heterosexual, gay and lesbian domestic violence. *Journal of Family Violence, 20,* 363–371. doi:10.1007/s10896-005-7798-4

Simpson, E.K., & Helfrich, C.A. (2007). Lesbian survivors of intimate partner violence: Provider perspectives on barriers to accessing services. *Journal of Gay & Lesbian Social Services: Issues in Practice, Policy & Research, 18,* 39–59. doi:10.1300/J041v18n02_03

Strömwall, L.A., Alfredsson, H., & Landström, S. (2013). Blame attributions and rape: Effects of belief in a just world and relationship level. *Legal and Criminological Psychology, 18,* 254–261. doi:10.1111/j.2044-8333.2012.02044.x

Sylaska, K.M., & Walters, A.S. (2014). Testing the extent of the gender trap: College students' perceptions of and reactions to intimate partner violence. *Sex Roles, 70,* 134–145. doi:10.1007/s11199-014-0344-1

*Please note that this is only an example. The time scales are very short and would often not be feasible within a real project, so keep this in mind when drafting your own timetable (see later section on project planning for more details).

Activity

Outline a research proposal for your research project, or a project idea. If you are not yet ready to specify the details of your study in some sections, outline the sort of information that you will include (e.g., specify IVs and DVs) so that you can easily and quickly add this information to your proposal when you are ready to do so.

Submitting your proposal

You should be now ready to submit your proposal. It is important to consider that you might need approval for your research from more than one organisation. If you are a student/researcher working at a university, it is very easy to focus only on the processes that are required for the university; however, the organisation(s) within which you wish to collect data, or which manage access to databases you wish to use, might have procedures for approving research projects/ designs (prior to seeking ethical permission) that you will also need to follow. Note that there may be specific deadlines that you will need to meet (e.g., an organisation might review proposals only once or twice a year). Do not assume that someone will tell you what these processes are (or that if you are not told about these processes that they do not exist). It is not possible for your supervisor/research tutor to know the procedures for every organisation within which it is possible to collect/use data, so you must actively seek out information about the processes *you* need to follow for the organisation within which you wish to collect data or whose data you wish to use/access. (It is still a good idea to discuss with your supervisor/tutor the best way of doing this.)

University timescales for the submission of proposals, particularly for projects that have to be completed in one year, are very tight. Submitting your proposal in line with the university deadline will leave you with just enough time to complete your study, so you might need to submit the research proposal to the organisation within which you wish to collect/use data before or at the same time as you submit the proposal to the university. Therefore, you will need to plan ahead to ensure that you can complete the project in the relevant timescale (and, as discussed in earlier chapters, you should have a plan B in case you are not granted approval). If this applies to your research project, discuss this issue with your supervisor/research tutor to determine the most appropriate way of dealing with this issue.

Project Planning

Throughout this book we have stressed the importance of planning ahead and thinking through the possibilities of what might happen in your research, so you should have a good sense already about the importance of project planning. It is quite common, particularly for university dissertation research projects, that there is a limited amount of time within which the research project needs to be completed and that there is a specific deadline for the final report (in whatever format is required). This means that carefully planning the research timetable is important. In this section we will outline some methods for documenting your planning and for carefully thinking through the potential risks involved in the project and how you can think through and document strategies that you might take to mitigate and/or avoid these. It is important to plan all research projects, including research dissertations. If you are submitting proposals for research (e.g., for a PhD application or funding application), then it is likely that you will need to include a proposed timetable and, in some instances, a risk assessment/ risk matrix. There are many ways in which timetables/risks can be documented, so it is important that you follow the method requested by the relevant organisation, if appropriate. If, however, no specific method is required, then you can use a Gantt chart and the risk table outlined in the following section.

Project schedule/timetable

The first step in planning your project is to think carefully through all the stages that are involved in completing the project. The key to successful planning is the level of detail that you put into the task list (without being too specific,

148   Designing and planning

e.g., you do not need to plan each individual email that you will send, but you need to be more specific than: obtain ethical approval, collect data, analyse data, write up). Following are some examples to demonstrate the level of detail that is appropriate:

- Drafting your ethics materials (i.e. participant information sheet, consent forms)
- Drafting your fieldwork materials (e.g. vignettes, interview schedule)
- Drafting your ethics application(s)
- Submitting your ethics application(s) drafts to your supervisor/colleague
- Revising your ethics materials/fieldwork schedules/ethics applications following feedback
- Submitting your ethics application(s)
- Revising your ethics materials/fieldwork schedules/ethics applications following ethics decision
- Resubmitting your ethics application(s)
- Contacting gatekeepers
- Producing/copying fieldwork materials for pilot study
- Recruiting pilot study participants
- Collecting pilot study data
- Analysing pilot study data
- Revising fieldwork materials following pilot
- Producing/copying fieldwork materials
- Recruiting participants
- Collecting data

As you can see, you will generate a long list of activities for each project. When you have listed the activities, you should consider which stages need to be completed before other stages can be started (e.g., you need ethical approval before you can begin asking participants to take part in your study or collecting your data) and which can be done over longer periods of time concurrently with other aspects of the project (e.g., you can draft your introduction and method sections of your write up from the start of the project until the first draft of your report is required). In this list, the first three 'drafting activities' could be completed in any order or concurrently, but each of these needs to be completed before a draft can be submitted to your supervisor/colleague; after that, most the stages need to be completed before the one that follows.

You should also consider when there might be periods of time in which some activities cannot be completed (e.g., when you are awaiting decisions regarding ethics) and which other activities can be completed during this time (e.g., reading up on the methods of analysis that you will use) so that you can use your time most effectively and avoid weeks of inactivity. You should also consider activities/commitments that need to be completed alongside your research (e.g., you might have other assessments that need to be completed or other work tasks to do) and personal activities (e.g., holidays, breaks, birthdays), so you can allocate time to your research project accordingly. Finally, you should consider the activities/commitments of key stakeholders and potential participants; generally, it is not a good idea, for instance, to plan to collect data in August (in the UK) because many people have holidays and/or child care commitments. If you are hoping to recruit students as participants, you need to consider when they will be available (teaching weeks) and when they won't (holidays/exam and assessment periods). You should discuss with your supervisor or research lead/colleagues the times that they are available/unavailable, and consider how long they would like/will need to complete tasks. There is no point sending your draft to your supervisor two days before the final report is due in, or when he or she is on holiday or otherwise busy, so you need to agree the dates that tasks will be completed across the research project team.

When you have listed the activities, you should then identify the earliest date that each activity can be started, the deadline for that activity, and the length of time you think it will take to complete. If you have any 'absolute' deadlines (e.g., deadlines for the dissertation thesis/research papers or for the completion of a PhD or funded project), then note these as crucial deadlines (e.g., bold/highlight) and work back from them, so that you know how much time you can spend on earlier tasks and when they need to be completed. You might produce a schedule (you could do this in whatever format you prefer: paper, Excel, Word or via project planning software) that includes the information shown in Table 8.1.

Table 8.1 Example of timetable for planning out the project process

Activity	Earliest start date	Deadline	Duration
Drafting ethics materials	10 October	15 November (draft to supervisor)	One day
Drafting fieldwork materials	10 October	15 November (draft to supervisor)	One day
Drafting ethics application(s)	10 October	15 November (draft to supervisor)	Half day
Revise ethics materials	22 November	29 November (ethics application)	Half day
Revise ethics materials	After ethics decision	One week after decision	Half day
Other deadlines			
Essay	10 October	7 December	
Presentation	1 November	10 December	
Personal activities			
Xmas holiday	22 December to 4 January		Two weeks

150 Designing and planning

At this stage there should be some flexibility about when tasks can be done (e.g., a task might one require one day, but there is a two-week period within which it can be completed). Where there is flexibility like this, you should schedule tasks as early as possible to allow for any delays. Similarly, your schedule should be based around completing tasks as soon as they can be done; your original schedule may mean that you have your draft ready two to three weeks before the deadline, for example, which allows time to take care of delays/problems as they arise. You will need to estimate the duration required for tasks based on your prior experience and advice from supervisors/colleagues and others. It is normal for people to underestimate the time that it takes to complete tasks, particularly when other people are involved. Ethics committees/panels may take a few weeks or a couple of months to respond. Bear in mind that it is most likely that you will need to make some revisions and resubmit your application, and there will be an additional period of time before you receive a response. Recruiting participants will also take time. Remember, your research is not a priority to potential participants in the way that it is for you, and you may need to be persistent in recruitment methods (whilst staying within the remit of your ethics applications/permissions).

Activity

- List all the activities involved in your research project or a project idea.
- Mark out the activities that can only be completed once other tasks have been done and note what these tasks are.
- Identify times when you are waiting on decisions/feedback from others and note activities that can be done during these times.
- Think about times/days/tasks that would be important to note due to the impact they would have on the project schedule (e.g., holidays).

Gantt Charts

Named after its inventor, Henry Gantt, a Gantt chart is a way of visually representing every task and phase of a project in a way that clearly shows what activities are being completed in each week (so you can see if more than one activity is required at a time). An example is shown in Figure 8.1.

As you can see, the activities that are required are listed on the left (note that the example does not contain all of the activities required to complete a research project) and the timeline for the project runs across the chart from left to right. You might find it easier to produce a Gantt chart with each week

	October	November	December	January	February	March	April
Project meetings/meet supervisor							
Draft ethics & fieldwork materials							
Draft ethics application(s)							
Submit draft ethics to supervisor							
Supervisor review drafts							
Revise ethics materials etc.							
Submit ethics application(s)							
Ethics application under review							
Revise ethics materials etc.							
Resubmit ethics application(s)							
Ethics application under review							
Contact gatekeepers							
Produce fieldwork materials (pilot)							
Recruit pilot study participants							
Collect pilot study data							
Analyse pilot study data							
Revise fieldwork materials							
Produce fieldwork materials							
Research paper/report							
Literature search/Literature review							
Draft Introduction							
Draft Method section							
Holidays/Unavailable							

Figure 8.1 An example of a simple Gantt chart

labelled with the date (e.g. 1/10 for the week of 1 October) so it is clear what activities should be completed each week. Using the dates/deadlines from your initial list, block out the weeks/blocks that you think you will need to complete each task. When tasks are dependent on previous tasks, it is easier/clearer to list these from top to bottom (as per the example), so that your blocks of activities move from left to right. Where you have different types of tasks (e.g., reading or drafting reports) that can be completed alongside other tasks, these can be listed together. Similarly, it is important to factor in meetings (e.g., with the research team or your supervisor) throughout the project, as well as periods of time when you or other team members cannot work on the project (as shown in the example). As discussed in Chapter 6, it is a good idea to have a plan B in case you experience difficulties with your plan A, and this should be included in your timetable/Gantt chart.

You can produce a Gantt chart in a variety of ways; the example (Figure 8.1) was produced with the table functions in Microsoft Word, but you might prefer to use a spreadsheet or another type of software. If you use project management software, you can normally produce a Gantt chart using this software once you have input all the elements of the project with respective date/duration information. It is most important that you plan your timetable and have a clear outline of the schedule that you can follow easily and that can be understood by others; the manner in which it is produced or the software you use to produce it are less important, so use whichever method you find easiest unless a specific method is requested.

152   Designing and planning

> ### Activity
>
> - Produce a Gantt chart for your research project or a research idea.
> - Make sure you include project team/supervisor meetings, activities that are clearly dependent on other activities, report writing, holidays and unavailable periods of time. You could also include deadlines for other assignments (e.g., you could produce a Gantt chart that includes the work you will do on all your assignments/tasks, so you can manage your time most effectively on a range of projects, if you find this helpful).

Monitoring and maintaining progress

It is important that you use your timetable/Gantt chart to monitor your progress throughout your project. If you are working as a member of a research team, then you should share your timetable with the members of the team; similarly, you should let your supervisor have a copy of your plan once you have agreed with him/her on the dates for the submission of drafts and provision of feedback. It is not unusual for people to spend a great deal of time producing a lovely detailed Gantt chart at the start of a project and then to never look at it again once it has been finished and perhaps reviewed by a supervisor or included in an research proposal.

You should try to keep to the schedule you outlined, so you will need to look at your timetable each week (and make a note of tasks that have been completed) to see what you should be doing. You may want to add this information into a diary or task list (or whatever method you use to plan your work schedule). If there are delays, then you should update the timetable accordingly, although it is important that you do not spend all you time updating your timetables to the detriment of the rest of your work! It would be very unusual for your project to progress exactly according to the schedule you outlined at the start of the project, so it is important not to panic at the first sign of a minor delay or change; however, it is important to consider each change to the schedule to determine whether it will have a significant impact on the timely completion of your project; most likely, you will need to adjust the schedule. As discussed in more detail later, you should identify key points by which certain tasks/activities should be achieved (e.g., ethical approval) so you can take timely decisions to revise your project or switch to plan B, if necessary.

It is unlikely that your research project will be the only project/task that you will be working on at any one time, so be prepared to work on your research when time becomes available. You might not have full days when you can read the papers you found in your literature search; it is more likely that you will need to read a paper or part of a paper when time becomes available. Similarly, even though you may estimate that it will take a day to complete your ethics materials, you do not need to do this in a single day. Success in your research project will be dependent on you using your time most efficiently, which is likely to mean that each day you will do some work on your research and some work on other tasks/activities. Where you can, try to set aside blocks of time for some tasks that require focussed/dedicated time (e.g., data analysis, writing) and schedule this and/or make any necessary arrangements (e.g., study leave) in a timely manner.

Risks and risk management

As we outlined in Chapter 6, research is not always a smooth process. You will need the help and support of a number of individuals, such as gatekeepers, stakeholders and participants, who are likely to be busy with a wide range of priorities of their own. Your research project is very important to you, but it is not likely to be such a high priority to everyone else; therefore, it is important to consider this at all times and at all stages in the research process. For example, you should plan to keep stakeholders informed about your progress and to take time to produce good-quality (e.g., typo-free) materials for potential participants. You should also consider the best method to approach participants and collect data from them so it is easier for them to take part in the study, even if this means that it involves extra effort on your part. Thinking these things through from the start will help you plan an appropriate schedule/timetable for your project. Considering these issues, you should also highlight stages/activities in the research project that could be more difficult to complete (e.g., data collection that is dependent on a number of participants agreeing to give their time to take part in your study) or might not work out as you would hope (e.g., a gatekeeper does not give permission for the research).

Some typical examples of risks for research projects are listed here; it is important to consider that risks are project specific, so you need to think carefully about the risks in each project.

- Gatekeeper permission is not granted.
- Permission is not given to use measures/tools.
- Ethical approval is not obtained.
- Ethical approval decision takes considerably longer than anticipated.
- There is a delay in obtaining the copies of the measures required.
- You run out of printing credits before you copy/print the required research materials.
- Recruitment of participants is slow or problematic.
- An error in the research materials is identified partway through data collection.
- You do not recruit the number of participants anticipated/the number required for the analysis to have sufficient statistical power.
- You, your supervisor or members of the project team become ill or unavailable.

154 Designing and planning

- Your computer crashes and you lose the data analysis/drafts you have been working on.
- The analysis you planned to run is not possible with the data collected.
- The printer breaks/you run out of printer ink.

It is important to remember that many research projects are completed successfully, so the aim of risk assessment is not to stop you from starting a project or to make you feel that your project is doomed to failure. However, if you think through the stages/activities where there might be difficulties, you can take measures to manage these risks. Many of the risks previously listed are relatively easy to manage/mitigate (e.g., if you do not leave printing your report to the day of the deadline, running out of printer ink is a minor irritation rather than a major problem). The purpose of listing the risks, therefore, is to enable the identification of risk management strategies that you should build into your schedule/timetable.

There are a range of other measures that you can take to mitigate risks if you think through the potential issues carefully. If, for instance, you think that potential participants might be suspicious about your research, then it might be possible for you to speak to them and outline your project and the reasons for it and to provide opportunities for questions, rather than relying on a 'dry' participant information sheet given to potential participants by someone other than you. The way in which this risk is managed, therefore, is by adapting your participant recruitment strategy in the design stage, which should be reflected in your research plan/timetable. Despite your best efforts to think through the potential problems in recruiting participants or collecting data, for example, some issues might present themselves, and these will need to be managed throughout the project; it is important, then, to build in time into your schedule to allow for a change to your recruitment strategies or data collection practices. Remember, it is likely that you do not have to collect all your data before you can start entering some of it into the statistical package you intend to use, or you can start transcribing your data (or you can start drafting sections of your report/thesis); as highlighted previously, it is important to consider what activities you can be completing at all stages of your research project to maximise the use of your time and avoid periods in which you complete no work on the project at all.

Activity

For each of the risks previously listed, identify one or two risk mitigation/management strategies that could be employed to limit the impact of the risks on completion of the project. In some instances, the risks can be managed by planning ahead (e.g., having spare printer ink and not

Research proposal 155

> leaving the printing of the report to the last minute), but others can be more difficult to manage because you are reliant on other people. Even in these instances, planning ahead, starting in good time and so forth can minimise the impact the risk has on the completion of your project. Not obtaining gatekeeper permission could clearly have a significant impact on your project; however, you could 'sound out' the gatekeeper at an early stage to see if he/she is likely to support the research. If a gatekeeper is set against the idea at this early stage, you can develop a new project, rather than persist with something that is unlikely to be supported/successful. Note, however, that it is *important to seek advice from your supervisor/colleagues to determine the best stage to approach gatekeepers/ stakeholders.* If you approach them too early, before you have a clear idea about the research, the proposed method and so forth, you are unlikely to be supported and it might not put you/your supervisor in a good light if you present a poorly thought out or vague idea. So, as we keep saying, it is important to think this through carefully, and approach gatekeepers at a stage when you have a clear idea/outline of your project but that is early enough to allow you to revise your plans if needed.

Having a plan B that you can use if you do not obtain gatekeeper or ethical approval or you cannot recruit participants for plan A is a risk-management strategy. It is important to consider some key dates by which you should have completed various tasks so you can identify dates when the decision to switch to plan B has to be made. Your research is unlikely to hit a total/sudden 'brick wall', although this might happen if you do not get initial gatekeeper permission. What is more likely to happen, however, is a series of small delays: for example, it takes a while to get gatekeeper permission, and then takes a while for the authors of the measure you want to use to give permission to use the measure and so on. Each of these processes might not take too long, but they can quickly have an impact on your ability to complete your project on time, particularly if you have a short period of time in which to complete it. It may be easy to sort out each issue in turn and hope that things will speed up and that you will be able to finish the project on time, but you may suddenly find that the research deadline is a fortnight away and you have only collected data from two participants. For this reason, it is important to bear in mind the time that plan B will require so you know when you need to make a decision as to whether you continue with plan A or switch to plan B. If you have built a Plan B into the 'main' project (which is a risk management strategy) – for example, you will include two groups of participants rather than three – then this decision is likely to be simpler than a plan B that involves a completely new project. Using your timetable/Gantt chart is important in this decision making, so you can see

Table 8.2 Example risk assessment for case study one

Risk	Likelihood	Impact	Mitigation	Revised likelihood	Revised impact
Ethics approval takes longer than expected	2	4	Appropriate time has already been planned into the Gantt chart. Should this be extended, additional tasks will be completed whilst waiting for approval, e.g., writing introduction for final report.	2	2
Ethics application is rejected	3	5	Feasibility of the project has already been discussed with the organisation that is reviewing the ethics application, so it is considered unlikely that an application will be fully rejected. However, it is recognised that amendments may be required before final approval is achieved. Time has been built into the Gantt chart to allow for this.	3	2
Web site instability	2	5	As data is being gathered through an online questionnaire, web site instability is a key concern. However, online questionnaire hosting sites have been examined and the most popular/established site host has been chosen for us within the project. This should minimise any likelihood of the questionnaire being unavailable for participants.	2	2
Poor participant recruitment	3	5	Strategies have been developed by the researcher to ensure that the required participant sample size will be achieved. These include a presentation to staff members at the start of the project so that potential participants understand the purpose of the project. The gatekeeper within the organisation has also arranged for the study to be published through several organisation information systems (e.g., daily news) and for posters to be placed within the organisation offices. Recruitment of participants will be monitored throughout the data collection period to ensure that the required number of participants is achieved.	1	1

Note: The rating scale of the risk is based on 1 = low impact/likelihood to 5 = high impact/likelihood.

how much you are delayed and how much time to have left (and whether you can reschedule the activities so you can complete your project on time).

In Table 8.2, we have included a risk assessment for case study one, based on the example proposal in section one of this chapter. This risk assessment includes a list of the potential risks (one the left) and also assessments of the likelihood that the risk will occur and the potential impact this will have on the project (e.g., not gaining ethical approval will have a much greater impact on the project than running out of printer ink). The mitigation is then outlined and a revised likelihood and impact following the implementation of the mitigation are also shown. You will not always need to include assessments of the likelihood or impact, but it is important to identify the potential risks for your project and the risk mitigation/management strategies that you will employ, even if you do not present these formally to anyone. The manner in which you document your risk assessment is not likely to be of major concern unless a specific format/style has been requested, in which case you should clearly follow the instructions/guidance given.

Summary and checklist

In this chapter, we have outlined the process for developing your research proposal and how to plan appropriately for carrying out your project. In completing this chapter, you should now understand:

1   The importance of the research proposal in providing you with the opportunity to explain and outline your project in full.
2   That that proposal should be the culmination of all of the processes that you have completed in developing your ideas, searching the literature, deciding on methods and so forth.
3   How to appropriately structure the proposal. Use the headings in section one as a guide to structure your proposal but remember that these should be adapted according to any required templates.
4   The importance of project planning, which is often overlooked with a research project. As you should now know, we strongly recommend that you properly plan out the time that you need to carry out your project. This will ensure that you know exactly how much time you have available for each task and will ensure that your final project is not rushed or late.
5   How to plan your project using a Gantt chart. This is an excellent method to help you in planning out this process, so give it a try for your project.

Further reading

Denicolo, P., & Becker, L. (2012). *Developing research proposals 1* (Success in Research). London, England: Sage.

158 Designing and planning

Denscombe, M. (2012). *Research proposals: A practical guide* (Open UP Study Skills). Maidenhead, Berkshire: Open University Press.

Punch, K.F. (2006). *Developing effective research proposals* (2nd ed.). London, England: Sage.

For more information about Gantt charts, see http://www.gantt.com

References

Braun, V., & Clarke, V. (2006). Using thematic analysis in psychology. *Qualitative Research in Psychology, 3,* 77–101. doi:10.1191/1478088706qp063oa

Heider, F. (1958). *The psychology of interpersonal relations.* New York, NY: Wiley.

Smith, J.A., Jarman, M., & Osborn, M. (1999). Doing interpretative phenomenological analysis. In M. Murray & K. Chamberlain (Eds.), *Qualitative health psychology: Theories and methods* (pp. 218–240). London, England: Sage.

Section 2

Conducting research

Chapter 9

Gaining ethical approval

Now that you have completed the planning for your research, and assuming that your research proposal has been given the necessary permissions, you can now begin conducting your empirical research project. The first stage of any empirical project is obtaining relevant ethical and gatekeeper permissions to conduct your research. You *must* obtain the relevant approval(s) before you approach potential participants and request that they take part in your research and/or before you collect any data (including piloting stages of your project). Note that as the lead researcher, it is your responsibility to ensure that you have requested/obtained the required permissions/approvals. If you are working on a project that someone else is leading, then you should be satisfied that the relevant approvals/permissions have been achieved (do not be afraid to ask for confirmation). Do not assume that someone will tell you what permissions/approvals you need to get, and do not assume that silence on this matter means that no approval is required. You must actively seek out information about these processes. Professionals who do not conduct research might not be aware of the ethical procedures that are required, so you need to make sure that you thoroughly check the approvals/permissions you need to obtain (speak to your supervisor, if appropriate, or experienced researchers in the area if you are unsure what is required). It is unlikely that no form of approval is required, and you might need to obtain permission from more than one organisation (e.g., from your university *and* from the organisation within which you are collecting data, such as police, probation or prison services). Each organisation will have its own procedure, forms and requirements that you must follow (some of which are overseen by national organisations, such as the National Offender Management Service [NOMS]). In the unusual event that permissions/approvals are not required, we would advise that you obtain confirmation (written/email) that approval is not required for the project from a suitable senior gatekeeper.

In this chapter, we will outline the processes required and appropriate codes of conduct and guidelines that should be followed in gaining ethical approval. We will explain how participant information sheets (PISs), consent forms and debrief information should be constructed with examples that would be appropriate for some of the case studies. It is likely that you will be asked to

162 Conducting research

respond to feedback and to make revisions suggested by ethical approval panels/
boards, so approaches to responding to feedback and revising proposals will
be discussed. It is important to note that while we will outline the processes
required, organisations constantly update their ethical guidelines/procedures
and the requirements for PISs, consent forms and debrief information change
over time. Furthermore, given the large number of organisations and countries
in which you might wish to collect data, it is beyond the scope of this chapter
to detail all the processes for every organisation/country in detail, so you must
consult the latest documents, ethical guidelines, university/organisation information and so forth and follow their instructions/guidance carefully.

Once you have read this chapter, you should be able to:

- list the key organisations/types of organisations whose ethical/research
  guidance and/or codes of conduct apply to you in undertaking your
  project;
- understand the key requirements of an ethical approval proposal;
- construct PISs, consent forms and debrief information;
- identify other documents that you need for your application;
- complete an ethics application; and
- appropriately respond to feedback and requests for revisions.

Ethical guidance/codes of conduct

As discussed in Chapter 7, it is most likely that you will need to follow the
guidance or adhere to the codes of conduct of a number of organisations when
you are carrying out your research. For example, you will need to follow the
codes of conduct and/or research/ethics guidance for:

- the psychology association(s) for the geographic area(s) within which you
  are studying/working and collecting data (see Chapter 7) *and*
- the professional registration body for which you (and your supervisor) are
  registered or are trainees (e.g., the Health and Care Professions Council)
  (see Chapter 7) *and*
- the organisation(s) within which you are conducting the research (e.g., the
  university where you are studying) *and*
- the organisation(s) within which you are practicing as a psychologist/
  trainee/assistant *and*
- the organisation(s) within which you are collecting/using data.

This might sound rather daunting, but is made easier by the fact that there is
usually a great deal of similarity between the general principles/requirements
(see Chapter 7) across associations/organisations. You must ensure, however,
that you are familiar with the requirements of each. This information should

be readily accessible (this is an ethical requirement for organisations) via the organisations' web pages and/or staff resources.

Activity

Look through the ethical codes of conduct/guidance for the psychological association(s) that are relevant to you (look at EFPA guidance in addition to the psychological association if you are researching in Europe) and the relevant registration bodies. List the core ethical principles/requirements of each and note areas of similarity/overlap, as well as any differences. Draw up a single list of the ethical principles that you should follow. Locate and read the research guidance/rules of all the organisations that are applicable to your research/practice. Identify areas of similarity and difference. Compare the requirements of the organisations with those of the psychology associations and regulatory bodies; add any new principles/rules to your ethical principles list and determine if there are any conflicts in the rules/guidance that are relevant to your research study.

In some instances you might find that there is a conflict between the codes of conduct/guidance of different organisations; for example, psychological guidance might state that when conducting research with children you should seek opt-in consent from the children and opt-out consent from the parents, but your organisation might require opt-in consent from both children and parents. In this instance this issue is fairly easy to resolve, as opt-in consent from both is the most stringent requirement and is not opposed by the psychological guidance; therefore, seeking opt-in consent from both is the simplest solution. If there are specific reasons why this is not possible, then you might be able to discuss this with the organisation and seek permission to make an exception for your study. Note, however, that this is likely to take time or might not be possible/feasible, so you need to consider this carefully after discussing it with relevant supervisors/colleagues/managers.

In other instances, you might find that the *guidance* of two organisations is different. In this case, bear in mind that the organisations are providing guidance rather than strict rules, so you should choose the most appropriate procedure bearing the general ethical principles in mind. It is always a good idea to discuss issues such as this with relevant supervisors/colleagues. Furthermore, in your ethical proposal, you should outline the issue with respect to the difference between the two sets of guidance and outline why you have chosen the proposed procedure. This issue can be more difficult to resolve when there are specific rules/legislative requirements (discussed later) that are at odds. Again, you should discuss this with colleagues/supervisors; it might be that there is a

164   Conducting research

way to meet the requirements of both that you have not considered, or there may be ways of dealing with the issue have been developed by others.

Ethical dilemmas

If you are faced with issues such as those previously mentioned, or something arises in the course of the research that generates an ethical dilemma or that you are not sure how to deal with ethically, there are a number ethical decision-making procedures and other guidance that you can follow (see 'Further reading' section). Most importantly, you should not ignore these issues simply because you are not sure what to do, and you should deal with the issue as soon as is practically possible. As highlighted previously, it is always a good idea to discuss the issue with a supervisor/gatekeeper/ line manager/colleagues. Bear in mind, if appropriate, that you can often find a way to discuss an issue without breaching confidentiality, or you can discuss the issue with a psychologist/professional on the basis that they will maintain the confidentiality of the individuals involved. As outlined in the decision-making processes/guidance, you should clearly document the issue that has arisen, the steps you took to resolve the issue and the decisions and actions taken, by whom and why.

Activity

Locate and read at least one ethical decision-making procedure/process. If you identified any conflicts relevant to your research in the previous activity, use this process to reach a decision to resolve the issue (remember to document this). If no conflicts arose in the previous activity, consider how you would resolve the following issue in relation to case study five.

In order to complete all the testing required for the study, participants will need to attend additional sessions to the treatment sessions. The principle of responsibility means that you should consider reimbursing participants' travel costs for the testing sessions. The guidance of your organisation, however, indicates that payments of any type are not permitted for individuals who have engaged in criminal activities (which they deem to include violence), and it does not have a procedure for processing travel claims for research participants. A further issue is that since there is no funding for the research, you, personally, would have to fund any travel expenses and costs of the research.

Legislation

In addition to considering ethical issues you will most likely also be required to conduct your research in adherence to the legislative requirements of the countries within which you are conducting research. If you are collecting data in more than one legislative jurisdiction/region, or using data that was collected across legislative regions, then you need to comply with the relevant legislation of all regions. If you are studying in one legislative region and conducting research in another, then again, you will need to comply with legislation in each region. It is your responsibility to ensure that you comply with the appropriate legislative requirements.

It is not possible to outline the details of all legislative requirements in this book; however, the areas and issues relevant to conducting research that are likely to be governed by legislation are:

- human rights;
- equality;
- practice (which includes research and contact/communication with clients/patients etc.) as psychologists/health and social care professionals;
- data protection; and
- mandatory reporting (e.g., of sexual offences or risk of harm).

Case study one

If this research project was being conducted with West Midlands Police (whose officers will be asked to participate) by a student at Coventry University, under the supervision of a forensic psychologist (registered with the HCPC) employed by Coventry University, using an online survey to collect data, the researcher would need to need to adhere to the following guidance and legislation:

1 BPS Code of Conduct, Code of Human Research Ethics and Guidelines for Internet Mediated Research
2 HCPC Standards of Proficiency
3 Coventry University's research ethics
4 West Midland Police research procedures
5 Legislation on

- human rights
- equality
- data protection

Ethical approval processes

As previously discussed, the first stage of seeking ethical approval is to determine to which ethical approval panels/boards the proposal needs to be submitted. This can be difficult to establish, as the procedures vary by organisation and often depend on the type of research project being proposed, so you will need to find and carefully read through information from a range of sources. If you are conducting research within (as a student, paid or voluntary researcher, member of staff) or in collaboration with a university, as a minimum you will need to obtain approval from your university. Processes vary across universities, and the process you need to follow is likely to depend on the type of project you wish to conduct; for example, projects deemed 'low risk' (perhaps because anonymous data previously collected will be used) might require different procedures than projects deemed 'high risk' (perhaps because they involve collecting data from offenders or victims). In addition, different procedures might need to be followed if the project only requires approval from the university than for projects that require approval from organisation(s) in addition to the university. If you are not conducting research with a university, then you will need to consider whether you need approval from the organisation for which you work, and you will need establish how you should obtain ethical approval in respect of the organisation from which you will collect/use data. Note that this can mean that you need to achieve approval from one organisation (e.g., your university) before you can apply to another (external board), so you need to factor this into your timetable.

The processes for seeking approval for studies conducted in the UK are outlined here; as previously discussed, remember that you will probably also need approval from your university in addition to these. You will need to determine the order in which the applications should be made (e.g., at Coventry University, approval must be sought from the university *before* external organisations) and the processes for applying. This information is correct as far as we can determine at the time of writing (November 2014). Please note that these processes are subject to change. Therefore, you must clarify the obligations that are required at the time of your application. The information herein should give you an idea of the sorts of processes required, even if the exact details have changed.

National Health Service (NHS)

If your study involves data collection in NHS settings and/or with NHS staff/patients or relates to health in prisons (NOMS, Northern Ireland or Scotland) or individuals over the age of 16 who lack (or lose) the mental capacity to give informed consent, you should apply for approval through the online Integrated Research Application System (IRAS) (see 'Further reading' section). Note that the IRAS system incorporates a number of national ethical approval processes, so you will need to answer questions that will be used to direct you to the correct forms/procedures.

Social Care

If your research concerns adult social care, intergenerational studies involving adults and children or families, or use of social care databases, you should apply to the Social Care Research Ethics Committee, via IRAS.

Prison, Probation, Young Offenders' Institutions (YOI)

England and Wales

If you intend to conduct research in a single prison (HM prison or 'contracted' prison) or YOI, you should follow the NOMS approval process (see 'Further reading' section) or apply via IRAS. You will need to download the NOMS form and complete it. The form should be accompanied by applicant CVs, any ethical submissions and approvals, and any questionnaires, consent forms or other documents. This form should be reviewed by the institution within which you wish to conduct the research, with NOMS being notified. The NOMS approval process excludes research in secure training centres, secure children's homes or with youth offending teams. Applications to conduct research in these areas should be directed to the Youth Justice Board. If your research has been commissioned by NOMS, relates to more than one establishment/trust or concerns extremism or a topic of 'national significance', you should apply via IRAS. The application will be reviewed by the NOMS ethics panel (i.e., at a national level, rather than an individual institution/trust level).

At the time of writing, during the reorganisation of community offender supervision processes, undergraduate and master's students are not permitted to conduct research within the National Probation Service or the organisations that have been awarded the Community Rehabilitation Company contracts. In the past, approval to conduct research in probation trusts has been via processes similar to those outlined (i.e., via NOMS, with applications approved by individual trusts and NOMS notified) for research conducted within a single trust, and nationally for research in more than one trust or on the topics previously identified. This process may change in time, so it is important that you check with the relevant organisations.

Northern Ireland

You should seek approval via the Northern Ireland Prison Service or the Northern Ireland Probation Service (as appropriate).

Scotland

You should seek approval from the Scottish Prison Service or, for community projects, from the relevant organisation (e.g., criminal justice social work service).

Police

You should apply via the relevant approval process for each police force. Most police forces have their own format of application form, so you will need to contact the police force to ensure that you complete the relevant form. The application process can also vary according to whether you want to access data that is routinely gathered by the police (e.g., in relation to reported crimes) or you want to recruit participants (e.g., police officers) within the organisation. Again, these processes can vary considerably from police force to police force, so you will need to familiarise yourself with the particular processes required for the police force with which you want to research. This information is often not published on publicly accessible police web pages, so you will need to contact the relevant individual within the organisation.

Courts

Approval to use documents from court cases is required from HM Courts and Tribunal Service. You need approval from the respective judicial offices for each jurisdiction in the UK to conduct research involving the judiciary. Note that approval is unlikely for student projects.

Remember, if you wish to collect data across contexts or organisations (e.g., if you wanted to conduct research regarding prisoners across the UK), you will need to apply to each relevant organisation (e.g., NOMS, NI Prison Service and Scottish Prison Service).

Activity

- For each of the case studies, list the approval processes that will be required before data collection can begin.
- Identify the approval processes required for your study.

Constructing Ethical Information

Before you apply for ethical approval, there is a significant amount of work required to develop all your research materials (interview schedules, vignettes, dependent variable measures etc.) and to construct the ethical documents that you will have to use. You will need to provide participants with information about your study using a PIS, seek their consent via a consent form or consent statements, and provide them with debrief information that you present when they have completed your study. In addition, you will require evidence of appropriate gatekeeper permission.

Gatekeeper approval

If you are conducting research in organisations, privately owned locations or particular situations (e.g., during lectures of classes), you will need gatekeeper approval. Gatekeepers are essentially senior people who are able to provide permission for research in the relevant context (e.g., the head of an organisation or service). In many instances, approval for research is required from the most senior people in organisations, but you should also make sure that you have approval from the most senior person in the specific area that you will be conducting the research (e.g., your research might need approval via senior staff in a specific police force, but you should also obtain permission from the police officer in charge of the station or section directly relevant to your project). Some examples of research contexts that require approval with appropriate gatekeepers are listed in Table 9.1. In your ethical approval application(s) you will need to provide evidence of this approval; this usually takes the form of a signed, headed letter. An email from the gatekeeper's organisational email account may be sufficient; however, you should check the requirements of the relevant ethics committee. In addition, you may need approval from the authors of testing materials/measures or other items, which you should also evidence in an appropriate manner.

Permission of this type will take time to obtain. Remember that your research project is not the priority of the head of a busy organisation, so you need to build in time for this. You might have to remind gatekeepers to send you the document, but remember, no one appreciates hourly/daily phone calls/ emails about the same issue! Think about how you can make this process as easy as possible for the gatekeepers (without making them feel that you have decided for them), by providing an example or template of a letter that would be appropriate. You should plan ahead and contact the gatekeepers as soon as you are able to allow time before you need to submit your ethics application(s). The gatekeepers will need information about your project (e.g., you might want to send them your proposal) so they can make an informed decision. It is important that you politely request permission to conduct research in the organisation; do not assume that your research will be approved or that it should be approved. It would be a good idea to stress the benefits of the research, particularly if there are benefits to the organisation, and also to state how you will communicate your research findings to the gatekeeper/organisation.

Table 9.1 Examples of research situations that require gatekeeper approval with suggested gatekeepers

Research situation	Gatekeeper
Prison, including use of prison records	Prison governor and, if input of psychology staff is required, head of psychology
School or college	Head teacher or principal
Shopping centre	Senior manager responsible for shopping centre
Employer (e.g., for employees to be participants)	Head of organisation (required if the research is about the organisation's service/provision) and/or head of local establishment
Forensic service provider	Head of organisation and regional/local head
Lecture/class	Lecturer/class tutor
Permission to use measure/ psychometric scale	Author(s) of the measure/scale and, where appropriate, the publishers

170 Conducting research

Activity

- For each of the case studies, list the organisations/individuals from which gatekeeper approval will be required.
- Identify the permissions required for your study and the gatekeepers you need to approach for approval for your study. Discuss these with your supervisor/line manager (or a colleague) and identify the best approaches for contacting gatekeepers about your study.

Research materials

In order for your research to be approved, the reviewers require information about all aspects of the research that will determine whether the research is appropriate/ethical. This means that they will need to see: (a) all the information that will be provided to participants during the research process, including vignettes, materials, views in computer experiments etc., and (b) all the questions that you will ask participants, including interview schedules, dependent variable measures and questionnaires. If you are using a published measure/scale, you may not be required to provide copies as long as you have provided the relevant references and it has established reliability/validity. Bear in mind, however, that some ethics committees require copies of all information that participants will be asked to complete, so you should be ready to provide this information.

Ethical approval is often seen as an early stage of the research process, and many people are surprised that copies of all materials are required (e.g., that interview schedules have to be developed at this stage). In case we have not stressed this enough already, this should reinforce just how much work is required on your research project in the design/initial stages. Changes to your research materials (other than correcting minor typos) will require reapproval from ethics committees, so it is important that you do not rush this stage. Remember, as we have emphasised previously, it is important in developing these materials that you consider the types and levels of data that will be produced and the impact of this on your potential analyses. See Chapters 3 and 4 for more information about developing these materials and for further reading suggestions (e.g., on writing questions/questionnaires).

Activity

- For each of the case studies, list the research materials that will be required.
- Identify the research materials required for your study.

Participant Information Sheets (PISs)

The PIS should provide a clear outline of your study. It should be presented in a style that is concise and appropriate for your participants. Remember that if you are collecting data from different groups of participants, it might be necessary to produce different information sheets for each group. Remember that words that you have become familiar with through your psychological studies might not be so readily understood by nonpsychologists, so be careful to ensure that you explain things clearly without using jargon, yet at the same time without being patronising. The briefing should always be written in a way that an 11-year-old child would understand. This means explaining any technical terms and avoiding complex language. It is a good idea to ask someone unfamiliar with your study to read the information. You should also carefully proofread your work to ensure that there are no typos or spelling or grammar mistakes.

Different organisations require PIS information to be presented in different ways, although the general principles are similar. You should follow the format that is requested by the relevant organisations. A PIS should always include the following basic information about the study:

- information about you as the researcher;
- contact information for you and/or your supervisor;
- information about the nature of the research about to be undertaken;
- a description of what the participants will be expected to do;
- acknowledgement of any sensitive issues relating to participating in the study;
- how long the study will take;
- who will have access to the raw data and any copies of the data (e.g., transcripts, statistical analysis files) and who will not;
- how long the different types of data will be stored, where will they be stored and when will they be destroyed;
- assurances regarding confidentiality or anonymity (not both);
- confirmation that participation is voluntary; and
- an explanation of the method by which participants can withdraw their data after the conclusion of the data collection session, including a deadline for doing this.

Common confusion

The terms *confidential* and *anonymous* are often used interchangeably, when in fact they mean different things. If data is collected *anonymously*, it means that it is not possible to identify an individual from that data; hence, if you say that you will store data anonymously, it will not be possible for you to

172 Conducting research

determine which data belong to which participants. *Confidentiality* refers to ensuring that you do not disclose the identity of the individuals; for example, if you store data confidentially, then the names or other identifying features are stored with the data. In reports and similar documents, you should ensure that the identifying details are not revealed. If you share data, you should ensure the data are de-identified (i.e., anonymous). In information you provide to participants and in reports about your study, you should be clear about the use of these two terms. Do not tell people that you are collecting/storing data anonymously if it is possible to identify individuals from it.

A good way of presenting this information is to organise it under the sub-headings that are shown in the example PIS created for case study one below.

Participant information sheet for case study one

Study title

What is the impact of victim sexuality and type of abuse (physical or nonphysical) on police officers' responses to intimate partner violence (IPV) victims?

What is the purpose of the study?

The aim of this study is to examine police officers' responses to IPV victims.

Why have I been approached?

You have been asked to take part in this study because you are a police officer in the West Midlands police force who responds to IPV victims.

Do I have to take part?

No. Participation is entirely voluntary. I have been asked to complete the study by West Midlands Police; however, I am an independent researcher. There will be no consequences if you decide that you do not wish to take part in the study. If you take part but change your mind, you can withdraw at any point during the research by simply closing the web browser. If you complete the research, you can withdraw from the study at any time in the two weeks after you complete the study. At the end of the study, you will be asked to provide a code that you can remember. If you wish to withdraw from the study, email me using the contact details at the end of this sheet, stating your code. Your responses will then be destroyed and not used in the study.

What will happen if I take part?

You will be sent an email that includes a web link to an online study. When you are ready to complete the study, click on the web link and follow the instructions on the screen. You can complete the study on any computer or tablet. Please note that the study includes a description of an IPV case, so it would be best to complete the study in private. You will first be asked to indicate that you agree to take part in the study, and then you will be asked to read an example of IPV. You will then be asked to respond to some questions about the example. In the final part of the study, you will be asked to provide some details about yourself (age, gender, ethnicity), your experience as a police officer and your experience in responding to IPV. The study will take approximately 20 minutes to complete.

What are the possible disadvantages and risks of taking part?

The study will take time to complete. I do not expect any other risks in taking part in the research. After taking part in the study, you will be provided with sources of information where you can find out more about IPV and sources of support, in case participating in the study raises any worries or concerns.

What are the possible benefits of taking part?

You will be contributing to a study that has been requested by West Midland Police managers so that they can determine how officers respond to different types of IPV victims. The aim of the study is to ensure that IPV victims are responded to equally and to find out if there any training needs.

What if something goes wrong?

If you experience any difficulties in completing the survey, please contact me using the contact details at the end of this document. If you change your mind about taking part in the study, you can withdraw at any point during the study completion and at any time in the two weeks after you complete the study by contacting me using the email below. If you decide to withdraw, all your data will be destroyed and will not be used in the study.

Will my taking part in this study be kept confidential?

Yes. You will not be asked to put any identifying details, such as your name, in the survey. Only I will have access to your survey responses. When the information is transferred to the statistical software for analysis, the secret code will not be recorded. The survey responses will be stored on my university password-protected computer, and they will be destroyed three months after the submission of the report to West Midland Police. The anonymous data file used for data analysis will be kept for a further two years.

What will happen to the results of the research study?

The results will be presented in a report that is given to DCI Smith. I will discuss the findings of the study at West Midland Police Headquarters at a date to be agreed upon, and you will be invited to attend. The results may also be presented at academic conferences and/or written up for publication in peer-reviewed academic journals.

Who is organising and funding the research?

The research has been commissioned by DCI Smith, West Midland Police. I [name of researcher] am organising and completing the research. This project is not externally funded.

Who has reviewed the study?

The Coventry University Research Ethics Committee and the West Midland Police have reviewed and approved this study.

Contact for further information

Name of researcher
Researcher's email address
Researcher's telephone number

It is important to note that although the standard practice is to present this information in a written format and to allow participants to keep this information, in some instances this might not be appropriate. With some groups of offenders, you might need to consider that they do not want to be identified as offenders (e.g., if they are in the community) or as a particular type of offender (e.g., as a sex offender in a mixed-offender prison). Similarly, survivors of crime might not wish for others to know about their victimisation. In these and other situations, you need to be sensitive as to how this information is presented and retained (and how you contact participants). A solution to this can be to provide a blank envelope within which to keep the information, which may be sufficient in some situations; in other situations, it might be best for individuals to not retain the written information and you should consider if there are other methods of making the information available. Written information for individuals with visual disabilities is clearly not going to be appropriate, and you need to consider how you will present this information to this group. For individuals with learning difficulties, you should consider explaining the study verbally on a one-to-one basis. Whenever possible, you should provide opportunities for individuals to ask questions and request additional information.

Activity

Construct a PIS for your study using the headings shown in the previous box, or according to the format specified by your university/organisation.

Consent Forms

When participants have read the PIS, you should seek their consent. Traditionally, this is done via a paper consent form that participants are asked to sign. This is the preferred method whenever you are collecting data face-to-face. When you are collecting data remotely (e.g., online), you will have to seek participants' consent in other ways (e.g., by asking participants to indicate their consent by responding to online questions). Whichever method you use, a similar approach should be used, in that you should check that participants understand key aspects of the ethical elements of the study (e.g., that they understand that they can withdraw) before asking them to indicate that they consent to taking part in the study. As a minimum, a consent form should include the following:

Participant Reference Code:_____

*I have read and understand the participant information sheet and by signing below I consent to participate in this study.
*I understand that I have the right to withdraw from the study without giving a reason at any time during the study itself.
*I understand that I also have the right to change my mind about participating in the study for a short period after the study has concluded (insert deadline here).

Signed:_____

Print name:_____

Witnessed by:_____

Print name:_____

Researcher's signature:_____

* Where a paper consent form is not appropriate, you should ask participants to agree to these statements and a further statement as follows: By completing this study, I am giving my consent for you to use my responses in this research study.

176 Conducting research

All signatures must be witnessed. You, as the researcher, can act as the witness. You must give all participants a copy of the signed consent form with the PIS. However, the consent form and information sheet must be on separate pages. Rather than photocopying signatures, you can produce two consent statements on one page, ask the participant to sign both parts, and give him/her the bottom half of the page. Make sure the participant's copy has the participant code on it, so he or she can withdraw data later if desired.

You do not need to obtain signed consent from participants if you are asking them to complete some paper-based scales or questionnaires. In this instance, instead of a consent sheet, you would put the following on the front page of your questionnaire. However, you do need to get signed consent if you are asking participants to complete this type of information in addition to another task or other activity.

I have read and I understand the participant information sheet
for this study. ☐
By handing this questionnaire back to you, completed, I am
giving my consent for you to use my questionnaire answers
in this research study. ☐
I understand that I have the right to withdraw my questionnaire at
any point, by contacting you using the details on the participant
information sheet and quoting the participant reference code
written at the top. ☐

Activity

Construct a consent form for your study, or list the statements that you will include at the start of your paper questionnaire/scale or the statements that you will include at the start of an online study.

Debrief information

In the debrief information you should do all of the following, with the exception of items six and seven, which might not be appropriate (but consider this carefully).

1   Thank the participant for completing the study.
2   Explain the study and its aims. Here you should explain the study in more detail than you did in the PIS; for example, if you have used a between-groups design, you should explain that the information that participants read (or condition they participated in) varied, explain how

it varied and indicate that the aim is to compare the responses of groups of participants so that you can identify the impact of the differences. In cross-sectional studies, you should explain the groups being compared and so forth. You do not need to go into lengthy detail here, but you should provide enough information so participants can understand the key aspects of the study.

3   Outline what you expect to find (e.g., that the groups receiving XX information will have more XX responses then the groups receiving YY information).

4   Provide one or more sources of information where the participant can find out more information about the topic. Remember to choose information that is in a suitable format for the participants (e.g., a meta-analysis is unlikely to be appropriate).

5   Remind the participant that he/she can withdraw from the study and indicate the deadline for this and how this should be done.

6   Provide information about sources of support, should support be needed.

7   Provide your contact details. (These should not include personal contact details, and it may be appropriate to use a gatekeeper as a point of contact, through which the participant can contact you.)

All the issues discussed in the PIS section about ensuring that the information is clear, presented appropriately and so on should also be considered in relation to your debrief information.

Activity

Write the debrief information for your study.

Ethical approval applications

Completing ethical applications is often a good test of your ability to follow instructions and use the information provided by organisations. If you carefully follow the information that is provided and answer the questions clearly, you should avoid difficulties that can arise if you did not follow the appropriate requirements or supply the correct information. This requires attention to detail and time. Although this should be reasonably straightforward, it is unfortunately quite common for individuals applying for ethical approval (and all sorts of other processes) to not follow the simplest of requirements (e.g., to complete the form in black ink and block capitals). By completing the processes carefully and reading all the relevant information, you will avoid unnecessary delays due to your application being rejected (e.g., because you did not supply all the information requested). Most ethical applications are now completed online (or via the completion of a computer document of some type, which

178   Conducting research

you then upload or email), and information for applicants is also online. Unfortunately, the online systems and processes vary widely between organisations, and you may find that you have to spend a great deal of time rewriting information about your study so that it is appropriate for different organisations/ethical procedures. Although this feels like a waste of time, there is simply no way of avoiding it, so you should plan for it in your timetable.

It is important to remember that the people reviewing your application know nothing about your study, why you wish to complete it and your ideas for how it will be designed and conducted. We have had many indignant conversations with individuals whose applications have been rejected where the applicant says things like 'but I have gatekeeper permission' or 'the XX scale is reliable and valid'. The frequent response to this is 'but did you note this/make this clear in the application?' This often leads to the realisation that this was either not included or was not clear within the application. Often this can be a result of spending a great deal of time working on a project, as then it can be difficult to step back and review it from the perspective of a person who knows nothing about it. However, it is important to try to do this, as it will enable you to explain the study more clearly to reviewers. It can also help to ask colleagues or a supervisor to look through your ethics application/documents to check that you have been clear throughout. This can often identify issues that you can become 'blind' to because you are familiar with your own project.

It is beyond the scope of this chapter to provide advice for all the ethical approval processes that you might need to complete, but bear in mind that forms often contain a combination of specific questions that you must respond to with fixed choice responses (e.g., Do you intend to conduct research with children? yes or no) and questions for which you have to provide written information (e.g., outline the background of your research). Some applications have strict word/character limits that you must keep to, and it is important to check this because sometimes this only becomes apparent when you upload/submit the application. This can mean that material beyond the limit will be omitted and your application will not be complete or make sense. It is important that you answer each question and, where an answer is not required or is not appropriate, then it is a good idea to indicate this (e.g., N/A) so it is clear that you have fully considered all aspects of the application. Following is some general advice for application processes, but remember to seek advice from your supervisor/line manager and/or individuals with experience in applying to the relevant committees:

- The background to your study and/or research justification should be relatively brief. You do not need to include a detailed literature review; however, you should include a brief summary of the relevant research that you used to develop your proposal and your justification for your study and its design. Remember to outline the relevance to theory and practice.
- Explain clearly how you will approach participants/ask them to take part in your study, not just who your participants will be.

Gaining ethical approval 179

- Include the PIS, consent forms/statements and debrief information.
- Include all research materials (vignettes, questions, interview schedules etc.).
- Explain how data will be anonymous or confidential, how and where it will be stored, when it will be destroyed etc.
- Include a priori power analysis and your proposed sample size. For qualitative studies, appropriate samples sizes for the specific methodology you are using should be outlined and justified using previous research studies/guidance.
- Demonstrate that you have permission to use the measures/scales and that they are reliable and valid for the population you are studying and, if they are not, why they are still appropriate to use.
- Include copies of gatekeeper permission.
- Include copies of the CVs of relevant researchers/supervisors if this is required.
- Do not forget to outline any pilot studies that will be conducted. Explain who the pilot participants will be, how they will be asked to take part etc.
- Explain how you will disseminate the findings of your results, not forgetting to consider how you will inform the participants/organisations involved about the findings of your study.

Responding to feedback

It is quite common for revisions to be requested before a study is approved. You need to take this into account in planning your timetable. You will most likely receive some feedback on your application, with specific revisions requested (e.g., some changes to your PIS or debrief), areas to consider further identified (e.g., the proposed sample size might be queried), and/or further information required (e.g., it might not be clear in your application how you will ask participants to take part in your study, or which social media sites you will use). Having your proposal rejected or being asked to make revisions can feel frustrating. (Remember that rejection might not be a final decision; it might just mean that it is rejected in its current form and you can revise and resubmit.) Often it is a good idea to read the information through but then put it away for a few hours or overnight and return to it when you are feeling calmer. When you read the feedback and look at your application in light of this, it is likely that you will notice that the information you provided was not as clear as it could have been or was omitted. Most likely, you will need to make the relevant revisions and resubmit the application. It is a good idea to discuss these issues with your supervisor and ask him/her, or another appropriate person, to review your revisions. Although you do not want to delay your application unnecessarily, it is important that you do not rush your revisions; revisions with many typos/errors or that look rushed will not create a good impression. You might need to write a letter noting the changes that you have made (which is a good idea if it is possible to submit this in the application process, as this makes it easier for the reviewers to quickly and easily see what you have revised) and/or note the changes in some other way (e.g., with a different colour font/highlights). No

180 Conducting research

matter how frustrated you feel with the process, it is important to be polite in communications with the reviewers/ethics committee. We would not recommend writing an email or phoning the committee immediately upon receiving your feedback/rejection. It is a better approach to speak to your supervisor and/or a suitable colleague to consider the feedback and your options carefully before you resubmit your application or contact the committee to request additional information and/or query the decision.

Summary and checklist

In this chapter, we have outlined the processes for seeking ethical approval for your research study and have outlined how you should construct ethical documentation (PIS, consent form and debrief information). Remember that ethical approval processes are subject to frequent change, and standards for ethical documentation are often revised. In addition, standards vary – sometimes significantly – between organisations. You should comply with the style, format and requirements of the relevant organisations at the time of your application. This chapter should provide you with core information and examples that you can use as a template/starting point. You should now be able to draft your ethics application using the following checklist. Remember that you should ask your supervisor to review this before you submit it. If you do not have a supervisor, then ask a colleague to review your draft.

1 Identify the ethical approval processes that you need to complete for your study.
2 Obtain written confirmation from relevant gatekeepers.
3 Write/construct your PIS, consent form or statements and debrief information.
4 Develop your research materials as appropriate for your study (e.g., vignettes, information participants are asked to read/review etc., interview schedule, dependent variable measures, predictor questions, questionnaires).
5 Draft your application.
6 Ask your supervisor or colleague to review your draft.
7 Revise in line with the feedback received.
8 Submit your application.
9 Respond to feedback/requests for revisions and resubmit as necessary.
10 When all approvals have been received, you can begin your study.

Further reading

Ethical decision making

The BPS Code of Ethics and Conduct has a decision making section in Chapter 2; this can be used to guide your ethical decision making process:

British Psychological Society. (2009). *Code of ethics and conduct*. Retrieved from http://www.bps.org.uk/system/files/documents/code_of_ethics_and_conduct.pdf

The following paper focusses on decision making when legal and ethical guidelines conflict:

Knapp, S., Gottlieb, M., Berman, J., & Handelsman, M.M. (2007). When laws and ethics collide: What should psychologists do? *Professional Psychology: Research and Practice, 38*, 54–59. doi:10.1037/0735-7028.38.1.54

Ethical approval resources

HM Courts and Tribunal Service: http://www.justice.gov.uk/about/hmcts
Integrated Research Application System (IRAS): https://www.myresearchproject.org.uk/Signin.aspx
National Offender Management Service (NOMS): http://www.justice.gov.uk/downloads/offenders/psipso/psi-2012/psi-13–2012-research-application.doc
Social Care Research Ethics Committee:http://www.scie.org.uk/research/ethics-committee/
Youth Justice Board: https://www.gov.uk/government/organisations/youth-justice-board-for-england-and-wales/about

Chapter 10

Setting up and implementing your study

By this point in your project, you should have a well-designed study with ethical approval and organisational permission (where necessary) to carry out your research. This is often the most interesting part of the research study, as you begin the process of actually gathering some data. However, you still need to engage in some careful thinking/planning at this stage, as it is easy to gain ethical approval and run headlong into data collection without thinking about the logistics of this process. Therefore, in this chapter, we will outline the key issues that you need to consider in setting up and implementing your study. As ever, a little more time put into this planning stage of data collection will hopefully save you time and energy (and misery) and will help avoid things going wrong in the data collection stage. There are no promises that nothing will go wrong, but we hope that the following guidance will address the most common issues that need to be considered when setting up and implementing your study. Once you have read this chapter, you should be able to:

- understand the importance of approaching research project stakeholders appropriately;
- understand how to communicate with professionals/potential participants most effectively and appropriately;
- plan the data collection process;
- identify the importance of completing any required security procedures (e.g., vetting); and
- complete the piloting process for your project.

Project implementation with external organisations

In Chapter 6, we discussed the importance of negotiating access to participants and emphasised with case study one that access to participants should be considered early on in the project. By this point in your research project, you should have gatekeeper approval to access your participants, but we need to return to this issue to discuss the importance of working carefully with the organisation with which you want to collect data, to ensure that this process runs smoothly.

Now that you have ethical approval and approval from the organisation, you should have a discussion with your gatekeeper to establish the exact logistics of how you are going to gather data and to whom you should speak to facilitate this. You may have gatekeeper approval from a governor of a prison, for example, but it is unlikely that the governor will be assisting you with the day-to-day data collection. This task might be assigned to the head of psychology (or similar) or to a psychologist or other member of staff in the prison who may know very little about your study. Please remember that although we would hope that you are (still) interested in your research and excited about your potential findings, it is important that you consider your research from the perspectives of others. Your research might be perceived as an extra burden on some; for example, you might have obtained gatekeeper permission from a manager who has assigned the task of day-to-day assistance/management of your project to one of his/her staff who is extremely busy. This person might not have had the purpose of the research explained clearly to him/her and might resent the time that will be required to help with the project and/or be worried about what the research might find. Therefore, you need to work respectfully and carefully to ensure that the people facilitating your research understand it, are clear about their roles (and your roles), and are engaged in the project and with assisting you in data collection. The first step to take is to arrange a meeting/phone call with the gatekeeper to outline the project; this might alleviate any fears/concerns. You should also be absolutely clear regarding any deadlines, so the gatekeeper (or other person) is aware of any limitations that you may have in achieving your data collection. However, this should be communicated extremely respectfully; remember that it is unlikely that the gatekeeper will directly benefit from helping you with your research, so you need to ensure that he/she is motivated to assist you in the data collection process.

Many of the organisations with which you may want to collect data are overstretched and have limited resources and time, so you need to keep this in mind when asking individuals to facilitate the gathering of your data. You should do as much as you are able. If someone has been assigned to help facilitate your research, that usually means helping you find the best times/locations to access the participants and ensuring you can access the building; it is not this person's role to collect data on your behalf. In some instances, it might be necessary for other people to collect or extract data for you (e.g., if you do not have permission to access a secure database). If this is the case, you should make this clear in your proposal, ethics application and gatekeeper request for access to the data. Trying to find ways to minimise the time your research requires of the person/people facilitating access to participants/data is always a good idea.

184 Conducting research

Case study one

As you will remember from case study one (see Chapter 8), we stated that participants would be recruited through a gatekeeper. Although you should already have had a discussion with the gatekeeper who has approved the project, this person is the manager of the organisation and you need to clarify who will actually assist with the data collection. You need to arrange a telephone call or a visit to the organisation to discuss this further. Let's assume that the manager says that it will be appropriate to send out an organisation-wide email publicising the study, with the link to the online questionnaire within the email. She thinks it would be best if the email comes from her, but her administrator will send this on her behalf and she says that you should liaise with him. You also need to consider how this is going to work in practice (e.g., you need to discuss the time-scales for when this will be completed). You should also consider whether you want to put any deadlines in place for following up this initial email and how many times you want to send out the email. It can be a careful balance between trying to remind people to complete the study and being too annoying and leading potential participants to just start delete the emails. There are some guidelines about this and some information about good/poor response rates and how to determine if your responses are representative of populations; see the 'Further reading' on this method in Chapter 3 as a starting point on this topic. It would also be helpful to the administrator if you sent him a draft email with the core information about the study and the link, so that all he has to do is adapt the writing and add in any organisation-specific information. Remember, the email should include the PIS, so you will need to give this to the administrator (in electronic format). Note too that the PIS has your contact details for people who have questions about the research, and you need to be available to respond to any questions; you should consider this with regard to the timing of the emails requesting participation. If your PIS includes your supervisor's (or other people's) contact details, you should also make them aware of when the emails will be sent, so they know to expect questions about the study. It would be a good idea to ensure that they have a copy of the email and other relevant information about the study. Basically, you should try to think through what might happen and when, and then do everything that you can to help make sure things run smoothly.

Communicating with supervisors/external organisations/participants

During the planning process, if your research project is a dissertation or a project in which you have a supervisor, you should have built a strong working

Setting up and implementing your study **185**

relationship with this individual. You should continue this communication through the setting up phase of your project. You should not take this relationship for granted, and you should keep this person informed as to your progress with working towards data collection. Remember that you can benefit from his/her knowledge and experience as a researcher in avoiding some of the common pitfalls at this stage of the project.

Common difficulties

It is important that you build a good relationship with your supervisor. There is a lot of advice available in books and on the web, but your supervisor is there to advise *you*, while *you* complete *your* project. It is not your supervisor's role to do your project, find the papers you need to read, design your project, collect your data, make the arrangements for your data collection, do your analysis, draft your dissertation/report and so on. In working with your supervisor, you can help the process by doing the following:

1. Communicate clearly, politely and appropriately with him/her, allowing reasonable time for him/her to respond.
2. Plan and arrange meetings at the start of the project and/or in good time (e.g., unless it's a real emergency, do not ask for a meeting late one afternoon for the next morning).
3. Attend meetings promptly, come prepared and bring a list of things that you wish to discuss.
4. Listen to what he/she says, and if you are not sure about something check with him/her first.
5. Allow him/her time to read through applications/drafts (do not send something at midnight and expect a response by 11:00 a.m. the next day.
6. Plan the writing phases of your project (including drafting ethics applications), identifying dates when you will send the draft to your supervisor, when she/he will respond, when you will make revisions etc. and agree to these with your supervisor.
7. Remember that supervisors have lots of things to do, many students to supervise and commitments that mean they may not always be at the university, and that they are entitled to holidays and weekends! As we have said in respect to stakeholders, while your project is your priority, it is unlikely to be the number one priority of your supervisor.

As part of the setting up of your project, you also need to consider exactly how you are going to phrase communications that you will have with potential participants and external organisations. In relation to working with external organisations, it should not have to be stated that you should phrase any communication using formal language (e.g., Dear Prof X/Dear Ms Y /Dear Mr Z, I am emailing to request. . . . I look forward to hearing from you). This can occasionally be forgotten, particularly if you are inexperienced in carrying out research projects with external organisations. You may find that as you build a relationship with your gatekeeper or other individuals within the organisation the language may become more relaxed and informal (e.g., you can use first names and less formal introductions). However, you should not assume this, and you need to remember how easy it can be for misunderstandings to occur in communication (e.g., when an email is phrased poorly). Therefore, it is best to remember to always behave professionally in any communication and to proofread any communications prior to sending. As a postgraduate student/ inexperienced researcher, it can be worthwhile to ask a supervisor/line manager/ colleague to read through written communications prior to sending. This can reduce the likelihood of any miscommunication or misunderstanding occurring, which will mean that your project should run more smoothly without having to problem solve any difficult situations. Wood, Giles, and Percy (2012) provided the following good guidance in relation to this issue:

- Remember to always be respectful in communication with any individuals related to your project. This is particularly relevant when working with external organisations, as they are likely to be essential in enabling you to gather your data. You need them to remain committed to your project.
- Never assume anything about your project. It is always better to be clear about any aspect of your project, and if you are not clear then ask. This does not mean that you should send your gatekeeper several emails a day, but if you do not understand how you are going to data collect, you need to clarify this.
- Engage with any concerns or issues that the external organisation raises with you. As we stated, it is very important that they remain committed to your project, so you need to make sure that any concerns about the project, or the findings that will result from the project, are allayed.
- Ensure that an identifiable gatekeeper is associated with your project, one who will be able to facilitate your data collection process. However, remember that this person has a job to which your research project will be adding duties, so you need to develop this relationship carefully.
- Always maintain a polite and grateful approach in any communication, even when you may perceive that the gatekeeper is not being as helpful as you wish him/her to be. Remember the essential role that he/she has in your project and that you need to build a functioning relationship.
- Visit any locations that you may need to access. However, make sure that this is not creating an additional burden on the external organisation. This step can be helpful in enabling you to work out any issues that may occur

as part of the data collection process. For example, a room that has been identified for you to carry out interviews in may turn out to be a room that people need continual access to, and so it would not be suitable for an interview to be carried out in.

Many of the above points also apply when you are recruiting participants. For example, you must always keep in mind that you are clearly benefitting from their participation in your project, whereas they may actually receive very little benefit from taking part in it. Therefore, you should do your best to make their participation as easy as possible with as little inconvenience as possible. The following activity is useful in applying this to your own project, so that you can identify all possible strategies that will help you communicate effectively with participants, as well as gatekeepers/external organisations.

Activity

Using case study two:

- Identify the key stakeholders that you should communicate with in setting up this project.
- Think about how you would explain this study to each of these groups.
- Identify strategies that may make this project run smoothly.

Common difficulties

When you communicate formally with people, you need to identify a person's title (Prof, Dr, Mr, Mrs, Ms, DCI, Inspector). Try your best to find out the correct or preferred title of the individual you wish to contact; this can often be identified from the web page of the organisation for which the person works (or social networking sites such as LinkedIn, Facebook and ResearchGate). In some instances you can infer the title from the job role and/or the person's qualifications. For example, a professor would generally have that title in his/her job role (Professor of XX), though this might less clear if he/she has a role such as Head of Department or Dean. All other academics with PhDs will be Dr. If you cannot identify whether it should be Prof or Dr, choose Prof; most people do not mind erroneously being called a professor! Note that the use of titles such as professor vary from country to country; in some countries many academics have titles such as associate professor or assistant professor, and individuals with these roles should be referred to as Prof X.

188 Conducting research

In organisations such as the police, you should identify and address people by their rank (e.g., DCI or Detective Chief Inspector X). It can be more difficult to establish whether someone should be Mrs, Ms or Miss; it is a good idea to clarify this in an early communication if you are not sure and cannot see it stated anywhere. Do your best to get it right (some people can be very put out by someone using the wrong title), but do not spend so long on this that you do not get around to sending the communication and/or that you start to engage in borderline stalking behaviours to find out!

Planning your data collection

It is also useful at this point to reexamine your Gantt chart or timetable of the project. It is likely that some adjustments are needed if earlier tasks (e.g., gaining ethical approval) took longer than planned. When planning your data collection time, ensure that you give yourself enough time at the end to be able to analyse and write up your data. If your project does not have a specific deadline this is less essential, but this is essential if your project has a clear submission point (e.g., for a dissertation). In planning your remaining time, you will need to give yourself enough time to complete the analysis and write up, and you also need to allow sufficient time for participants to be recruited and take part in the study. This is not always a quick process and can take longer than expected, particularly as people tend to overlook the management aspect of this (e.g., finding a time suitable for you and the participants, sending emails making arrangements, rescheduling).

Case study five

As you will remember from case study five, this project involves a small number of participants, but a design where the data needs to be gathered at three specific time points. Planning your data collection is particularly important in this study as you need to gather data before the start of the intervention. Missing this time point would be a fatal flaw to the current design of the project, so it is vital that you are aware of the start data of the intervention and that you make arrangements to collect data prior to this date. As data will also be gathered at the midpoint of the project, you also need to plan when exactly this will be and how you will gather the data. Finally, you need to ensure that you have considered how you are going to gather data at the end point and how you will contact participants to facilitate this. This can often be overlooked but might be the most tricky, as once participants have completed something (i.e., the intervention), it can be difficult to get them to return to take part in research. If you have all of this planned out, you can outline this clearly to participants when you are recruiting them to take part in the study. This will mean that they will have a fuller understanding of the time commitments required to take part in the study. You should also consider the best way in which to collect data to avoid any difficulties (i.e., if possible, it might be best to collect data at the end of the last treatment session, rather than to have participants attend a specific posttreatment data collection session, though if the treatment and data collection sessions are long, this is unlikely to be appropriate).

Remember that when you are planning your data collection, you can also be working on other aspects of the project; for example, dependent upon how time intensive the data collection phase is, you may also be able to complete some writing up of the project (e.g., the introduction and method sections). This will ensure that you are making the best use of your time.

Vetting/security approval

Although you have already achieved ethical and other required approvals, if you are working with external organisations, they may require you to go through additional security or vetting procedures. This should be something that you are already aware of, as this should have been discussed within the planning stages of the project. This can be overlooked, however, and you may find yourself waiting to start data collection because you have not passed security vetting. The easiest way to avoid this is to have a clear discussion during the planning stage to understand whether any further vetting will be needed. This will mean that you can possibly start the vetting procedures during the time when you have submitted your ethical approval and are waiting for a decision. If vetting does not occur in the earlier stages, you are going to be delayed for a period of time prior to being able to collect data. The key here is to use the time as efficiently as possible. You should discuss what parts of the project you can start whilst completing security vetting. For example, some organisations may allow you to start recruiting participants during this stage, but not to actually start data collection, whereas others may require you to wait until you have received your final approval before you start recruiting participants. Furthermore, you should also plan out other aspects of your project that can be completed (e.g., you can write your introduction, or draft your methods section).

190 Conducting research

Activity

Identify whether you will need any vetting procedures for your project. For example, look at the Disclosure and Barring Service (DBS) web site (provided here) and identify the activities and roles that require DBS checks. Remember, there are many other vetting processes specific to organisations, such as the police, and you will need to ask your supervisor/gatekeeper/colleague about this.

https://www.gov.uk/government/organisations/disclosure-and-barring-service

---

Piloting your project

Even if you do not need to formally pilot your project, it is always a good idea to go through the procedures that you will use to collect data to identify any potential issues. For example, if you are carrying out an experiment using a computer-mediated task, it is useful to ask a colleague/peer to act as a dummy participant to check that everything works smoothly prior to using these processes on actual participants. Although this may seem like an unnecessary additional task (and a delay) to complete before getting to data collection, it can help remove any unfortunate errors that may have an impact on the quality of the data that you collect. Obviously, you want to be able to use all data that you gather, so it would be unfortunate if you could not use a participant's data because of an unforeseen error that could have been addressed with piloting/dummy runs.

Equipment issues do just occur in experimental studies. Relatively simple equipment, such as Dictaphones or psychometric testing kits, can be tricky to use and/or be problematic (e.g., a Dictaphone may not be working, or elements of the psychometric testing may be missing). Therefore, you should familiarise yourself with all the equipment that you will use. For example, if using a Dictaphone, make sure you can turn it on, pause, restart and stop the recording, copy the recoding to a computer and remove the recording. (Remember, you should not keep interviews on the Dictaphone for long, for data protection reasons. If it is a shared Dictaphone, you should check carefully that your interviews have been fully removed before giving it to another person to use.) You should also try to record a dummy interview to identify the best place to locate the Dictaphone during the interview so that it records the conversation clearly. In addition, consider the likelihood of equipment breakdown and think about whether you want to have a backup piece of equipment, should your original equipment not work. Make sure you have spare batteries and/or chargers for all equipment that requires them.

In addition, you may be using a technique with which you are not familiar (e.g., interviewing or psychometric testing). Therefore, if you can, it is a good idea to run through practice interviews and testing. For example, if your project involves interviewing offenders, you may want to plan out some strategies to ensure that you maintain an appropriate level of language when talking to participants (this should already have been considered in relation to your ethics documentation, but it is important to consider it here again). Also, you should think about how you will respond if you have a participant who does not provide sufficiently detailed responses to your questions (e.g., yes/no responses when longer responses are desired). Again, you should have already considered prompt questions in the schedule that you submitted for your ethics proposal, but this is the point to consider exactly how you will respond if answers are not sufficient. If you are not familiar with interviewing or testing, ask some peers/colleagues to be dummy participants and interview/test them. Ask one or two people to be difficult (you do not need to specify how), as this will give you some practice in dealing with different people and different levels of cooperation.

Remember that if you do make any changes to your project on the basis of this piloting, you may need to consider whether you need to submit a revision to your ethics proposal. You should seek guidance about this issue and not assume that everything will be fine. Your supervisor can be an excellent guide in this respect, but if your project is not a dissertation, you need to seek out the relevant individual with whom to address this concern. Even if your project does not need additional ethical approval, it may still be a good idea to repilot your project. For example, returning to the example of an experimental study, if there was a process that did not work very well and you have now changed this to address this concern, it is not enough to assume that this will work fine now. You may have changed a process, but this may not necessarily have been a positive change! Therefore, you should run through the procedure again with a dummy participant to ensure that the change has improved the data collection procedure. This applies equally to the piloting of any materials; for example, if you pilot a vignette in which there was a floor effect, a change may produce the opposite effect, so you will need to pilot, revise, pilot, revise, pilot and so on, until the materials are appropriate. Again, although this takes time at this stage, this piloting and running through the procedures of your study can save you valuable time in the long run and save you the heartache of thinking you have collected useful data when for some reason you have not (e.g., the recordings on the Dictaphone are indecipherable, the data has a significant floor effect, a key aspect of the experimental design was not recorded on a piece of equipment, there are no scoring instructions for the psychometric test). As you collect data, it is also a good idea to check for these issues as you go along; losing one interview because there was a problem with the Dictaphone is annoying but manageable, but getting to the end of data collection and finding that there is a problem with all of your interviews for the same reason is potentially very problematic, especially if there is a limited time period for the project.

192 Conducting research

Activity

You should now be in a position to setup your data collection. Use the checklist in the following section to guide you through this process.

Summary and final checklist

In this chapter, we have summarised the key concerns that you need to think about before you start the data collection process. As we have emphasised, do not run headlong into your data collection process. Taking a little additional time to think about the logistics of exactly how you are going to collect data should ensure that the process runs smoothly. The key points that we have emphasised within this chapter are as follows:

1   Review your timetable for the project. Make sure that this now reflects the time that you have left for the project.
2   Meet with your supervisor (or research team) to discuss the project and plan future meetings.
3   Build strong relationships with your stakeholders.
4   Plan your data collection carefully.
5   Communicate appropriately with all individuals involved in your project. This can be as simple as remaining professional and polite in any communications that you have. Always keep in mind how important these individuals are to the success of your project.
6   Pilot your project materials and revise and repilot as appropriate.
7   Practice and prepare for your data collection – test all equipment, run through the study with dummy participants. Revise as appropriate and retest/practice.
8   Start data collection, remembering to check the quality of your data as you progress, i.e., that the interview has been recorded, materials (e.g., questionnaires, online survey) have been completed appropriately, experimental study data have been recorded and so on.

Further reading

Robson, C. (2011) *Real world research* (3rd ed., pp. 399–406). Chichester, England: John Wiley and Sons.

Reference

Wood, C., Giles, D., & Percy, C. (2012). *Your psychology project handbook: Becoming a researcher.* Harlow, Essex: Pearson Education.

Chapter 11

Collecting data

After all of the planning and preparation that we have encouraged you to do, you have finally reached the point where you actually get to gather some data. This should be where all of the work you have done so far pays off, and (hopefully) you experience a problem-free data collection process. In this chapter, we will discuss things that you should consider during your data collection, highlighting issues that arise with both qualitative and quantitative data, as well as more general considerations. Once you have read this chapter, you should be able to:

- recognise issues associated with quantitative data collection;
- recognise issues associated with qualitative data collection;
- understand the importance of keeping track of participants;
- identify and implement strategies to deal with poor participant recruitment; and
- appreciate the importance of working professionally and ethically throughout your research project.

Data collecting with participants

We outlined in the previous chapter how to approach and communicate with participants when you are recruiting them to take part in your study. Remember that much of this guidance remains important when you start to gather data from these individuals. Therefore, it is essential that you remember to present yourself professionally. It is particularly important that you think carefully about what clothing would be appropriate for the organisation in which you will be collecting data and the sample of people from whom you are collecting data. For example, Wood, Giles, and Percy (2012) suggested that if you are going to be collecting data from children, you should consider whether very formal clothing would be too intimidating. Similarly, if you are collecting data from offenders, you should consider the appropriateness of your clothing (i.e., if you are collecting data in a prison). If you have any concerns about what clothing you should wear, it is best to dress in formal business attire. You can always adapt your clothing as data collection continues.

194 Conducting research

Planning

The time taken to gather data can vary considerably according to the mode of data collection. For example, an online survey can gather data very quickly and easily, with little effort on your part. In comparison, gathering data in a lab can be much more time consuming because you may have to gather each participant's data individually. Therefore, it is important that you plan your time appropriately (e.g., using your Gantt chart). You will need to plan your timetable so that you are prepared for the start of the data collection period. As discussed in the previous chapter, by the time you come in contact with participants, you should have tested the processes of gathering data carefully. If you have overlooked this stage, we strongly recommend that you retrace your steps and pilot the processes that you are going to use. If you are not prepared, you risk things going wrong with your study (e.g., collecting data that you are not able to use), and you may make an unfavourable impression on your participant, which has ethical implications. One participant may well know other potential participants, so it is important that you do not create a bad impression, as this may affect your recruitment of future participants.

You should always be fully prepared to complete your data collection when it has been scheduled to take place. It is a good idea to take a contact number for the participant if you have scheduled an interview or testing session, so that you can contact him/her should an unforeseen/unexpected event affect your ability to collect data. Contact the participant as soon as you know that there is likely to be a problem and try to reschedule, or cancel the session if necessary.

Case study one

You will remember that case study one involves the use of an online survey to collect data in collaboration with a local service provider. You should test the online survey with dummy participants before it is sent to actual participants to complete. However, throughout the course of the data collection process, it is important to check through the survey and the data being collected to ensure that no technical errors have caused any difficulties. You should also have your data collection timetable organised such that you and the gatekeeper know when participants will be sent the original email and when this original email will be followed up with a reminder email. Now is the time to implement this timetable. Remember that your gatekeeper has other priorities within his or her daily work and may need a reminder of these time points. Do not rely on the gatekeeper to remember this.

Collecting data   195

Building rapport

It is vital that, no matter what method or design you are using, you understand the importance of building rapport with your participants; many of the topics that are researched within forensic psychology are sensitive and/or involve participants who are considered vulnerable. Developing methods to establish rapport should be considered in the design stages of your project. Strategies should be built into the manner in which you will approach people to ask them to take part in your study, your PIS and your research materials, such as the interview schedule. It is important to clearly explain the scope of the project, exactly what will be asked of participants, and issues regarding confidentiality and withdrawing from the study. You should also address any questions that the participants may pose.

Case study two

This case study involves asking crime victims questions about their well-being and the crime and its impact on them. A method of data collection has been chosen whereby victim support charities ask individuals to participate on your behalf, and the victims receive the information and research materials by mail. In this study, you need to think very carefully about all the stages of contact with the potential participants. It would be a good idea to write information materials for the service providers who are going to ask their service users to take part in your study (i.e., the individuals who will speak to the service users, not just the gatekeepers). In this material you can stress that participants are free to choose to take part in the study and that the information should only be sent to those who request it. Remember that the service providers are taking time to assist you with your study, so this information should be worded in a friendly, helpful and grateful manner. You should think carefully about how your postal communication will be received. It is not a good idea, for example, to have VICTIM SURVEY written in large letters on the envelope, as this identifies victims and is likely to make them feel very uncomfortable. The information that you provide about the study will need to be carefully worded to avoid unnecessary distress and to explain the purpose of the study and the ethical processes. You should consider whether it is appropriate to include a telephone number through which potential participants can contact you to ask questions and seek clarification. If you do this, it is important that you are able to respond to these calls promptly. Because participants will be completing the study without direct support, the information you provide about the study needs to be exceptionally clear. It is important that participants can understand what they need to do to, what questions need answering and what sort of response is required. You should ensure that the instructions for returning the research materials are straightforward and clearly explained. You can test all of these things prior to the start of data collection. Do not just test the materials on another student or colleague, as it is likely that students/colleagues will have a good understanding of what you expect; rather, test the study on individuals most similar to the potential participants. Ask the dummy test individuals to be really critical and to highlight everything that they were not sure about and/or did not understand. Since you will have no input into the data collection process once it has started, you need to very confident about your materials and that appropriate data will be produced. For example, if you put the wrong address on the information, or do not consider how return postage will be paid, you risk receiving no responses, which clearly has serious implications for the study.

Interviews and focus groups

Building rapport and making participants feel comfortable is particularly important in interviews and focus groups. In the previous chapter, we discussed the usefulness of practising interviewing techniques; this should make you more comfortable and relaxed, which in turn will help make the interviewees feel more comfortable. In addition, think through how participants might feel as they take part in your study. No matter what topic you are discussing, you should make every effort throughout the research process to make your participants feel comfortable. For example, interview/focus group schedules are often drafted where the first question is about the topic of concern ('Can you tell me about the abuse you suffered?'), without any consideration given to approaching a topic carefully and leading the participant into talking about aspects of the topic that are likely to be difficult to discuss. It might be useful, for example, to understand the make-up of the family at the time of the abuse, so you could start by asking questions about where the participant lived as a child or who lived in the house before you ask about details of the abuse. Remember that you do not need to launch straight into the interview schedule as soon as the participant arrives; you can ask some general questions about how the participant feels, how his/her journey to the location was, and so forth to put the person at ease. If the topic of your interview/focus group is sensitive, or if a participant is finding it difficult to discuss the topic, consider offering to take a break or other strategies that enable the individual to take part in the study in a supportive manner.

Case study four

This case study involved getting groups of participants together to take part in a group task. In most studies that involve groups in a research activity, it would be appropriate to consider an 'ice-breaker' task to ensure participants feel comfortable with you and with each other. In real juries, however, jurors are placed together and given a 'group task', without a researcher asking them to undertake an ice-breaker task. In this instance, therefore, you might decide that it would be more like a real-life setting if you did not make any effort to ensure that participants felt comfortable with each other. The key issue here, however, is that you think about which is the best approach and that you have a justifiable reason for the approach that is used. These details should be included in your ethics application(s).

As you conduct your research, you will probably experience a range of interviews or focus groups (including a stilted and awkward interview!), and you will learn how to develop rapport and ensure that participants feel comfortable. It will be beneficial for you, your participants and the quality of your data if you can learn these skills prior to data collection; however, this is a skill that you can always improve. Even experienced researchers learn from each interview/focus group they conduct. It is important that you develop reflective practice skills, where you consider how each interview felt, what worked well, what did not work as well, and what you can do differently in future interviews to make the process smoother and/or more comfortable.

Dealing with distress

You should also consider how you will behave if a participant becomes distressed during data collection. You should be aware of the limitations of the support that you can offer participants; remember that you are there to collect data and not to offer support/counselling, even if this may be within your area of expertise. This is where it is very important that any dual roles are clearly explained to participants. It is natural to want to offer support to participants when they become distressed, but you must recognise that there are limitations to the support that you can offer. As we have mentioned, your debrief should outline any sources of support that participants can access. This should be where you direct participants, rather than attempting to deal with the issue that has caused distress.

In group tasks, dealing with the distress of an individual participant can be challenging, especially if you are leading the task alone. It is important, therefore, that you consider prior to testing how you would deal with such a situation. In research based on group tasks, you also need to carefully consider issues such as withdrawing from a study and consent. For example, it might be appropriate to explain to all participants at the start of the session that they should keep the content of the session confidential. You might need to limit the ability to withdraw, in that, although you should allow a participant to withdraw from your study, it will not be possible to withdraw the impact of what the participant said on how the discussion evolved and/or what was said by the other participants. It might be that if one participant withdraws that you have to consider withdrawing all the data from the group that the participant was in. This can be a tricky issue if the other participants particularly want their data to be included in the study. Again, the key point is that you need to think these issues through carefully.

Keeping track of participants

This is an important issue as you need to be able to identify a participant's data should he/she wish to withdraw. Also, this becomes a critical issue when your study design requires that you gather data from your participants at different time points. There are a number of methods that you can use to keep track of participants. It is very likely that you will be using an anonymous participant identifier so you do not need to collect the names of participants that are involved in your study. If you allow participants to self-generate an identifier, this can result in them not remembering their identifier in future testing sessions. This is obviously very problematic should you need to match data across time points, or if a participant wishes to withdraw his/her data. It can therefore be helpful to think up a method that will be memorable to participants; for example, you could ask participants to use their initials as the identifier. However, the problem with this is that more than one individual or many individuals in a study can have the same initials. This may seem really obvious to state, but you would be surprised how many researchers have fallen foul of such a difficulty. One of the easiest ways of identifying participants can be to use a combination of their initials and their date of birth. For example, John Smith who was born on 5 November 1985 would be participant identifier: JS051185. When you collect the first set of data, however, it is important to check that this method produces different identifiers for each individual. As ever, the point here is to think about how you are going to do this before you start to collect data.

Case study five

This project involves a small number of participants, and the data needs to be gathered at three specific time points. As recommended within the previous chapter, you have planned out exactly when you are going to collect data. However, it is important to remember that you need to have a consistent method of identifying participants so that you can match up the data collected at the three time points. If you have not thought about this process before gathering the data, you may find that although you have correctly gathered data, you have no way of knowing to whom the data belong. This emphasises one of the key pitfalls that can befall researchers when they do not adequately plan out the logistics of gathering data.

Monitoring

Even if you have piloted your study and carefully tested all the materials, it is still a good idea to monitor your data quality throughout the data collection process to ensure that an issue has not arisen. For example, you should check that data is being stored by online survey software, that the computer program being used to collect data in an experimental study is recording data as expected, that your interviews can be heard clearly in digital recordings, that participants write their identifiers clearly on research materials and so forth. We would also strongly recommend that you back up your data. If you are using online software or a lab/shared computer, then download your data regularly and store it carefully in line with data protection requirements and the processes you outlined in your ethics application(s).

Difficulties in recruiting participants

There can be many reasons why you have trouble gathering a sufficient number of participants. For example, you may require a very specific type of person or a person who is very difficult to recruit. One important point to emphasise is that you need to be very proactive about gathering data. For instance, if you are using an online questionnaire, then you need to do all that you can to promote the internet link to possible participants. Think as creatively as you can about how to advertise this, but remember to stay within the constraints of your ethical approval. Also, remember to seek all necessary permissions when using things like email list servers. Do not automatically assume that it is fine for you to email everyone in a particular organisation or university. Similarly, with more traditional methods of gathering data, you need to be proactive while acting within the constraints of your ethical approval and ensuring that you do not cause any problems with any external organisation with which you are working. Even if you are a university student wishing to gather data within a university building, there is often an approval process or permissions that need to be granted before data collection can occur. It is your responsibility to make sure that you gain this prior to gathering any data.

200   Conducting research

Common difficulties

The gatekeeper to my organisation has stopped responding to my emails.

You need to approach this issue carefully. Remember that this person is often a key access point to you gaining your data, so you need to manage this relationship cautiously. Do remember that your research is often not the top priority of that individual and that, frequently, the individual is likely to be managing a substantial workload. You need to be particularly careful about how to phrase emails to ensure that no offence is taken. Remember that comments can be very easily taken out of context in an email. A reminder email can be a useful way to encourage the individual to get back in touch with you. It may be useful in this email to identify any deadlines that have been previously agreed upon. It might be better to call, rather than to send an email, as it can be easier to discuss these issues by phone. Again, this needs to be approached sensitively; you cannot just demand to know why the individual has not responded to your emails. All of this advice seems simplistic, but researchers can sometimes be guilty of focussing on their own project needs/requirements rather than balancing those with the needs of others involved.

If you are experiencing difficulties recruiting your participants, speak to a supervisor/line manager as soon as a problem arises. It is easier to identify strategies to remedy the situation the longer you have available (e.g., you could revise your ethics proposal to use another method of data collection), so identifying the problem early and taking appropriate steps may allow you to limit the problem (see previous discussions about contingency plans in Chapter 6). Ignoring the situation is very unlikely to help, so if you find that recruitment is difficult, speak to someone as soon as you can and carefully consider the range of options that are available to you to try to remedy the situation.

If you have made all attempts to gather more participants but do not manage to recruit the sample size that you identified in your proposal, it is likely that this will have an impact on the analysis that you can carry out on your data. The impact can be greater in quantitative studies, as there is an increased risk of a type two error (refer back to Chapter 6); however, low numbers of participants can also have an impact on qualitative studies. For example, if there is a wide range of views/perspectives in the participants that you have recruited, this could lead to questions regarding the saturation of the data (see Chapter 6).

In quantitative studies, you may need to reconsider what analyses would be most appropriate for the data that you have collected. For example, if you have a 3×3 between-groups design, you may find that simplifying the design (particularly if you have unequal numbers of participants across your conditions) enables you to carry out some analyses with sufficient power. This may mean that you need to make some alterations to your research questions, and you will need to reflect on whether this is appropriate for your aims. However, in some situations, making alterations may be unavoidable. If you have a specific deadline that requires a research report (e.g., for a master's course), then making such adjustments will enable you to complete the assignment.

Remember that in research assignments for undergraduate or master's courses you are being assessed on a number of things, so a lower-than-anticipated number of participants, whilst not ideal, does not mean that you cannot write a good report. Although there may be some impact on the mark you receive, please do not think that all hope is lost and that you should not submit your assignment, or that you will not be able to submit it. The key thing to remember if you need to write up a research report with less-than-ideal participant numbers (whether quantitative or qualitative) is that you draw conclusions appropriate to the sample size and that you clearly outline the limitations in your discussion (see Chapter 15).

Data collection that does not involve participants

It is very easy to assume that if you are using data from established datasets, databases and other sources (news accounts, discussion forums, blogs) that you do not need to worry too much about your data collection phase; however, it is important that you are not complacent, as depending on the nature of your study, these processes could require significant planning and organisation.

Planning

It is unlikely that the data you require are going to appear on a memory stick in the exact format that you need to conduct the analysis. If you are using data from a large dataset, you need to allow time to understand the data and to read the coding manual (or similar) to understand the data/variables you have. If you are using data collected by an organisation, bear in mind that the data may be in different files/locations. You might not be able to take data away from the organisation, in which case you will need to make arrangements to work at the organisation (see case study three discussion) at specific dates and times to ensure you can gain access to the data. If you are using data from sources such as news accounts, forum postings or court cases, then you need to plan the time to locate and collate the relevant data. It is likely that there are far more data than are possible to analyse, so you will need to develop a justifiable and clear strategy for selecting the data to include in your study. The key point, as we have stressed many times, is that you need to think all these things through carefully and plan ahead.

Case study three

The service provider has indicated that it has collected the data that are required for this study; however, in discussions with them following ethical approval, you realise that they have a data set of the recidivism data, which does not contain the age at time of sentence, sentence length and number of previous convictions, which are details that you need. These details are in individual case files. The service provider is clear that the recidivism dataset can be matched to individual case files, but you realise that one type of person identifier is used for the recidivism dataset and that the files are categorised and stored according to the offenders' names. Although with the service provider's assistance you are able to work out a method for matching the data (the identifier used in the recidivism file is located in one part of each offender's file), this will involve you looking through the offenders' files to find the relevant information. This has to be done at the premises when one of the two members of staff who has access to the files is available. In addition, while you are using the identifier, you are required to store the information on a secure computer at the service provider's premises (i.e., you cannot remove identifiable data from the premises). You will therefore need to identify times when you can collect the data and make the relevant arrangements for each and every visit to the service provider's premises.

Keeping track of data

No matter what your data are, you need to carefully and appropriately collate the data. If you are using large numbers of text extracts (e.g., from news accounts, forum postings), you will need to develop a clear method of labelling these; you need to be able to identify which data came from which original source and how each extract meets your data collection strategy (e.g., if you said you would take the first and last news account each week, you need to know which extract is the first and which the last and which week both accounts are from). Considerable time could be lost if you lose track of your data, so it is important that you have a clear strategy for these processes and that you are very methodical in applying it.

Ethics

Conducting research in an ethical manner is an active process that takes place throughout your study. It is not just a process that you complete to get permission for your study. It is during the data collection phase of your study that you are likely to have to make a number of decisions to ensure that you conduct your study ethically. It is very easy to read about all the processes and think that there will be no difficulties, but these processes are challenging, and you should be prepared to deal with issues that arise in your own study.

Research advice

The following is taken from an email from one of our students:

"Working with vulnerable participants . . . all those ethical issues you learn about academically suddenly become a reality. I can think of at least 4 incidents (so far) where informed consent, protection from harm and diversity issues have suddenly become very real and very important to deal with in the correct manner, and I've been challenged by them despite working in the Service for 5 years. And that's just with a questionnaire based study!"

As we discussed in Chapter 7, there are many guidelines and decision-making processes that you should follow during this stage. It is important that you do not ignore problems – remember that it is an ethical breach to not respond to an ethical issue. After careful consideration and appropriate discussion/advice, it may be appropriate to do nothing – but there is a difference between an active decision to do nothing and simply ignoring the situation. Remember, seeking advice from a supervisor/colleague is a feature of these ethical guidelines/processes, so this is a good place to start if you experience any difficulties or do not know how to deal with a situation that arises during your research.

If you make any changes to any part of your project, you need to check whether this impacts on your ethical approval. It can be very easy to forget about ethical approval and the method that you have permission to use, especially if you are struggling to recruit participants. However, it is very important that you continue to think about ethics as an integral part of the research process. If you wish to change anything about your data collection process (or any other part of your project), you need to check the ethical implications. This can mean that a brief amendment is required with no further review, or it may mean that your application needs to be reviewed again. Your prior planning about data collection should mean that this is not a problem within your project timetable; however, circumstances can change and therefore amendments may be required. As always, it is your responsibility to ensure that you check whether any further review of your ethics application is required.

Other ethical issues that need to be considered are falsification of data or tampering with data. It is not currently known to what extent this occurs within forensic psychology; however, it must be recognised that it does occur. As you will recall from Chapter 7, the ethical principles of respect, competency,

204　Conducting research

integrity and responsibility should guide the research process. It should be obvious that any individual who engages in the falsification of data or in tampering with data is clearly violating the integrity principle (and aspects of the other three principles).

Activity

Using the further reading list of ethics resources in Chapter 7, consider the ethical principles of respect, competency, integrity and responsibility. For each principle, identity how falsifying or tampering with your data, or massaging your data analysis, violates these principles.

Research advice

Tampering with and/or falsifying your data (or statistical analyses) are deemed to be considerable breaches of ethical principles; therefore, the consequences of such activities can be severe.

If a dissertation project was found to contain falsified data, the impact is likely to range from failure of the dissertation, at a minimum, to not being able to complete the course and possible disciplinary procedures. If such ethical breaches are identified post-award, the award can be removed, which could have implications for employment. Papers published in academic journals would be retracted/withdrawn, which would be clearly identified to readers of the journal and in professional circles. Such behaviours will also be reviewed, with appropriate action taken by professional bodies. There are obvious career consequences. In references, for example, writers are required to indicate the level of trustworthiness/honesty of an individual. Clearly the individual you list to provide a reference would not be able to indicate that you are trustworthy and honest if ethical breaches had been identified.

Research advice

Falsification of data

Over recent years, there have been a number of high profile cases where researchers in academic institutions, including psychologists, have been found to have falsified or massaged data to provide outcomes that would promote their work. It is frequently cited that the underlying reasons for falsifying or altering data were personal benefit (in terms of promotion) and recognition as a key researcher within the field. However, once found out, these academics have frequently been sacked from their academic positions, and questions have been raised about the validity of *all* of their research outputs. These cases highlight the impact falsification of data can have on individuals' careers, and they should serve as examples for why this should not be done.

There is no justification, however tempting it may be, for falsifying results or data. As a researcher, you have to accept that there may be occasions when you cannot carry out the analyses that you want to, perhaps because you have not managed to gather enough participants or you have not found any significant results in your data. The correct response to this is to reflect on the research process and the design that you used. What you learn from this reflection will be useful to you in developing your research skills, and you can use this in future research projects.

Common confusion

It is often assumed that a study has failed or is of no value if the results of the analysis are not statistically significant. In fact, important findings and theoretical developments can arise when the predicted hypotheses are not supported. To use a fairly silly example to illustrate the point, if my hypothesis is that the world is flat and my research finds nonstatistically significant findings (i.e., the world is not flat), that might lead me to develop a theory that the world is in fact an oblate spheroid, or perhaps a nonperfect oblate spheroid!

Summary and final checklist

In this chapter, we have summarised a number of key issues that you should consider in your data collection processes. You should now be ready to collect your data, taking care to consider and do all of the following in this important aspect of your research study. Hopefully, by taking care to follow these steps, you should collect data that ensures that you can complete your study as anticipated.

1   Plan your data collection carefully and think about how you will deal with unexpected situations, participant identification, participant withdrawal and distress in your participants.

206 Conducting research

2 Behave professionally and ethically at all times, and be considerate to all involved in your research.
3 Consider and ensure that you make every effort to build rapport with your participants and make them feel comfortable throughout the data collection process.
4 Continually monitor your data collection process and keep back-ups of data in line with data protection and ethical approval.
5 Act quickly if you identify problems, and consider the range of contingency strategies that could be implemented to limit potential problems.
6 Speak to supervisors/line managers/colleagues if you experience difficulties, and seek advice regarding the most appropriate actions to take.

Further reading

Fanelli, D. (2009). How many scientists fabricate and falsify research? A systematic review and meta-analysis of survey data. Retrieved from http://www.plosone.org/article/info%3Adoi%2F10.1371%2Fjournal.pone.0005738#s1

Reference

Wood, C., Giles, D., & Percy, C. (2012). *Your psychology project handbook: Becoming a researcher.* Harlow, Essex: Pearson Education.

Chapter 12

Data analysis

In this chapter, we will outline the data analysis methods that you should carry out on your data. You should have already planned the form of analysis that you are going to use before you reached this point. Therefore, you should already know exactly what tests/analyses you are going to conduct. In this chapter, we will work through the steps that you should take once you have input all of your data and you are ready to start the analysis. The purpose of this chapter is to facilitate your data analysis, rather than to work through every single possible statistical test or qualitative analysis that you can complete on your data; therefore, this chapter should be read in conjunction with a statistics text, such as Field (2013), or a relevant qualitative analysis text, such as those in the 'Further reading' section. It should be obvious to even the most novice researcher that each type of analysis is only appropriate for certain types of data. This is why we have emphasised the planning of analyses before you get to this point in your project. One of the major issues that novice researchers can experience is gathering a lot of data and then being unsure what analysis to carry out, or even worse being unable to carry out any sophisticated methods of analysis. As ever, prior planning is key in this respect. However, certain changes may have to be implemented within the course of the project, and this may mean that you now have to change or amend the analyses that you initially planned to carry out. Once you have read this chapter, you should be able to:

- appreciate the importance of working with accurately recorded data (both qualitative and quantitative);
- understand the importance of assumption testing for quantitative data;
- identify the appropriate quantitative analysis for your data;
- recognise the basic processes used in qualitative analysis; and
- know how to check the quality of this analysis.

Data cleaning and assumption testing

Data cleaning can be an overlooked process, as researchers often want to dive straight into carrying out their statistical analyses to determine whether they

208 Conducting research

have any significant results or emergent themes. Cleaning is usually a process that is associated with quantitative data; however, this does not mean that you should omit checking that your qualitative data is correct. For example, after transcribing an interview, you should listen to the interview again and check that you have not left out any data and that the transcription is correct. The data cleaning process is essentially ensuring that your data has been correctly inputted, so that any analysis/findings are based on reliable data. This section is going to examine this process for both qualitative and quantitative data.

Qualitative data

It is very likely that if you have gathered qualitative data (interview or focus group data, for example) you will need to transcribe that data from an audio format to a written one. This is the usual process to allow you to carry out your chosen qualitative analysis. It is easy to underestimate just how much time transcription will take you, but take our word that it is not a quick process. As a general rule of thumb, it takes six hours to transcribe one hour of one-to-one speech, unless you are a very skilled typist and/or transcriber. Transcribing focus groups or data with several speakers can take more time, as it is difficult to identify who is speaking and because people speak at the same time (see case study four box later in this section). There will also be variation depending on the type of transcription (e.g., noting the length of pauses and type of speech will be more time consuming). Therefore, you need to carefully plan out how and when you are going to complete all of the transcription that your project may require. Transcribing equipment, such as foot pedals that are used to pause and restart the recording as you type, can speed up the transcription process, so it is worth investigating whether this is equipment is available to borrow, or to purchase it if you are going to be conducting lots of transcribing.

Remember that for some qualitative approaches you should transcribe and analyse your interviews/data as you complete the data collection process, with the insights provided by earlier participants informing the way in which you interview later participants. For other approaches, it is possible to complete all your transcription after you have collected all your data. So you need to build data collection, transcription and analysis into your project timetable as appropriate. Unless you specifically need to collect all your data before you transcribe it/analyse it, we recommend that you do not leave all of your transcription to do at the end of your data collection. It is a better approach to do this as you continue to gather data. Unless you have exceptional concentration, it is unlikely that you are going to be able to transcribe for very long periods of time. It can be a better approach to block out two to three hours to transcribe data and then do a different task. You can attempt to transcribe data all day, but it is recommended that you take frequent breaks.

Before you start any transcription, remember that the analytical approach that you have chosen to complete on your data may mean that you need to use a specific transcription style. Some approaches, such as discourse analysis, require very detailed transcripts, including the length of pauses and speech intonation, whereas for other approaches, such as thematic analysis, this level of detail might not be required. You should have considered this in the design phase of your project, but remember to check before you start transcribing, so that you use the most appropriate approach from the start and avoid having to spend time redoing you transcription.

Braun and Clarke (2013) identified some of the common errors that occur within the transcription process that you should attempt to avoid.

1   *Sentence structure errors:* As you start to transcribe, you will realise that participants rarely use complete sentences that are evident in written language. Instead you will find partial and unstructured wording. You may be tempted to include punctuation to give meaning to the words being said; however, this should be avoided as meaning can be changed quite significantly just by (mis)placing punctuation within a sentence. If you are struggling with understanding what is being said, then return to the audio and include punctuation where it is clear that there is a pause in speaking; otherwise limit the use of punctuation.

2   *Quotation mark errors:* Quotation marks are required when participants are reporting the speech of others. Make sure that you pay attention to the audio recording and ensure that if your participant reproduces someone else's speech that you place this speech within double quotation marks. This will highlight to you later that these are not the participant's own thoughts/attitudes, but are another's speech.

3   *Omission errors:* This is where the transcriber misses words or utterances spoken by the participants. This highlights why it is important not to attempt to transcribe for long periods of time – the longer you transcribe, the more likely it is that you will make errors. Missing a word in a sentence can mean that the meaning is lost, which obviously has an impact on your data and potentially your findings. Make sure that once you have transcribed a section of your data that you go back and listen to the audio to ensure that you have not made any errors.

4   *Mistaken word/phrase errors:* This issue is similar to item three, but occurs when something a participant says is unclear. If anything a participant says is unclear, make a note of this within the transcription, using something like '(unclear)' next to the text where the wording is inaudible. This will highlight to you that you need to be cautious about drawing inferences from that particular piece of data. You also need to take care with the spelling of words that sound the same but have different meanings (e.g., there, their).

If you have financial support, there are companies that will transcribe your data for you. You should consider carefully whether you wish to use such a service. Experienced transcribers can complete transcription quickly, and clearly

210 Conducting research

it will save you time; however, the transcribers will probably not have a clear understanding of your topic, which might mean that errors are made. If you do use professional transcribers, it is important that you plan for time to review the transcriptions. Another thing to keep in mind is that although transcription is tedious and time consuming, it is very useful in informing your understanding of your data. Familiarisation with the data is a key stage of many qualitative analytical approaches, and the transcription process will enable this. Therefore, you may wish to transcribe your own data as it can be helpful in getting started with identifying key themes.

Case study four

Data collection can be particularly challenging in this instance because you will need to test where it is best to place the Dictaphone, and you might need to use more than one. Transcription can also be challenging because you will find that people do not always wait for others to finish speaking, so there may be overlapping speech. It may be difficult to work out exactly who is saying what within the room. If you have the support available, it can be a good idea to have someone sit in on the session to record who speaks when (with some key parts of speech noted), as this will be really helpful when you transcribe the data.

Braun and Clarke (2013) suggest that where there is overlapping speech, you should include '(in overlap)' before the start of the speech that is overlapping. If speech is inaudible, then use '(inaudible)' if you cannot make out any of the wording or '(inaudible)' and the speech that you can make out, when you can identify some of the words. If you are not sure who is talking, then include a question mark in place of the speaker's name within the transcription, and an M or F if you can tell whether the individual is male or female. If you think you know which participant it might be but you are not sure, then include some identifier (e.g., 'Judy?'). Refer to the 'Further reading' section for more information of how to deal with these particular issues when transcribing your data.

Quantitative data

Ensuring that your data are accurate is a key component of the data analysis process; just one incorrectly inputted number can skew data and lead you to draw incorrect conclusions about your study. For example, imagine a situation where you have questioned participants about a particular attitude and asked them to respond on a five-point Likert scale (1 = strongly disagree to 5 = strongly agree). Of the ten participants that have responded, the data are 1, 4, 3, 5, 2, 2, 4, 5, 4 and 3. The mean for this data is 3.3 and the standard deviation 1.3. However, should you enter a number incorrectly, such as *11*, 4, 3, 5,

Data analysis 211

2, 2, 4, 5, 4 and 3, you will find that the mean is 4.3 and the standard deviation 2.6. The impact of an incorrectly inputted number can therefore have a substantial effect on the statistical analyses that you carry out, so you should always check your data to make sure that no data have been incorrectly inputted. With small data sets, it is possible to check through each participant's data to ensure that the numbers are correctly inputted; however, this can be time consuming. Therefore, it is often easier to use the descriptive data functions within SPSS to examine the data. Selecting Analyze > Descriptive statistics > Frequencies will enable you to check the mean, median, mode, standard deviation, variance, range, minimum number value and maximum number values for your data. All of these are invaluable for identifying incorrect data as well as outliers within your data. When examining the output from these analyses, you should check whether all of the values are within the expected ranges. For example, returning to the example of the five-point Likert scale, if you have a maximum value that is greater than five, then this suggests that something has been incorrectly inputted.

Missing data

One issue that you may come across while cleaning your data is missing data. This is quite a frequent problem, so do not let this overly concern you. It may be that participants decide that they do not want to answer a question or that they get bored with answering questions. There are several different types of missing data that can occur within your data set: missing completely at random (MCAR), missing at random (MAR), and missing not at random (MNAR). The pattern of your missing data reflects how much of an issue missing data can be to your data set. MCAR data is the least problematic, whereas MNAR data is the most problematic because, as the name suggests, there is a pattern to the data that is missing. Chapter 4 in Tabachnick and Fidell (2013) will help you to identify what type of missing data you have within your data set (see 'Further reading' section). Do not worry if you find that there are missing data within your data set; there are several different methods that you can use to deal with this situation (e.g., deleting cases, mean substitution, expectation maximization). It is beyond the scope of this chapter to explain all of these methods; however, we have included sources that deal with this issue in depth in the 'Further reading' section to help you resolve this problem.

Case study two

As you will remember, case study two involved gathering data from victims of crime to examine the impact of the type of sentence on their psychological well-being. You have gathered data from 100 participants, which means at the moment, you have sufficient power to carry out the hierarchical regression that you intended to use to analyse the data. However, when you complete the data screening, you realise that ten participants did not fully complete items across the questionnaire. You have carried out an SPSS missing values analysis and this has determined that the missing data are MAR. You have two options at this point. First, you could simply remove the participants that have not completed all the questions. This is a satisfactory approach when you only have small number of missing data and also where you are sure that the data is MAR. However, you are concerned that this will reduce the level of power in your analysis; therefore, you decide to use expectation maximisation to estimate the missing values. This method is available in SPSS under Analyze > Missing value analysis. Having selected the variables where you have missing data, you then select the EM tick box. This then generates a new data file with the inputted variables, and your missing data has been dealt with. You can then progress to examining the descriptive statistics, assumption testing, and the inferential tests as appropriate. Remember to outline this process in any reports about the study.

Assumption testing

The testing of parametric assumptions should be a process that is familiar to you from your undergraduate studies. As with data cleaning, this is a process that can be overlooked in your eagerness to get some analysis completed. However, if you miss this step, the end result may be that you use a test that is inappropriate for your data. As such, this means that the conclusions that you draw could be incorrect. Therefore, we recommend that you spend the necessary time completing assumption testing, so that you can be sure that you use the correct test on your data.

The first assumption that we are going to outline is independence. This means that the data in one variable should not influence the data in another variable. Independence also relates to the cases within your data set as well, in that the data gathered from one participant should be independent from the data gathered from another participant. The second assumption of multivariate normality should be fairly familiar to you. It is generally considered that this is an important component to allow parametric statistical tests to be carried out on the data. However, Field (2013) highlighted that there are situations where we can assume normality even if the shape of the data does not suggest a normal distribution. In fact, Field (2013) argued that once samples are large enough (generally considered to be $n > 30$), central limit theorem means that the distribution of samples will approximate a normal distribution anyway. This particularly applies to where you are going to use tests that group data (e.g., using ANOVA) (Tabachnick & Fidell, 2013). However, it is still good practice to examine the normality of your data even if you have a large sample, so we would recommend that you carry out this process or at least provide a justification for why you have not.

Please read the original sources cited in the previous paragraph (or other publications that provide information on these analyses), rather than simply citing what we have stated; it is important that you understand why you are making the decisions you are in relation to the normality assumption testing of your data. To establish the normality of your data, you can use several processes, including visual inspections of the data in a histogram or via the Kolmogorov-Smirnov test. Field (2013) will guide you through how to carry out these processes.

The third assumption of parametric tests is homoscedasticity (for ungrouped data, e.g., regression type designs) or homogeneity of variance (for grouped data, e.g., ANOVA type designs). This assumption relates to the variability of the scores in your data set. For ungrouped data, homoscedasticity is the assumption that variance in the scores in one variable is similar to the variance in another variable (Tabachnick & Fidell, 2013). For grouped data, homogeneity of variance is the assumption that the variance will be similar across the groups that you are using within your analysis. Field (2013) suggested several processes that you can use to examine homoscedasticity/homogeneity of variance within your data set. For example, you can use graphs or the Levene's test within SPSS, although with the Levene's test some caution should be used, as large samples can ensure that this test is significant even when there are only small variances within the data (Field, 2013). See the Field (2013) in the 'Further reading' section for how to examine this using SPSS. If this assumption is violated, you may decide to transform your data (as you may also decide to do if your data is non-normal). This decision should not be taken lightly as there has been substantial debate within the statistical literature regarding whether it is ever appropriate to transform your data. Tabachnick and Fidell (2013) suggested that you should always transform your data under these circumstances unless there is a rationale why you should not do so. However, Field (2013) highlighted several concerns that have been raised regarding the process of transformation:

1 Central limit theorem suggests that large samples will approximate the normal distribution anyway.
2 By transforming the data, you are changing your variables and thus the hypotheses that you are testing within your data.
3 In small samples, it is difficult to accurately determine normality.
4 There is a possibility of using an incorrect transformation, which would have a more substantial impact than the violation in the first place.

Should you decide to transform your data (see 'Further reading' for help on this process), you should not forget that you need to check your assumptions again with the newly computed variables. You should not assume that the transformation has corrected the issues with your data. When writing the results, summary statistics of the raw data should be presented, but the transformation also needs to be clearly reported, along with the reason for doing this (Manikandan, 2010).

At this point you may think that you have completed the assumption testing phase of your data. In fact, you have, in terms of establishing whether you can carry out parametric tests of your data. Examining the three previous assumptions will enable you to make a decision as to whether parametric tests are appropriate for your analysis. However, this does not necessarily mean that you have finished all assumption testing. Many of the statistical tests that you may have chosen for your project include additional assumptions that you will need to examine to ensure that it is appropriate to use them. This can be a frequently overlooked step in statistical testing, so it is important you remember when you have chosen your test that you need to check the assumptions of the particular test and ensure that you can still use this test.

Treating ordinal data as interval-level data

One of the assumptions that you will see for some tests is that the variables need to be at the interval level and above (refer back to Chapter 4 if you do not understand these terms). You may remember that Likert scale data (and other similar types of data) are considered to be at the ordinal level. This would mean that all studies in which this type of data was included should only be analysed using tests appropriate for ordinal-level data (i.e., nonparametric tests). However, it is very likely that you will have seen many published papers in which this type of data has been analysed using parametric tests. In fact, there has been quite a substantial debate regarding whether it is appropriate to treat ordinal-level data as interval data. Without getting too specific about this debate, Fife-Shaw (2012) argued that, assuming the quality of the scale/questionnaire you are using is sufficient, it is very likely that a parametric test will find the same conclusion as a nonparametric test would. This is helpful advice to a certain extent, as there is not always a nonparametric alternative to your chosen parametric test. However, this argument comes with the suggestion that it is good practice to carry out both the parametric and nonparametric versions of the tests (wherever possible), as you will not be able to determine whether your analyses will definitely draw the same conclusions between the two tests. Should there be any difference in the two solutions, then you should opt for the nonparametric results because this is the appropriate test for your data (Fife-Shaw, 2012).

Data analysis

This is the point at which you can finally carry out your analysis. Hopefully you are still feeling fairly excited about this process! One of the challenging issues

Data analysis   215

at this point is the choice of analysis. As we have emphasised earlier, this should have been decided long before this point, when you developed your research proposal, so we will assume that you are reading this section to inform the writing of your proposal! Broadly speaking, the decision process will be guided by the type of data that you have gathered and your research question(s). We will now work through some of appropriate forms of data analyses that you should carry out on your data, whether qualitative or quantitative.

Quantitative data analysis

This section is going to give you a broad overview of what statistical tests can show you with regards to your data. We strongly recommend, however, that once you have decided on your particular test that you then seek out one of the more specialised texts, e.g., Field (2013) or Tabachnik and Fidell (2013). These have been specifically chosen to provide a detailed overview of the tests that you are likely to be using. Choosing the correct test to analyse your data can be a daunting experience, but it is a process that with a little bit of practice can become a relatively easy part of the research process. The important thing to know before you attempt to choose your test is the type of data that you have gathered, the number of independent/predictor and dependent/criterion variables there are within your design, and the type of design that you are using (a between- or within-groups design). If you know this information about your design, then your choice of test should be a relatively easy process. A very broad overview of the more commonly used statistical tests is that they tend to fall into two groups. The first group of tests tends to be used to explore relationships within the data and amongst variables. These types of tests include correlation, regression and factor analysis.

Examples of statistical tests that examine relationships

Correlation: This test is one of the simplest analyses that you can carry out on your data, particularly bivariate correlation. The parametric version is called Pearson's correlation coefficient, whilst the nonparametric version is called Spearman's correlation coefficient. Essentially, the tests are a measure of the association between two variables and they provide you with a determination of the size of that relationship. Correlations can be either positive or negative, and these determine how the variables relate to each other. A positive correlation means that as the scores on one variable increase, the scores on the second variable also increase. In a negative correlation, as scores on one variable increase, they decrease on the second variable.

> *Regression:* There are multiple forms of regression analyses and the type of regression that is appropriate for you will depend upon the type of data that you have gathered. These tests are more sophisticated than correlations, in that they can be used to examine whether a score on a variable predicts a score on another variable. Multiple regression is generally used when there are continuous predictor and outcome variables, whereas logistic regression can be used where there is a combination of continuous and categorical variables. There are variations of both of these tests, so it is important that as well as determining the actual test that you are going to carry out on your data, you also need to determine which version of that test you are going to use.

The second group of tests examines the differences between groups; examples of these are *t*-tests, analysis of variance (ANOVA) and multivariate analysis of variance (MANOVA).

> ## Examples of statistical tests that examine differences
>
> *t-test:* This test is one of the simplest analyses that you can conduct. It is used to examine whether a variable differs between two groups. A *t*-test is a parametric test; a between–groups *t*-test (or independent *t*-test) is used for a between-groups design, and a related *t*-test is used for within-groups designs. The nonparametric versions are the Mann–Whitney test for between-groups designs and the Wilcoxon for within-groups designs. In essence, these tests examine the mean values for each group and determine whether the difference between these values is statistically significant.
>
> *ANOVA:* This is essentially a more sophisticated version of a *t*-test, whereby differences in a number of variables can be tested. For example, you may remember that case study one uses a 2×2 design. ANOVA enables us to examine the difference in the groups but also the possible interaction between these two variables. There are multiple forms of ANOVA, as well as versions for testing a number of dependent variables (MANOVA) or for including control variables (ANCOVA and MANCOVA). You need to choose the appropriate test according to your design, usually by whether it is a between-groups, within-groups or mixed design.

In addition to this information, there are many statistical test decision trees available that will help facilitate this process. Field (2013) has a particularly useful and easy to use decision tree to help you choose your test, and it also provides alternatives should your data not met parametric assumptions.

Activity

If you are intending to gather quantitative data, examine your research proposal and determine the following:

1   whether you are testing that there is a relationship between your variables, or whether there is a difference between groups;
2   that you understand the variables that are being tested within your study (i.e., IVs and DVS); and
3   that you understand the level of data that you will gather.

If you understand these aspects of your study, then you should refer to the decision tree in Field (2013) to determine the test that you should use for your analysis.

Effect sizes

At this point you should be beginning to understand the type of analysis that is appropriate for your quantitative data. One final area of good practice is in relation to effect sizes. This should be a term that is familiar to you, but it is possible that you have not come across this term before. When you are carrying out your statistical analyses, it is very likely that the main thing that you will be focused upon is whether any of the tests are statistically significant (e.g., $p < .05$). However, it is important to note that although p values are of obvious importance, you should also take some time to consider the level of importance of that statistically significant result. Effect sizes provide us with a method of reporting on the size or importance of the result. For example, you may want to examine whether an intervention affects reoffending, and you have one sample that completed an intervention and one matched sample that did not. You have a very large sample, and you measure recidivism one year after the intervention. You may find a statistically significant difference in the levels of reoffending between the two groups, suggesting that those who received the intervention offended at a lower level. However, when you examine the mean values, this determines that three individuals in the sample that received the intervention reoffended and four in the matched control sample reoffended. Although the analysis has determined this difference to be statistically significant, the size of that difference is actually quite small, as there is only one offence difference between the two groups. Hopefully you can see from this

218 Conducting research

example why it is important to report the effect size of any statistical analysis that you have found to be significant. There are different methods of calculating effect sizes depending on your data and type of analysis, so you will need to read a statistics book such as Field (2013) (or other publications) to select the method you need for your study. Cohen's d provides us with a method of determining the size of effects. It is generally accepted that when $d = .2$, this is considered a small effect; when $d = .5$ this is a medium effect; and when $d = .8$ this is a large effect.

Qualitative data analysis

As with the previous discussion, we will provide you with a broad overview of qualitative analysis processes; the 'Further reading' section on this topic will guide you to more specific resources that you should use in developing a detailed analysis of your qualitative data. By this point in the book, we hope that you know the form of analysis that you are going to use. If you do not, we recommend that you refer back to Chapter 3. As a general overview of the processes required for qualitative data, once you have transcribed or collected the data, you should fully familiarise yourself with your data. Basically, this means that you should read through your data several times. You may feel like you just want to start the analysis; however, this familiarisation stage is crucial in identifying the initial ideas that are relevant to your research question(s) that are apparent across your data. This will also mean that when you analyse the data, you will be familiar with what the participants have said or what is contained in the text extracts, so instead of trying to understand the words, you will be able to examine the content for meaning. Therefore, the familiarisation reading should be active and critical, examining the meaning of the participants' words (Braun & Clarke, 2013). If you notice anything that you think may be important within your data, then note these points in a research diary, as they may be useful when you begin your analysis later on.

Most forms of qualitative analysis now progress to some form of coding, although the approach used can vary considerably from one analysis type to another. This is why it is important to seek out a dedicated text that relates to your chosen analysis method. The process of coding is where you identify extracts within the data that contain some meaningful information in relation to your research question. You will usually find it useful to work through a process where you identify all of the important data within your dataset and then start to slowly organise the initial codes into more developed categories or themes. This process is very developmental, and you should continue to organise and reorganise the themes as you understand more about how the data relate to each other. You should be able to see patterns, similarities and differences in the way in which participants discuss particular topics, which means that you are completing the analytical process. You will usually discover that there are broader themes that are overarching to several subthemes. The roles of themes and subthemes should be made clearer in the following example.

Data analysis 219

> ### Case study four
>
> You are completing thematic analysis on the jury deliberation data examining how mock jurors use DNA evidence within a court case to determine the guilt or innocence of a defendant. One of the key overarching themes that you identify relates to the credibility of DNA evidence. Within this theme, there are conflicting subthemes, where DNA evidence is either perceived to be a 'useful investigative tool' compared with a subtheme of 'unreliable'. The manner in which mock jurors use DNA evidence varies, in that those who think DNA evidence is 'unreliable' dismiss the usefulness of this evidence and instead rely on other evidence presented within the case. Mock jurors who perceive DNA evidence to be a 'useful investigative tool' rely more heavily on it and use this evidence within their decision making.

The purpose of this section is to only give you a brief overview of the qualitative analytical process. If you are using a qualitative method of analysis, you should now refer to the 'Further reading' section to find materials that will provide more details about carrying out this type of analysis. In the following section we discuss some of the issues that are frequently levelled at qualitative research in relation to reliability and generalisability.

Ensuring quality in a qualitative analysis

Qualitative research is often criticised (unfairly in many cases) regarding the quality and 'unscientific' nature of the analysis. Indeed, as an inexperienced researcher, it is fairly common to feel uncertain about your qualitative analysis and whether you have analysed the data properly. There are several quality processes that you can use to ensure that the themes/codes/categories that you have drawn from the data truly represent what is held within the data. However, you must be careful, as terms such as *validity, reliability* and *generalisability*, although important in qualitative research, do not represent exactly the same concepts as they do within quantitative research. As such, you should be careful about trying to impose quantitative ideals on your qualitative data. There are many processes that you can use to ensure the quality of your data; two are described here. Read information on qualitative research to explore the range of techniques that can be used.

Participant checking is a process through which you provide the analysis to the participants and discuss with them the authenticity of your analysis. This can be very useful in clarifying your thinking about the themes and the way in which you have structured the findings. However, you must also be prepared for the possibility that participants may disagree with the meaning that you have drawn out of the data. Therefore, before engaging in this process, you need to

220 Conducting research

be clear on how you will deal with this situation. For example, if several participants challenge your interpretation, are you willing to return to the data and analyse it again? Remember that the purpose of participant checking is not to prove your analysis 'correct' but instead to ensure that you have represented what your participants stated within your analysis.

Another process for quality checking is triangulation. If you want to engage in triangulation, this will need to be planned into your project early on, as it is likely that you will need to gather several different sources of data to examine the same phenomenon. For example, Walker, Bowen, Brown, and Sleath (2014) examined the process of desistance from intimate partner violence (IPV). The method of data collection involved interviewing perpetrators of IPV, victims of IPV, and treatment programme facilitators for IPV programmes. As such, the issue of desistance was examined from multiple participant perspectives. Triangulation can also be achieved by gathering different types of data or by using different researchers to gather the data. However, this process is nearly impossible to implement after you have gathered your data, so if you want to engage in the process of triangulation, then you need to think about it in the project planning stage.

Summary and final checklist

In this chapter, we have given you a broad overview of both qualitative and quantitative processes of analysis that you should complete. Given the range and number of different types of analyses and the different processes required for each, we are not able to cover these in detail. We hope, however, that combined with information in the 'Further reading' section and publications you are able to identify yourself, that you now feel relatively confident about choosing and conducting the appropriate analyses for your data. Remember that this is not an easy process and it can be difficult to feel confident about it, but as long as you actively engage in this decision-making process (and seek advice when required), you should not go too far wrong. This does mean that you have to do the reading and subsequent learning to understand why you are making the choices that you are. This knowledge will not spontaneously develop, but instead with experience you will learn to identify tests/analytical processes that are appropriate for your data. Use the steps below to successfully implement your own data analysis.

1   Identify the appropriate form of analysis for your project early on in the project planning stage. This will avoid you gathering the wrong data or data that you cannot analyse.
2   Research your data analysis technique in detail so that you understand any requirements that will impact how you need to gather your data. This will ensure that the data that you gather are appropriate for your intended research question and analysis.

Data analysis 221

3　If you are undertaking quantitative data analysis, make sure that you screen and carry out assumption testing on your data. Again, this will ensure that you are using the most appropriate test(s) for your data.
4　If you are carrying out qualitative analysis, make sure that your analysis is carried out according to the designated analysis method. Do not be tempted into thinking that all qualitative analyses are the same; there are specific requirements for each approach. Consider including quality checking procedures in your study.

Further reading

Missing data

Howell, D.C. (2008). *The treatment of missing data*. Retrieved from http://www.uvm.edu/~dhowell/StatPages/More_Stuff/Missing_Data/MissingDataFinal.pdf

Tabachnick, B.G., & Fidell, L.S. (2013). *Using multivariate statistics* (6th ed.). Harlow, England: Pearson Education. (Chapter 4)

Normality

Field, A. (2013). *Discovering statistics using IBM SPSS statistics* (4th ed.). London, England: Sage. (Chapter 5)

Transforming data

Pallant, J. (2013). *SPSS survival manual: A step by step guide to data analysis using IBM SPSS* (5th ed.). Maidenhead, England: Open University Press. (Chapter 8)

Tabachnick, B.G., & Fidell, L.S. (2013). *Using multivariate statistics* (6th ed.). Harlow, England: Pearson Education. (Chapter 4)

Homogeneity of variance/homoscedasticity

Field, A. (2013). *Discovering statistics using IBM SPSS statistics* (4th ed.). London, England: Sage. (Chapter 5)

Choosing the right statistical test

Field, A. (2013). *Discovering statistics using IBM SPSS statistics* (4th ed.). London, England: Sage. (Decision tree on the back page)

Pallant, J. (2013). *SPSS survival manual: A step by step guide to data analysis using IBM SPSS* (5th ed.). Maidenhead, England: Open University Press. (Chapter 10; this chapter is very accessible if statistics worries you)

Qualitative data analysis

Charmaz, K. (2014). *Constructing grounded theory* (2nd ed.) (Introducing Qualitative Methods Series). London, England: Sage.

Glaser, B.G., & Straus, A.L. (2009). *The discovery of grounded theory: Strategies for qualitative research*. London, England: Aldine Transaction.

Saldana, J. (2012). *The coding manual for qualitative researchers*. London, England: Sage.

Smith, J.A., Flowers, P., & Larkin, M. (2009). *Interpretative phenomenological analysis: Theory, Method and Research*. London, England: Sage.

References

Braun, V., & Clark, V. (2013). *Successful qualitative research: A practical guide for beginners*. London, England: Sage.

Field, A. (2013). *Discovering statistics using IBM SPSS statistics* (4th ed.). London, England: Sage.

Fife-Shaw, C. (2012). Introduction to quantitative research. In G.M. Breakwell, J.A. Smith, & D.B. Wright (Eds.), *Research methods in psychology* (4th ed., pp. 17–38). London, England: Sage.

Manikandan, S. (2010) Data transformation. *Journal of Pharmacology and Pharmacotherapeutics, 1*, 126–129. doi:10.4103/0976-500X.72373

Tabachnick, B.G., & Fidell, L.S. (2013). *Using multivariate statistics* (6th ed.). Harlow, England: Pearson Education.

Walker, K., Bowen, E., Brown, S.J., & Sleath, E. (2014). Desistance from intimate partner violence: A conceptual model and framework for practitioners for managing the process of change. *Journal of Interpersonal Violence*. Published online. http://jiv.sagepub.com/content/early/2014/10/10/0886260514553634

Section 3

Dissemination of your research findings

Chapter 13

Purpose of dissemination

In Chapter 2, we outlined the importance of your research having a purpose and of building on the evidence base so that your research contributes to forensic psychology knowledge. Hopefully, it should be easy to see that you cannot do this unless you tell people about your study (i.e., you must disseminate your research findings). Therefore, it is important for you to recognise that dissemination is an integral component of the research process, as without it there will be no benefits to service providers or service users and no theory or knowledge development. Broadly speaking, *dissemination* refers to communicating or broadcasting information to an audience, although the type of audience may vary considerably (e.g., your participants, service providers, academics). In this chapter, we will discuss the aims of research dissemination, your audiences, the messages you wish to convey to them and the different methods of communicating with them. Once you have read this chapter, you should be able to:

- appreciate the importance of research dissemination;
- understand the aims of communicating your research findings;
- consider your audiences and the messages that you wish to convey in your dissemination;
- identify a range of methods that can be used to share your results; and
- plan the dissemination of your research study.

Aims and importance of research dissemination

It is very easy when conducting research to simply see it as a means to an end. That end might be that you submit an assignment for your course or your thesis to the examiners. After all the hard work involved in the project up to the submission date, it is perhaps understandable that you breathe a huge sigh of relief, celebrate and then forget all about the research project. However, although a break at this point is sensible, your study is far from complete. If you were asked by a service provider to evaluate its provision, submitting your assignment does not complete this task. If you developed your research to build on the knowledge base or to develop a theory further, then again, your assignment/thesis/dissertation will

226 Dissemination of your research findings

not meet this purpose. Remember that only a very small number of people read work submitted for an academic course, and although your dissertation/thesis might be placed in the university library, it is unlikely that many people, especially those outside the university, will ever access this information. So you need to develop a plan to complete the research project. This may well mean that you need to continue working on your project when you are no longer a student and have perhaps moved away from the area in which you conducted the research. You are probably bored with us saying this by now, but it is important that you give this aspect of your study full consideration in your planning stage, so that you have a clear strategy and timetable for your dissemination work. As you will see here, you need to consider that you will most likely need to communicate with a number of audiences in a number of different ways, and each form of communication will take thought, planning and effort.

Not providing an opportunity for your participants to obtain the results of your study, or not communicating your findings to the stakeholders who requested the research or who helped you gain access to data or participants, is not in keeping with the ethical principles of respect and integrity. Furthermore, the principle of responsibility is not fulfilled if you do not communicate the findings to appropriate audiences who may be able to use the results to enhance service provision or minimise harm. That is not to say that you should communicate each and every study to every individual/organisation that you can contact. If you experienced difficulty in recruiting participants, for example, then your study may not be suitable for scientific reasons for dissemination to academic and practitioner audiences; however, you should still explain the outcome of your study to the participants and stakeholders involved in it. So you need to develop a dissemination strategy that is appropriate for your research study and its outcomes, taking into account your ethical and professional responsibilities.

Impact

In recent years it has become more common for researchers and research policymakers to talk about research impact – that is, that research should have impact. Broadly and simply, if a research study has impact, this means that the research findings led to some kind of change. Some examples of this could be: a service provider revised its programme or policy based on the findings of a study; members of the public changed their behaviours following the widespread dissemination of research findings; a national organisation rolled out an intervention nationally following research that demonstrated that the pilot delivery of the intervention was effective; or policymakers introduced or revised policy following the findings of a research study. Hopefully you can see that in order for a research study to have an impact, the findings need to be communicated to people who are in positions to use them. We are not explaining this because we expect all your research studies to have an impact. However, universities, research funders, charities and other organisations are increasingly assessed on the basis of the impact of their research and/or service delivery. Hence, impact has become of great importance. So we are explaining this, so (a) you understand what is meant when you hear the term being used and that you understand the context in which it is used and (b) you understand the importance of disseminating findings to appropriate people in order that research generates impact where appropriate. It is vital to note that simply disseminating your findings is not impact; you need dissemination to produce impact, but if you put your findings on a web page that no one reads or present your findings to a group of students who are really interested in your findings but are not in positions to use them, then your dissemination will not lead to impact. Communicating your findings to academics might lead to academic developments (e.g., your findings could contribute to theory development), which is also an important aim. Note, however, that academic developments are commonly distinguished from impact, with *impact* being used to refer to change/developments outside of academia.

Identifying and understanding your audiences

Hopefully you can see from the previous section that it is important that you identify the audiences with which you wish to communicate, as you will need to tailor your communication strategy for each type of audience. It is not appropriate, for example, to give copies of your 80,000 word PhD thesis to the participants of your study as a method of dissemination. Similarly, giving your dissertation to a service provider is not the best or most appropriate means of communicating to this organisation. So the first thing you need to do is to list all the groups of people (audiences) to whom you should communicate your study.

Case study one

In this example, the results of the study should be communicated to the following audiences (at a minimum):

1 Service provider (e.g., the gatekeeper/manager who requested the study)
2 Participants (note that giving the results to the service provider/ gatekeeper does not ensure that the results are communicated to the

participants, so you will need to discuss with the service provider the best method for communicating the results to the staff, many of whom were participants)

Depending on the outcome of the study and with the permission of the service provider, you could also consider disseminating the findings to other similar service providers. You can also consider dissemination to academic/forensic psychologist audiences.

Case study two

In this example, the results of the study should be communicated to the following audiences (at a minimum):

1   Charities/service providers who provided access to staff
2   The staff of the above organisations who asked service users if they would take part in the study
3   The service users/victims who were asked to complete the study

Depending on the findings of the study and the number and spread of organisations, it might also be appropriate to disseminate the findings of the study to service providers who provide support, health and well-being services to victims (e.g., if more support was needed to particular types of victims, or if victims' well-being was poor then the study might be useful for these groups to help provide appropriate services). It might also be appropriate to communicate the findings to sentencing policymakers. Finally, since the study evaluates sentencing theory, and assuming the study is scientifically reliable and valid (e.g., it has a good sample size), it should be disseminated to sentencing theorists/academics.

Activity

List all the audiences to whom you should communicate the findings of your study. When you have done this, identify the most appropriate form of communication with each group and think about how you would deliver this and ensure that each audience was provided with the relevant information.

Once you have listed your audiences, you need to identify the key messages that you wish to give to those audiences. For example, in case study two, the key message that you wish to communicate to sentencing theorists is likely to be different from the key message that you wish to communicate to victims/service users. The Agency for Healthcare Research and Quality (AHRQ, see further reading section) suggests that you list your major findings and that you select one key finding and consider how this should be disseminated. If you want to share your findings with stakeholders (including participants), it can be helpful to list the key findings from your project in bullet points. You can then consider what dissemination strategy would be most appropriate for each of these points and how you are going to communicate these findings to your audience(s).

Traditionally, academics and researchers have tended to rely on written forms of communication to disseminate the results of their studies. However, developments in social media and increased attention to the importance of impact have led to a broader and more innovative range of communication methods being used in recent years, a trend that is likely to increase in future. For example, Keen and Todres (2007) conducted a review of the dissemination of qualitative research studies and found that drama, dance, poetry, video and evocative forms of writing had all been used. Remember, the aim for your study is not to use the most innovative method possible, but to select a method that is most appropriate for your audience. Bear in mind that it is likely to be most appropriate to use different communication techniques with each audience (e.g., a report and follow-up meeting might be appropriate for the service provider manager in case study one, whereas presentations delivered at different times [to allow all to attend] might be appropriate for the staff in this organisation, who could also be sent a copy of the report or the summary, if requested).

Case study five

A dissemination strategy for case study five could be as follows:

1   A face-to-face meeting or phone call to each participant to explain the key findings. You could also consider a short (one- or two-page) summary that you can send to them in addition to this.
2   A professional-style report written for the service provider and a presentation of the findings to relevant staff (e.g., the manager, intervention lead, intervention providers).
3   Presentation(s) (poster or oral, see Chapter 16) at appropriate conferences, such as for practitioners delivering interventions to the same or similar service users.
4   An empirical research paper (see Chapter 15) written for an appropriate source, such as a journal with a practitioner audience.

Activity

Revisit the case study one and two boxes in this chapter and identify the most appropriate method of communicating with each of the audiences listed. When you have done this, revisit the list of audiences you made for your study in the previous activity, and consider the most appropriate method of communicating with each. Remember that you do not need to use the same method for each audience, and in some cases, more than one type of communication might be appropriate.

Methods of communicating your research findings

As you can see, there is a wide range of methods available to you to disseminate your research findings. It is not possible for us to outline them all in detail, but we have selected some of the more common methods and we will discuss some of the key areas. We have provided some useful web resources in the 'Further reading' section that contain useful information and advice about disseminating your findings and writing publications. In many ways, the principles for good communication are the same, even though how you will communicate for each will differ. For example, you should be clear about the following for each method of dissemination:

1   Who is the audience? What can I assume that they will and will not understand? For example, for academic audiences you can say 'a quasi-experimental approach was used' because you can assume some knowledge of research methods, but this would not be appropriate for nonacademic audiences, for whom you would need to explain the design of the study clearly and simply.

2   What are the key messages that I am trying to communicate? Think carefully about what people will be interested in and what they *need* to know. For example, do you need to tell your participants about all the research that was conducted prior to the study, or all the details about how the measures you used were developed and how you scored them, or how the analysis was conducted?

3   What language should I use? This is related to both of the previous items. Should you refer to the fact that, for example, you conducted a hierarchical logistic regression? Most people will not know what this is, so it is unlikely that you need to provide these details unless you are writing an empirical research paper, your research thesis/dissertation, or presenting for an academic conference (and at a conference, unless it is statistical, you most likely need to do no more than state that this is the method that you used; see Chapter 16). Having spent a number of years studying psychology or

related topics, it can be difficult to understand what others do and do not know about your topic, but you should try to do this and ask people from outside academia to proofread or listen to practice presentations that you plan to deliver to nonacademic audiences.

4   What format should I use? What sections and subsections are appropriate? What formats/styles are commonly used for this type of communication method? Generally speaking, unless you have a clear reason to be innovative/different, it is a good idea to use published examples as guides, templates, professionally tailored/appropriate advice etc.

Summary of your results

If you require a summary of your results for your participants or other stakeholders (whether you do this in written or some other form), the key things to remember are that this does not have to be long, does not need a lot of detail, and needs to be targeted appropriately (i.e., given their knowledge, background, level of understanding). A written summary of your results aimed at your participants, for example, should be no more than one or two pages. You could start by stating the aim of the research, remembering to make sure that this is written appropriately for your audience in a single sentence. Then state clearly what you did, avoiding the use of research methods jargon, in a short paragraph (you probably do not need to explain the method of analysis used). You can then outline what you found, which should be the focus of the summary. You could end with a short paragraph on what this means, remembering to focus on the participants' or stakeholders' perspectives and considering ethical issues (see case study one example). As with the debrief (see Chapter 9), you should provide your contact details so you can answer questions. In many instances, it would also be a good idea to restate the sources of support and/or information that are available.

Case study one

In a summary of the results given to police officers in the organisation, many of whom took part in the research, you might say something like what is quoted below. Note that information about training is provided so that officers do not feel worried about their current practice, and note that you provide information that they can use until this training is available. Remember ethical duties in respect to harm, risk and responsibility (see Chapter 7). Note that you would first need to discuss the training and information that you want to provide with the gatekeepers/managers of the organisation.

"Police officers identified interpersonal violence (IPV) equally well, whether the victim was a lesbian or heterosexual. However, officers

232 Dissemination of your research findings

> identified IPV more often when the violence was physical than when it was not, for example, when there were bullying and controlling behaviours. This suggests that training is needed to highlight the presence and impact of nonviolent IPV behaviours, so that officers can identify these more accurately in future. Such training is currently being developed and will be offered in XX. Attached to this summary is an information leaflet that provides more details about the range of IPV behaviours, the impacts of each on victims, and the links between these behaviours."

Professional reports

If you have been asked to evaluate an intervention/service or conduct research for a service provider or organisation, then summarising your study in a professional report is likely to be appropriate. Note that it might also be a good idea to discuss/present your findings in person as well. There is a lot of advice available about writing professional reports, and there are many templates (e.g., for software packages) that can be used. If available, have a look at other reports written for the organisation and use these as guides; if there are no reports available for that organisation, have a look at reports written for organisations such as the Ministry of Justice and NSPCC, which are available via the organisation web sites. The key sections that are frequently used are shown in the following box. Note that the style and layout of these reports are different from the style/layout that you would use in academic documents. As previously discussed, remember to carefully tailor your writing to your audience.

> ## Research report sections
>
> Contents
> Acknowledgements
> Summary
> Introduction/background
> Method
> Findings (including key findings)
> Conclusion and implications and/or recommendations
> References
> Appendices (where appropriate)

Presentations

It might be a good idea to present the findings of your study to participants and stakeholders, rather than relying on written materials. This method has the advantages that individuals have the opportunity to ask questions and that

Purpose of dissemination   233

you can see when you are discussing your results how they are being received and whether people understand what is being said. Many of the principles previously discussed apply to such presentations. Although you may have more control over the length of the presentation and the session in which the presentation is delivered, these presentations are similar to those given at conferences. Please refer to Chapter 16, in which these are discussed in more detail. Note that the organisation might not have facilities or equipment for presentations (e.g., projectors), so you will need to determine the best form of delivery for your presentation. You will need to negotiate with the organisation/gatekeeper when the best time to give the presentation will be, where it should be held, and how relevant individuals will be invited, so plan this into your timetable and remember the advice we have given in previous chapters about planning, organisation and communication.

Social media

It is becoming more and more common for people to share their activities, including research developments and findings, via a range of social media formats. Academics are increasingly using social media to share their research findings, and such resources can be useful in keeping abreast of the latest research developments in a field. This form of communication is easy to use, inexpensive and provides easy access to a range of individuals (academics, practitioners, public), often via the same resource. Care is needed, however, when disseminating your results via social media (see the following boxes), but this can be a valuable resource for sharing your findings (and is most appropriate when you have collected data via social media). It is likely to be most useful as a method of sharing a publication (for example, you can share a link to a report of your research published on an organisation's web site, or share your journal article when it is first published) or presentation (e.g., to tell people that you will be presenting at a conference), rather than as a way of directly disseminating your research findings.

Social media and ethics

Individuals often compartmentalise activities/locations, so that although they carefully consider confidentiality and ethics when collecting data and writing formal reports about research, they forget about ethics and professionalism when they are communicating on social media. If, for example, you have promised anonymity or confidentiality to your participants and the organisation where you are collecting data, you breach this if you put a status update on Facebook that says you are looking forward to collecting data in XX prison, or if you say in one post that you are looking forward to collecting data for your research that day and in another you say that your train to XX is delayed. Remember that many social media sites include the location of your posts/pictures, so you can breach confidentiality inadvertently. Once you have posted information to social media platforms, it can be very difficult to remove it, so you need to think very carefully about all the things you post to social media forums *before* you post, rather than after. This is good advice generally, but is particularly important when conducting research and when working in forensic psychology contexts. There are numerous examples that have received media attention when a post or status change in social media platforms that took an instant to write/send have had huge consequences for individuals, so think carefully about your social media presence at all times. Rarely is social media a 'private' conversation between you and one other person, so regardless of whether you are at work or home, or think you are primarily interacting with 'friends', you need to think carefully about what you say. Ethical practice applies to communication via social media even if you do not think you are 'working' (i.e., employed) when you use it. For example, if you are conducting research about the well-being of victims/survivors and you make a crass comment about a crime, victim or organisation on a social media site, that could be the end of your research project (i.e., you will not be able to get participants, the organisation might withdraw its support), and there might be a number of other serious consequences (e.g., for your employment and career prospects).

Copyright

Copyright rules are complex, and you should look into these further if you intend to publish your research in journals and books. Here, we want to highlight that you need to consider your publication strategy overall and decide what information you want to release via the various sources you have available to you. If you make your detailed dissertation available on a public web site, for example, then it is unlikely that you will be able to publish this later as a book chapter or journal article. Hence, thinking about the message that you want to give to each audience and the information that is appropriate for each audience is important for this reason, as well as those discussed throughout this chapter. If you produce a short summary for your participants and make this available to them, it is unlikely that this will have an impact on your ability to submit a detailed discussion of your paper in an empirical article to a journal. If you are unsure about any of these issues, seek advice from your supervisor/line manager or an experienced researcher.

Dissertation

Strictly speaking, a dissertation or thesis is not a method of dissemination. It is something that you need to complete and submit for a course/doctorate. The information in your dissertation/thesis will need to be adapted for use in disseminating your findings, as per the discussions in the rest of this chapter. There is a great deal of advice and a number of publications available about writing dissertations, and we recommend that you use these. Your organisation will have its own requirements that you must follow (e.g., in respect to format, word length). If you think of a dissertation/thesis as a long empirical paper, most of the information in Chapter 15 is also relevant.

Summary and final checklist

In this chapter, we have stressed the purpose and aims of disseminating your research findings, and we have highlighted a number of issues that you should consider in doing this. You should now be ready to develop a dissemination strategy, and once you have completed your research you can begin to share your findings. When doing this, make sure that you are clear about each of the points in the following checklist to try to ensure that your communication with all your audiences is successful.

1 Identify the purpose for your communication.
2 Identify the audience for your communication.
3 Identify the key message(s) that you intend to communicate.
4 Select the most appropriate method and format for your communication.
5 Think about the language that is appropriate, given the knowledge and expertise of your audience and other issues such as age, learning/reading abilities etc.
6 Carefully plan your publication and the way in which it will be delivered.
7 Take care to ensure that you are behaving professionally and ethically throughout.

Further reading

AHRQ dissemination planning tool: http://www.ahrq.gov/professionals/quality-patient-safety/patient-safety-resources/resources/advances-in-patient-safety/vol4/planningtool.html

Discussion of research impact: http://www.esrc.ac.uk/funding-and-guidance/impact-toolkit/what-how-and-why/what-is-research-impact.aspx

Guidance on producing a publication: http://www.esrc.ac.uk/funding-and-guidance/impact-toolkit/tools/publications/producing/index.aspx

Social media for researchers: http://www.rin.ac.uk/our-work/communicating-and-disseminating-research/social-media-guide-researchers

236   Dissemination of your research findings

Top tips for producing publications: http://www.esrc.ac.uk/funding-and-guidance/impact-toolkit/tools/publications/top-tips.aspx

Reference

Keen, S., & Todres, L. (2007). Strategies for disseminating qualitative research findings: Three exemplars. *Forum: Social Qualitative Research Sozialforschung, 8*(3), Article 17, September. Retrieved from http://www.qualitative-research.net/index.php/fqs/article/view/285/625

Chapter 14

Literature review papers

In this chapter, we outline the process of submitting journal article papers to journals for review and the structure of literature review papers. Since there are different types of literature reviews and a range of approaches that can be used to present them in journal article format, this section provides an overview of the keys issues to consider. As there is a great deal of overlap between conducting a literature review and writing it, you may need to refer back to Chapter 2 as you read this chapter. In addition, the information presented in Chapters 13 and 15 is also relevant. Please also use the resources in the 'Further reading' sections of all the chapters and other publications that you identify as relevant. When you have read this chapter, you should be able to:

- select a journal appropriate for your review;
- identify who should be listed as authors of the paper and appreciate the importance of agreeing on the order of authorship;
- identify who and/or which organisations should be acknowledged;
- recognise the core components of literature review papers and the importance of having a clear argument and purpose;
- draft a literature review paper; and
- appreciate the submission and anonymous peer-review processes.

Journal article publishing

In order to write literature review and empirical papers, you need to have some idea of the process of journal article publishing, which typically includes an anonymous peer-review process. At the start of the process of writing a paper, it is a good idea to select the journal for which you are writing the paper, as journals have different requirements in terms of word limits, formatting styles and required sections. Therefore, if you choose your target journal before you have written your paper, you will know exactly how to format and structure the paper according to the journal requirements, thus saving you time in the long run. Hence, in this section, we will provide some advice about selecting

238 Dissemination of your research findings

appropriate journals, provide information about some writing processes that you may not know about, and explain the review process that your manuscript will likely be subjected to. First we will provide some guidance about agreeing on the authorship of papers.

Authorship

It is important to agree the authorship of a paper before you submit it; however, it is a good idea to discuss this at an early stage in the research process. This can be a tricky thing to determine and negotiate, and there is some guidance (see the 'Further reading' section) about determining (a) who should be an author on the paper and (b) the order of authorship. Generally speaking, in the case of student projects, the person who conducted the study and drafted and redrafted the paper should be the first author. Someone who had a more supervisory role would be the second author (if there are several supervisors, these should be listed in an order that reflects each person's level of input into the paper). However, if person A did the study and drafted the original paper but the paper required substantial work by person B to make it suitable for publication, then it might be agreed that person B should be the first author and person A the second author. Decisions like these have to be agreed upon and dealing with conflicts with regards to authorship order can be tricky. It is best to approach any discussions about authorship carefully, wording all communications appropriately to avoid any chance of miscommunication. This is particularly important if you disagree with decisions that have been made regarding authorship. You should also refer to the principles that we have already highlighted in the book regarding communication with external organisations and supervisors (see Chapter 10).

Selecting a journal

There are a large number of journals that address the range of topic areas, types of methods, audiences, and locations within psychology and beyond. Selecting a journal can be tricky, particularly for those new to publishing, as some information about a journal (e.g., how long it takes to process reviews) is not publically available and is learned by experience. Therefore, it is a good idea to seek advice from someone experienced in publishing papers in your area of research. There are a number of things that you should consider that will help you narrow down the list of potential journals that would be appropriate for your paper.

1 Identify journals that accept either literature review or empirical papers as appropriate. You may also find that journals limit the types of review articles that they will consider (e.g., only systematic reviews or meta-analyses) or the types of empirical papers they will consider (e.g., only qualitative research, or only quantitative).

Literature review papers   239

2   Look at the 'aims and scope' information provided by each journal to select those that fit the topic of your review or research. This is particularly important because journal editors will reject articles that do not fit with the aims or scope of the journal.

This should provide you with a 'short list' of journals. At this stage, you should seek advice, as you will need to select a journal based on a combination of issues, such as the perceived quality of the journals (see impact factor box), the journals' audiences and the journals' requirements (e.g., if you have a long paper, perhaps a systematic review, a journal with strict, small word or page limits is not likely to be suitable). Since journals have different formatting requirements, it is a good idea to select a journal before you begin to write your paper.

Activity

Find the websites of five journals relevant to forensic psychology. You can identify these by looking at the papers you searched to design your project, or for other forensic psychology work, or you can use the accompanying list as a starting point. Each journal should have an 'aims and scope' section or another type of outline of the papers that it aims to publish (look in the 'about this journal' or 'for authors' sections).

1   Read this information for the journals and note:
   A: the topic of the papers accepted;
   B: whether literature review and/or empirical papers are accepted; and
   C: whether there are particular types of methodological designs and/or reviews that are accepted.

2   Find the 'instructions for authors' for each journal and note:

   A: the word or page limits of the journal; and
   B: the instructions for formatting the paper.

Examples of forensic psychology journals

Legal and Criminological Psychology
Psychology, Crime and Law
Aggression and Violent Behavior
Trauma, Violence and Abuse
Criminal Justice and Behavior
International Journal of Offender Therapy and Comparative Criminology

240 Dissemination of your research findings

Impact factors

An *impact factor* is the measure of the number of times that journal articles are cited in other journal articles, most commonly within a two-year period. For example, if journal X published ten papers in its 2010 volume; and these papers were cited in twenty other papers published in 2011 and 2012, the two-year impact factor is 20 (number of citations)/10 (number of papers), which is 2. A difficulty is that there are different indexes of journals (e.g., Scopus and Thomson Reuters) and the total number of citations usually includes only the citations in journals included in a specific index (and it does not include the number of times the paper was cited in publications such as books and reports). The Thomson Reuters Social Science Citation Impact Factor is the most commonly cited (e.g., you will notice this on many journal web pages). The higher the number, the better the journal is considered to be in relation to quality, as this indicates a higher rate of citations (seen as an indicator of academic impact – see Chapter 13). Thomson Reuters collates journals into subject grouping, such as Criminology and Penology (which at the time of writing contains 52 journals) and Psychology (which has 111 journals), to account for the variation in citation practices between topic areas. At the time of writing, *Sexual Abuse: A Journal of Research and Treatment* has a two-year 2014 impact factor of 2.280, which places it fifth in the Criminology and Penology group and thirty-third in the Psychology group (there is a larger range of impact factors in psychology journals).

Formatting

As you will have noted when you completed the previous activity, journals have different requirements for the formatting of papers. Bear in mind that some journals will reject a paper on the basis that it is too long or not formatted as requested, so it is important that you follow all the journal's instructions. The APA publishing guidance (see 'Further reading' section) is the most commonly used, but you need to confirm that this is the style required by your chosen journal. Many people think that APA formatting only relates to the formatting of references; however, the APA guidance contains information in relation to writing styles (e.g., whether you should use 'whilst' or 'while', 1 or one, and the use of gender neutral language), the use of punctuation, the format of tables and figures, the format of headings and subheadings, the manner in which statistical information should be presented and so on. When a journal requests APA (or other) style/format, therefore, it is important that you refer to the guidance and follow it carefully and consistently throughout the whole of the article, not just in the references and citations.

Common difficulties

In order to present your review or research study in a clear and concise manner, you need to be able to write well, use punctuation appropriately, and follow grammatical rules. You do not need to be an expert on grammar, but you should be able to write clear, properly constructed sentences and use punctuation correctly. When talking about the views of participants, for example, you need to understand the difference between the participants' views (i.e., the views of many participants) and the participant's views (i.e., the views of one participant) and use these correctly. When people are asked to do presentations (see Chapter 16), they often put a great deal of emphasis on presentation skills and can worry so much about the format of the presentation that they pay too little attention to the content of the presentation. The opposite tends to be the case with writing; people pay a lot of attention to the content but not to the style/format of writing. While people recognise that presenting is a skill that can and should be developed, many do not apply this view to writing. It is common for people to say, for example, "I just don't get colons and semicolons" or "I always write long sentences; that's just what I do". In fact, time spent developing your writing skills will pay dividends, no matter where you work. Being able to write clearly and to adapt your style according to the purpose of the communication, audience and message you are trying to convey is an important skill that requires development and practice. If you have received comments that your writing requires attention, or you are not confident about writing or using punctuation, you should spend some time developing these skills. A key aspect as to whether a literature review will be accepted for publication, for example, is the manner in which arguments are made about the papers included in the review, which is reliant on good writing skills. Similarly, a well-written empirical paper (see Chapter 15) has a greater chance of publication than a poorly written paper describing the same study.

Audience

As we highlighted in Chapter 13, it is important to think about your audience in writing literature review and empirical papers (see Chapter 15). Journals have different audiences, and you need to think about this in regard to the way you write your paper; for example, a greater focus on the implications of a review or research study might be more appropriate for a journal with a practitioner audience. Most journals have an international audience, and it is important to keep this in mind when you write your papers. Do not assume that a reference to a particular issue will be understood by all; remember that

242   Dissemination of your research findings

there are differences in legislation, criminal sentences and between organisa-tions. Although you can assume that the readers of research papers have some research knowledge (which does not tend to be country or culture specific), you should think about the way in which you explain issues that vary inter-nationally. If your study is very specific to a particular jurisdiction and/or type of organisation, then it likely to be most appropriate to select a journal that is similarly focussed.

Peer review

Peer review is considered to be a marker of scientific quality because papers are independently scrutinised by experts in the subject area. Most commonly, this process is conducted anonymously (i.e., the authors of a paper do not know the identities of the reviewers and the reviewers do not know the identities of the authors). Many journals use a process of peer review, and papers published in such journals are generally more highly valued in academia than papers published without such independent scrutiny. As discussed in Chapter 11, there have been a number of recent cases where the peer-review process has been violated, or where papers containing falsified or manipulated data were pub-lished even though they were subjected to peer review. This has sparked debate about the value of the peer-review process; however, this remains a standard process for most of the journals that would be suitable for the publication of your papers.

Two or three suitable reviewers (usually experienced researchers and authors of research papers) are selected on the basis of their knowledge of the topic area and/or methodological design. These reviewers read the paper and indicate whether they think the paper should be published as it is (very rare), published with minor or major revisions (more common) or rejected (rejection rates for journals vary; typically journals considered to be of higher quality have the highest rejection rates). Reviewers provide their views of the paper and the research described within it and they make suggestions for ways in which the paper can be improved. An editor or associate editor of the journal will consider the reviewers' comments and will decide whether to either: (1) reject the paper, (2) request that revisions are made (in which case the paper can be revised and resubmitted) or (3) accept the paper. Revised papers are typically rereviewed if possible by the original reviewers and a similar process is com-pleted. A paper could be revised a number of times before it is accepted for publication, though it would be expected that revisions are more minor as the paper is revised and rereviewed.

In terms of writing papers for peer-review publication, there are a number of things that you need to bear in mind: (a) papers need to be written so that you and your co-authors cannot be identified; (b) papers can and often are rejected if the journals' instructions are not followed; and (c) the research or review described in the paper needs to be of good quality, as does the paper. This does not mean that it is not possible for you to publish in peer-review journals, nor that student research will not be accepted. A number of our students have published literature review and empirical papers based on their undergraduate and postgraduate research projects. Therefore, the above advice should not deter you or make you feel that this is an unattainable goal; rather, we want to ensure that you understand the processes involved, so that you can maximise your chances of success.

Writing literature review papers

How you structure a literature review paper will depend on the type of literature review that you are completing. In the following section, we will outline the different approaches that you should take depending on whether your review is a systematic or narrative review. We will then provide some general guidance about the sections that a narrative style review should contain and the content that should be discussed within those sections.

Systematic Reviews

The format required for writing systematic reviews is quite rigid, since you should follow the guidance for writing such papers (see the 'Further reading' section). If you use the guidance for completing these reviews, the information required in each section should be fairly clear. We would also recommend that you find published systematic reviews (it does not matter what the topic of the review is, or even if the topic is a field other than forensic psychology, as the requirements are not subject specific) and use these as a guide. See the 'Further reading' section of Chapter 2 for a forensic psychology example. Other useful resources to help you are listed in the 'Further reading' sections of this chapter and of Chapter 2. Given the specificity of the information required in each section and the difficulty of recapturing the information once you have completed the process, it is a good idea to draft the sections of a systematic review as you complete the review (e.g., to record the number of papers identified by your search, the number of duplicates and the inclusion/exclusion criteria and so on). Some of information about writing narrative reviews outlined later (e.g., in relation to the title, abstract and introduction) will also be helpful in writing systematic reviews.

A potential difficulty with this type of paper is that the required sections, tables and figures result in a relatively long paper, which is often beyond the space limitations of many journals. Some journals will relax their normal space restrictions for systematic reviews; however, you might need to contact the editor or journal administrator (or equivalent) to determine this. If a journal has recently published a systematic review, then you can assume that it accepts this type of paper; however, you should also check the journals instructions for authors, as this might be specified there also. Seek advice from your supervisor/line manager and/or from those with experience of publishing in forensic psychology.

244 Dissemination of your research findings

Narrative reviews

> **Activity**
>
> Find five published narrative reviews and read them, noting the similarities and differences between them.

In reading a number of review papers, you will probably have noticed how the format and style of the papers vary. It is difficult, therefore, to explain exactly how narrative review papers should be written. This might mean that you have limited confidence about writing the paper, but try not to be put off by this. We have noticed that completing and writing narrative literature reviews are the parts of the research process that students often find most challenging. However, many of our students who struggled with this process have published literature review papers, so it is something that is worth your perseverance. Many of the skills required to write good literature review papers (e.g., an ability to be analytical and critical) are important skills to develop because they will also enhance your research and practice abilities.

As discussed in Chapter 2, it is important to be clear about the purpose of your literature review. Although you may have an idea what you will find in the review when you start the review process, you will need to carefully read all the papers that you select to include in the review before you are able to determine the key findings. When you have identified the key findings, you can form an overall argument that you wish to present in your literature paper. Your argument might be that practice is not supported by the research evidence, or that there is research evidence to support a new or revised practice. Perhaps there are methodological issues with the research studies, and your argument is that there are too few robust research studies to be able to draw conclusions about a topic/issue. The argument will clearly depend on the findings of your review. It should be easier to write the paper if you have a clear idea about your argument and the purpose of the review, as this should lead you to structure the main text of the review into sections and subsections and will also determine how you introduce the review, discuss the findings and formulate recommendations.

General structure of a narrative review

The review should be presented in a logical manner. Think of the structure as if you are: (1) outlining the need for the review; (2) explaining how the review was conducted; (3) summarising what the papers included in the review show and how reliable and methodologically sound these findings are; and (4) the implications of the review for research, theory and/or practice. Note that the format and subheadings of a review paper might be specified by the journal. If this is the case, then obviously you should use the required format.

Title

For review papers, it is a good idea for the title to clearly indicate that 'a review' or 'systematic review' of the topic is the focus of the paper. See Chapter 15 and its 'Further reading' section for more detailed advice about titles.

Abstract

Chapter 15 and its 'Further reading' section provide you with detailed advice about writing abstracts. The structure of these is largely the same for review and empirical papers, with slight variations. For review papers, the 'method' refers to the way in which you searched for papers to include in the review, and 'results' refers to the key findings that you drew from the papers that were included in the review. The conclusions should be based on the underlying argument that you are presenting (e.g., that there is not enough good quality, methodologically robust research studies to answer the review question, or that there is confidence about aspect A but less confidence about aspect B, leading to the recommendation that more research is required into aspect B).

Keywords, research highlights and acknowledgements

This content is largely the same as for empirical papers, so please refer to Chapter 15 and its 'Further reading' section for information about these sections.

Introduction

The introduction for narrative and systematic reviews does not need to be long; it is likely to be shorter than an introduction for an empirical paper. The key purpose is to make an argument for the need for the review. Take care not to discuss information that is included in the main part of the review and/or to preempt the findings/conclusions.

Method

Not all narrative reviews have this, but this section is becoming more common (see the examples in Chapter 2 for the range of ways in which the literature search method is described). The same level and amount of information as would be appropriate for systematic reviews is not required for narrative reviews, but it is a good idea to summarise the following details as a minimum: the databases that were searched; the search terms used; the inclusion and exclusion criteria; and the number of papers that resulted/were included in the

246 Dissemination of your research findings

review. You can provide this information in a separate subheading or provide it after you have outlined the justification for and purpose of the review.

Findings

This should be the most substantial part of the paper. Generally, in narrative reviews, the introduction, method and discussion parts are shorter than in empirical papers. Not all narrative reviews include a table of the studies included in the review (see the Clements et al. [2014] and Sandhu & Rose [2012] examples in Chapter 2 for reviews in which tables of studies are included) but this can be a good idea, as it enables you to include the detail of each of the papers, allowing you to focus on the key arguments in the text.

When you have carefully read and perhaps reread all the papers included in your review, you need to identify the similarities, differences and patterns in the studies. In some ways, conducting a literature review is like conducting qualitative analysis. It is important to be critical in your review of the literature. It might help to think about why you would read a review paper – perhaps to save you the need to read all the individual papers and to get a good overview of the studies included in the review and what the findings suggest for practice, research or theory. Your aim, therefore, is to give your readers a good understanding of the research included in the review and the weight or confidence that can be given to these findings. So in conducting your review, you should consider the methodological quality of the research outlined in each paper (see Chapter 3). The findings from studies with the greatest methodological rigour can then be given more weight, or you can express more confidence in them, particularly if the findings are consistent. If there are differences in the findings, consider why these may have occurred. For example, are the differences across countries, cultures, contexts or locations? Were there differences in the findings of studies in which different designs were used? By asking questions such as these and many more, you can identify some themes and perhaps subthemes in the results that you would like to present. These can then be used to structure the core part of your paper and might be used as headings and subheadings.

It is important to discuss the *literature* in your paper, not to simply include a list of studies. In an annotated bibliography, a number of papers/reports are described and critiqued one paper at a time. This is generally not an approach that should be taken in a literature paper, in which you should be discussing the patterns/themes that you find across studies.

Activity

Return to the literature review papers that you read for the previous activity. Notice how the authors summarise the studies in their reviews. For example, a section might begin with a summary of a number of papers:

> "The majority of studies were conducted in prisons in the USA, with one study (reference) conducted in a prison in the UK and another (reference) conducted in the community in Australia. Quasi-experimental designs were used in all studies with samples sizes ranging from X to Y, raising concerns about the statistical power of the analyses. . . ."
>
> Identify places where authors described a single study and think about the purpose in doing this.

Discussion or conclusions

Discussions/conclusions in literature review papers tend to be fairly short in comparison to empirical papers (see Chapter 15). This is largely because a great deal of discussion about the findings should be provided in the core/main section of the paper. In the concluding section, the purpose is to summarise the key findings from the review and to discuss the implications of these for research, theory and/or practice. It might be appropriate to make recommendations in line with these findings.

References

All sources should be cited appropriately in the paper, and you should list all the sources you have cited in the reference list. It is important that you carefully and consistently follow the referencing guidelines specified by the journal. It can be helpful to put an asterisk before the references that indicate the papers included in the review. If you do this, you should explain this to the reader in an appropriate place (e.g., when you specify the number of papers that were found and were selected for inclusion in the review, at the end of the method section or paragraph in which you describe the method).

Appendices

It is unusual to have an appendix in a narrative review paper, and we cannot think of information that would be useful to include here in this type of paper. That does not mean that you cannot have one, if it is appropriate, though keep journal space restrictions in mind.

Tables and Figures

To enable the publishers to place tables and figures in the paper in a way that makes best use of the space available, it is conventional to mention the figure/table in the following way where you want the table/figure to be presented:

TABLE [FIGURE] XX ABOUT HERE

The tables and figures should then be compiled at the end of the document (after the references and appendices), with each table or figure presented on a separate page. There are only a small number of journals that request that you do not do this, so unless this is specified, the approach described here should be used. You should format tables and figures as per APA guidelines, unless the journal requests a different style. Try to arrange any tables so that you make the best use of the space in them (i.e., minimise 'white' spaces in which there is no text by reducing or increasing the width of columns). Consider whether a portrait or landscape layout works best. Given journal space limitations and the space required to present a table, it is important to make sure that you are not presenting too many separate tables that could be easily combined. At the same time, don't include tables that are overcrowded and present too much information such that it is confusing for readers.

The submission process

Publishing ethics

It is important to note that you can only submit a paper to one journal at a time; you will probably be asked during the submission process to confirm that you understand this and that the paper has not been submitted elsewhere. If you submit a paper to a journal and it is rejected, then you are free to submit the paper to another journal. Please see the 'Further reading' section for resources outlining publishing ethics, including avoiding conflicts of interest.

Online submission

Most journals have online submission processes. These can be a little tricky if you are not used to them, but most have instructions. Read these to help you and/or seek advice from those accustomed to using such processes.

Cover letter

It is common practice to write a cover letter to the editor(s), which you will need to submit where it is requested in the submission process. Because this letter contains information that will identify you, it is important that you submit this information in the correct place, so that it is not included in the information sent out for review. This letter does not need to be long. You should simply state that you wish to submit a paper (list the title) to the journal. You can outline briefly why you feel that it is appropriate for the journal and/or what is novel about it and/or any other details that you feel are important.

Author details

Although the peer-review process is anonymous and you will need to ensure that there are no details about the authors included in the paper, when you submit it, you will be asked to provide the names and contact details of each author, so make sure you have these available.

Corresponding authors

The corresponding author is the person who communicates with the journal (the person who submits the paper, receives the decision email, checks the proofs of the paper, and whose email/contact details will be included in the paper). One author should be nominated to do this. This person does not have to be the first author. Decisions on paper authorship should be made on the basis of input into producing the paper and the study on which it is based (see above and further reading section). Selection of the corresponding author can be made on the basis of who is most able to submit the paper and/or will be available to receive and respond to communication from the journal and readers of the paper when it is published.

Journal decisions and responding to feedback

Much of the information provided in relation to dealing with feedback on ethical applications in Chapter 9 also applies to dealing with feedback on journal articles (or other processes). It is extremely rare for papers to be accepted as submitted, so to some extent you need to develop a thick skin to deal with the review process. You can learn a lot from the review process; usually, if you respond to the feedback as much as possible, the end result is a stronger paper.

If you are given an opportunity to revise the paper, it is common to note the changes you make to the paper via a 'track changes' facility or some other method. You will also need to explain how you have responded to each of the reviewers' comments. Therefore, it is important to keep track of the changes that you make as you work on the paper. You do not need to write lengthy comments in response to each suggestion (e.g., you can say 'revised' in response to simple typos or comments that are easy to revise). Your responses to the reviewers, like your paper and the revisions, should not include any details that will identify you or your co-authors. Sometimes you might need to challenge a reviewer's suggestion; perhaps what was requested is not possible, or something has been misunderstood about the study (bear in mind, though, that this probably means that it was not clear in your paper, so you at least need to clarify the issue in your paper). Any challenge to a reviewer's suggestion should be phrased respectfully, and it is appropriate to provide a short justification for why you

250 Dissemination of your research findings

believe it is not appropriate to make the requested change. Although you might find it frustrating to have to make changes to your paper, try not to let this show in your comments to the editor or reviewers; keep in mind that the editors/reviewers receive similar comments/requests about their own papers. It is useful to note that experienced authors/researchers have their papers rejected from journals and/or are asked to make revisions – this is simply an important part of the peer-review process. Remember that the purpose is to ensure the quality of scientific publications and the development of the evidence base. Nevertheless, it can be challenging to deal with at times, so do not be afraid to talk to your supervisor/line manager or colleagues about this for support and advice as to how to respond to the reviewers/editors.

There is normally a time limit for the resubmission process, so note this when you receive the decision and plan time for the revision process accordingly. The date for the resubmission may not be included in the decision email; you might need to log into your online account to find this information. Revised papers are submitted though a process very similar to the original submission. It is important that you enter it as a resubmission of the original paper and not submit it as a new paper. In addition, make sure that you submit your response to the reviewers in the appropriate place in the online submission process. If you do not, the reviewers might not be able to see the information that you have provided. Hopefully, the reviewers will feel that your paper is much improved and your paper will be accepted after the first or second revision. If the paper is accepted, it will be copyedited and you will be asked to check the proofs of the paper before it is published. It is important that you check the proofs very carefully, as any mistakes will be included in the published paper. Once published, it is extremely difficult, if not impossible, to make any changes. When your paper is published, you can then promote it (see the Further reading' section).

Summary and final checklist

In this chapter, we have outlined a number of important issues and processes that are important to understand if you wish to publish a literature review or empirical paper. We have also explained the key points to consider when writing systematic or narrative reviews. Since narrative views can vary considerably, it is not possible to be very specific about the structure that you should adopt in your paper, although we have given you guidance about the general sections that should be included. However, with the information provided here and in the 'Further reading' sections in this chapter and in Chapter 2, as well as the information in Chapters 13 and 15, you should now be able to select an appropriate journal and draft a literature review paper. When doing this, make sure that you are clear about each of the points in the following checklist.

1 Identify a journal and read the author guidelines carefully.
2 Agree on the authorship of the paper and identify whether acknowledgements are required.

Literature review papers 251

3 Find published systematic review papers or narrative review papers as appropriate and guidelines for formatting (e.g., APA guidelines). Use these to guide you throughout.
4 Draft your paper, taking time to consider the argument that you are presenting and the purpose of the review.
5 Ask someone with good grammar and writing skills to proofread your draft.
6 If possible (e.g., if it is not an assignment where review of a draft is not permissible), give your paper to your supervisor/co-authors to read and revise or recommend changes.
7 Revise, review and revise until all authors agree that it is ready to submit.

Further reading

Authorship

Discussion of why authorship matters and who should be defined as an author: http://www. icmje.org/recommendations/browse/roles-and-responsibilities/defining-the-role-of-authors-and-contributors.html
Elsevier's guidance on how authorship should be determined: http://www.elsevier.com/journal-authors/ethics
A guide for inexperienced researchers when conflict arises in relation to authorship: http://publicationethics.org/files/u2/2003pdf12.pdf

Selecting a journal

A publisher's guidance on how to choose an appropriate journal to submit your work to: http://journalauthors.tandf.co.uk/preparation/choosing.asp

Impact factors

An explanation of impact factors and how these should be used to assess the quality of a journal: http://journalauthors.tandf.co.uk/beyondpublication/impactfactors.asp

Peer review

Peer review and the acceptance of new scientific ideas: http://www.senseaboutscience.org/pages/peer-review.html
http://www.senseaboutscience.org/data/files/resources/17/peerReview.pdf

Systematic reviews

Centre for Reviews and Dissemination. (2009). Systematic reviews: CRD's guidance for undertaking systematic reviews in health care. Retrieved from http://www.york.ac.uk/inst/crd/pdf/Systematic_Reviews.pdf
Cochrane Handbook for Systematic Reviews of Interventions: http://www.cochrane.org/handbook
Moher, D., Liberati, A., Tetzlaffi, J., Altman, D.G., The PRISMA Group. (2009). Methods of systematic reviews and meta-anlyses: Preferred Reporting Items for Systematic Reviews and Meta-Analyses: The PRISMA Statement. *Journal of Clinical Epidemiology, 62,* 1006–1012. doi:10.1016/j.jclinepi.2009.06.005 (Note that these guidelines have been

252 Dissemination of your research findings

published in a number of journals, so you might find slightly difference references for them. They are sometimes referred to as the 'PRISMA guidelines'.)

Sense about systematic reviews: http://www.senseaboutscience.org/data/files/resources/52/Sense-About-Systematic-Reviews.pdf

Torgerson, C. (2003). *Systematic reviews*. London, England: Continuum.

Publishing ethics

American Psychological Association's guidance on publishing and authorship: http://www.apa.org/research/responsible/publication/

Committee of Publication Ethics: http://publicationethics.org/

Elsevier's ethics toolkit on publishing: http://www.elsevier.com/ethics/toolkit

Elsevier's ethics toolkit, information on conflict of interest: http://www.elsevier.com/?a=163717

Elsevier's conflict of interest form: http://help.elsevier.com/app/answers/detail/a_id/286/p/7923

Graf, C., Wager, E., Bowman, A., Fiack, S., Scott-Lichter, D., & Robinson, A. (2007). Best practice guidelines on publication ethics: A publisher's perspective. *International Journal of Clinical Practice, 61* (Suppl. 152), 1–26. doi:10.1111/j.1742-1241.2006.01230.x

Taylor and Francis's guide to ethics in publishing: http://journalauthors.tandf.co.uk/preparation/ethics.asp

Wiley's guide to ethics in publishing: http://authorservices.wiley.com/bauthor/publicationethics.asp

Promote your research

Sage's guidance on how to promote your research using social media: http://www.sagepub.com/authors/journal/10ways.sp?utm_source=authors_readership&utm_medium=nav&utm_campaign=10ways

Sage's guidance on how to promote your research through the internet: http://www.sagepub.com/authors/journal/discoverable.sp?utm_source=authors_readership&utm_medium=nav&utm_campaign=discoverable

Taylor and Francis's guide on how to promote your research: http://journalauthors.tandf.co.uk/beyondpublication/promotearticle.asp

Publishing advice and guidelines

American Psychological Association. (2009). *Publication manual of the American Psychological Association* (6th ed.). Washington, DC: Author. (See also http://www.apastyle.org)

Producing a publication guidance: http://www.esrc.ac.uk/funding-and-guidance/impact-toolkit/tools/publications/producing/index.aspx

Top tips for producing publications: http://www.esrc.ac.uk/funding-and-guidance/impact-toolkit/tools/publications/top-tips.aspx

Writing your article: http://journalauthors.tandf.co.uk/preparation/writing.asp

Literature review examples

See the 'Literature review examples' section of Chapter 2.

Chapter 15

Empirical papers

In this chapter, we outline the structure of empirical papers. Since there are a wide range of types of studies and methodological designs, this section provides an overview of the requirements of each section of an empirical paper, highlighting the key things that should be included and the issues to consider. You should read this chapter in combination with the resources listed in the 'Further reading' section and other publications that you find. Please note that many of the issues associated with writing empirical papers were discussed in Chapters 13 and 14, so please read these chapters together. When you have read this chapter, you should be able to:

- select a journal appropriate for your study;
- identify who should be listed as authors of the paper and appreciate the importance of agreeing the order of authorship;
- identify who and/or which organisations should be acknowledged;
- recognise the sections and subsections of empirical papers and understand what information should be included in each; and
- draft an empirical paper.

Writing empirical papers

Although it might seem daunting to write an empirical paper, there are a large number of resources available to help you through this process. Most notably, published papers will help you identify the structure, style and type of information that should be included in your paper. You can identify a selection of appropriate papers based on the following criteria to use as a guide in writing your own article:

- Research papers that you have read to develop your research idea and study design
- Papers in which studies with the same design and/or methodological approach as your study have been reported

254 Dissemination of your research findings

- Papers in which the same analysis that you have used have been reported
- Papers recently published in the journal that you have selected

Empirical papers, especially for quantitative studies, have a fairly rigid format that you should use; hence, there is a clear template to follow for most studies. The format for qualitative studies is less uniform, so it is useful to seek out a number of published papers in which studies with the same design/approach as yours have been used (these do not have to be forensic psychology studies) and use these as a guide. If there is a range of styles/formats to choose from, use the approach that has been employed in papers published in the journal that you have chosen, as this is most likely to be considered appropriate by the journal's reviewers and editors. In addition to using example published papers, there are a number of resources that you can use to help you write empirical papers, a selection of which are listed in the 'Further reading' section.

Preparation

Select a journal

As discussed in Chapter 14, and using the same procedures to guide your decision, you will first need to select an appropriate journal for your paper (see also the 'Further reading' section of Chapter 14). Make sure that the journal accepts empirical papers and studies with the design that you have used. Some journals, for example, focus on qualitative studies, and others focus on experimental studies. This might be clear from the title of the journal, or it might be specified in their 'aims and scope'. For some journals, although the aims and scope might suggest that a broad range of papers are accepted, a particular type of study is most frequently featured. To determine this, you will need to look at recent issues of the journal; you can find these on the journal's web page. It is a good idea to do this for any journal that you consider suitable for your paper, and you should look at the format (e.g., the sections and heading used) and style (e.g., the degree to which the writing is scientific, or is less formal and perhaps targeted towards a particular type of audience) of the papers and try to replicate these in your paper. Follow all the instructions for authors and the journal guidelines carefully and precisely.

Agree upon the authorship of the paper

As discussed in Chapter 14, you should agree upon this early in a research study, but be mindful that this might change (also see the 'Further reading' section).

Structure of the empirical paper

The following sections should be included in empirical papers.

Title

Titles for empirical papers (and dissertations) should be concise and informative. This will be the first piece of information about a paper that potential readers will use to determine if it is appropriate for them. Titles are used in search engines to extract appropriate papers, so your title should include words for which readers will search, without making the title too long. If you have an experimental study where you are testing the impact of variable A on variable B, then the title could simply be: 'Impact of variable A on variable B'. It can be important to include other details, such as the type of design, location/setting or participants. For example, a title for case study one could be: 'Impact of victim sexuality and type of abuse on police officers' identification of intimate partner violence'; and a title for case study four could be: 'A qualitative analysis of mock jurors' use of DNA evidence in deliberations'. Note that in order to ensure that titles are concise, words such as 'the' (i.e., 'Impact of. . . .' when grammatically it should be 'The impact of. . . .') and phrases such as 'a study to show' are not included.

Activity

Write a title for each of the case studies.

Abstract

An abstract should provide a clear summary of your study, whether for an empirical paper, literature review paper (see Chapter 14), dissertation or conference presentation (see Chapter 16). It is not an introduction to your research or review. The title and the abstract are the most common sections that a person will read to identify if a paper is relevant to them; hence, your abstract needs to provide the key relevant details about your study. These include: why it was conducted, the design of the study, the participants recruited and/or data used, what was found, and what this means for research, theory and/or practice. Journals normally have strict word limits for abstracts (you may not be able to submit an abstract electronically if it is too long), so you need to be concise. The abstract should be in the past tense, as it is summarising a study that has been completed (e.g., 'the aim was to', 'participants completed').

No matter what the purpose of the abstract (empirical or review journal paper, dissertation, conference presentation), it is a good idea to construct it as follows (also use the resources listed in the 'Further reading' section and other published abstracts to guide you):

1   Start with one or two sentences that sum up the background and/or purpose of the study. Most journals/publishers prefer that you do not use

citations in abstracts. This does not mean that you cannot include information for which you would normally include a citation (the citation should be in the paper); however, note that the purpose here is not to give a thorough literature review, but rather to place the study in context. For example, for case study two you might say: 'It has become evident that many victims experience secondary victimisation during their contact with the legal system; yet, many victims report some level of satisfaction and/or resolution when the perpetrator is punished. Little is known about the impact on victim well-being when the perpetrator receives different outcomes associated with the sentencing aims of punishment, retribution, and rehabilitation. The purpose of this study was to investigate this using. . . .'

2   Describe the design and method used in one or two sentences. It is important to outline the overall design of the study. In empirical papers you should be precise about the number of participants and/or type of data and the variables that were measured. In a review paper, this should include the method employed for the review (e.g. a summary of the databases searched), search terms and key aspects of the inclusion/exclusion criteria (e.g., peer-reviewed empirical papers in English).

3   Summarise the results in one or two sentences. In empirical papers, state clearly what was found from quantitative analysis and/or state the themes/key findings that were identified from qualitative analyses. You do not need to include any of the statistical data (e.g., p values or qualitative data extracts). For example, for case study one, you might say that 'police officers were significantly more likely to rate scenarios as IPV when physical violence was involved, compared to when scenarios included nonphysical violence'. Or for case study four, you might say that 'during deliberations, mock jurors stated that DNA evidence was: confusing, unreliable and of crucial importance to the determination of guilt or innocence'.

4   End with one sentence that summarises your conclusions and/or the implications/recommendations that arise from the study. Try to avoid sentences such as 'The implications of the results are discussed'; instead try to be specific about the key points that you included in your discussion. For example, for case study five you might say: 'It was recommended that the programme be extended to include additional work on decision making and to provide more opportunity for the changes in the expression of anger noted during treatment to be established in order to achieve a long-term change in behaviour'.

Some journals require structured abstracts; for example, *Legal and Criminological Psychology* specifies that abstracts are presented in four sections: purpose, methods, results, conclusion. You should be able to see that these sections require information that is in line with the four points previously listed, so the approach to writing these abstracts is very similar. Where journals request abstracts with a particular style or structure, look on the journal web page to see if there is advice for writing the abstracts and use papers in recently published issues as a guide/template for writing yours.

Activity

Choose one of the case studies and write an abstract for it. The information in Chapters 5 and 6 will help you write the first part of the abstract as per points 1 and 2 of abstract previously outlined. You will need to assume some likely findings to write point 3; then think about what the implications of these would be to write point 4. When you have done that, select another case study and write a structured abstract using the sections: purpose, methods, results, conclusion.

Keywords

You will be asked to list some keywords for your empirical paper (these will most likely not be required for a dissertation or thesis). Key*word* is actually misleading, as these are often key*phrases* or combinations of words (e.g., sexual offender, intimate partner violence). The purpose of keywords is to enable potential readers to find papers that are relevant to them in search engines or databases. Keywords or phrases in the title will be included in searches, but it is often not possible or appropriate to include all the phrases that are relevant in the title; hence, you are asked to provide keywords that will enable others who should be interested in your study to find your paper. Note that you should not use keywords and phrases that are in your title; the keywords provide you an opportunity to provide information in *addition* to the title.

Choosing good keywords can be tricky if you are new to this, and it is often something that people do in a rush at the end of writing the paper; however, it is worth spending time on this to ensure that people are able to find and read your paper (which, after all, is the key purpose of writing the paper). Thinking about the following should help you identify appropriate keywords for your paper (also note the resources in the 'Further reading' section):

- What would I type into a search engine if I was looking for a paper on this topic?
- What keywords are used by the authors of the papers that are most similar to my study (i.e., those cited in my introduction)?
- What are the characteristics of the topic of my paper (not in the title) for which people might search (e.g., cognitive-behavioural, controlling behaviours, one-to-one intervention)?
- What are the characteristics of my participants or data that people for which might search (e.g., juvenile offenders, police officers, online news forums)?

258 Dissemination of your research findings

- Are there any important geographical or location characteristics (e.g., forensic mental health, young offenders' institution, community, Europe)?

> **Activity**
>
> Identify five keywords for each of the case studies.

Research highlights and other
journal-specific summary sections

It is becoming more common for journals to request specific information or research highlights that summarise key aspects of the paper or study that aid the use of the paper by the journals' audiences. For example, a journal that has a readership of practitioners might ask for a bullet point list of the practice implications of the study. Other journals request a list of research highlights or key findings. This will be clear in the journal guidelines for authors, which is why we emphasise that you need to find this document and read this carefully at the start of the writing process. If you are not used to writing the information that is requested, it will probably take you longer than you think to decide how you should summarise it or to identify the key practice implications, so do not forget about these sections or rush through them as you near the deadline for the submission (if there is one).

Acknowledgements

For papers that you intend to submit to journals, your acknowledgements should be based on thanking the people that provided direct assistance to the actual project and production of the paper. In academic papers these are kept to a minimum and are succinct. Gushing acknowledgements in which you thank all your friends, family and pets for their support, inspiration and motivation are not appropriate for journal papers, but you can gush as much as you want in dissertations/theses (remember, though, that these may be lodged in university libraries/department collections). If the research was funded by an organisation or a grant-awarding body, this should be stated, and you will need to check the guidance from the funder/body in respect to the details that should be included. Participants are rarely thanked in academic papers, and you should not thank the journal's editors or peer reviewers. If you had substantial feedback and help from someone in proofreading a paper (and this person was not included as an author), then you could acknowledge that contribution in this section. When naming individuals, you should have their permission to be named in the paper. Because most journals employ an anonymous peer-review process, you need to follow the journal's instructions for the submission of acknowledgements (e.g., you might need to submit these in a separate document), as the information within them might reveal the identities of the authors.

Activity

Look through the academic papers that you have collected for your research project and/or course. Search for acknowledgements in these papers and note the tone/style of the acknowledgements.

Introduction

In Chapter 2, we discussed the importance of your research being grounded in relevant literature and/or theory. The purpose of the introduction of an empirical paper is to outline the literature context in which your research is based and to state your argument (or rationale) for your study. Although the introduction should contain a critical review of the relevant literature, it is not a literature review (see Chapter 14). Sometimes when students are asked to do a literature review and an empirical paper, they think that the literature review should be used at the start of the empirical paper. This is not the case. Although there are a range of purposes and arguments that you might have in writing a literature review paper, it is very unlikely that a journal would publish a review written solely for the purpose of justifying a specific single study; this is reserved for the introduction of an empirical paper. If you have done a literature review on the same topic as your research, then it is likely that you will refer to many of the same studies in each paper; however, the use you make of the studies and the way in which you discuss them will be slightly different for each paper (so you should not have to worry about self-plagiarism issues).

In Figure 15.1, we have outlined the structure of an empirical paper. You will see from this that the introduction should be structured as a sort of funnel: you begin by broadly introducing the topic, then you critically review the relevant literature. This should be followed by a clear justification for, and outline of, your study. Finally, you should state the aim(s) and/or research question(s) and where appropriate, your specific research hypotheses (null hypotheses are not normally included in research papers). Many journals have a word limit around 5,000 words for empirical papers; this means that you need to state this information in around 1,200 words. Therefore, you will need to develop a concise writing style. Word counts for dissertations vary; work out how many words you can have for each section before you start to ensure you do not exceed the word limit.

Although you need to broadly introduce the topic area, be aware that this should not be too broad, instead keep the attention on introducing the specific area of focus of your research. A good starting point for case study four, for

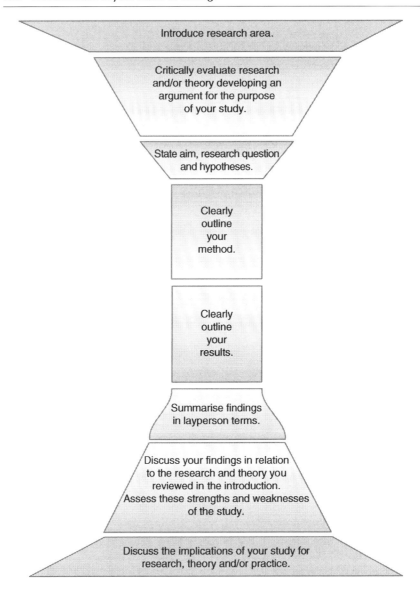

Figure 15.1 Structure of an empirical paper

example, would be to outline how DNA evidence has been used in criminal courts. In empirical papers, you do not need to write a long history about the discovery of DNA or the way in which DNA has been used in investigations and by whom. In dissertations, there may be a requirement to write a longer and broader introduction than would be appropriate for an empirical paper; even here, however, you should remember that the focus of this section is to introduce your study.

Empirical papers 261

In the main part of the introduction, you should critically discuss the research and/or theory relevant to the design of your study. In addition to discussing the topic area (e.g., the impact of variables on perceptions of IPV), you might also need to discuss the literature pertaining to the design/approach you have used (e.g., vignette design). Unless you are replicating a particular study, it is unlikely to be appropriate to describe each study in detail. You should avoid describing a study, then critiquing it and then describing another.

It is important that you critique the literature/theory in some way, as it is this critique that should form the basis of the arguments for your study. For example, you might say that: 'Although a number of research studies have shown that variable A is related to variable X (references) and variable B is related to variable X (references), there have been no published studies in which the impact of variables A and B together on variable X has been examined' (this being the aim of your research study). You could then say that: 'The majority of studies examining variable X have been conducted on psychology students (references), but since X is most relevant to police officers, it is important to examine this group' (i.e., the aim of your research is to examine the impact of variables A and B on X in a police officer sample). This critique should all work towards identifying a strong rationale for why you needed to carry out your project in the way that you did.

Be careful to ensure that your argument is logical throughout the paper. If you raise the issue that many studies have small samples sizes but then conduct a study with three participants (as in case study five), then this is inconsistent and looks bizarre and as if you did not adequately think through the study. If, however, you argue that quasi-experimental evaluations of interventions with small samples sizes are problematic due to the analyses having insufficient power, and then suggest that an ABA experiment design is more appropriate, then your argument would be consistent and appropriate.

By developing this type of argument throughout your introduction, the readers of your paper should not be surprised by the idea of your research study at the end of the introduction. You should structure your argument in this section, so that you end with a clear overall justification or rationale for your study. This should lead you nicely into saying what the aim(s) (purpose) of your study are and for outlining the research question(s) and/or hypotheses as appropriate. Remember that since you have conducted the study, you should be using the past tense, as in the abstract (e.g., 'the aim of the study was to . . .').

For some qualitative approaches, the data that you collect should be examined without prior assumptions tainting your analysis of the data (e.g., without prior reading of the literature relevant to the specific topic being investigated). There is debate about the extent to which it is possible to research a topic without prior knowledge of the literature or other factors that might influence your analysis of the data (see the qualitative publications listed in the 'Further reading' section). Furthermore, even if this approach is taken, there are different ways in which the introduction is written; for example, some people write an introduction without reference to such literature to logically reflect the

262 Dissemination of your research findings

approach used, whereas others include the literature (that they identified after collecting the data and conducting the analysis) to produce a report more in line with the conventional format. If using this type of qualitative approach, seek out published papers in which this approach has been used and use these as a guide; also seek advice from your supervisor/line manager/colleagues. In introductions not including reference to topic-specific literature, the purpose is to introduce and justify your study and the approach/design used. It is likely that you will reference literature in which the same approach has been used (e.g., to demonstrate that the approach will be useful to investigate the issue you are addressing) and/or literature about the qualitative approach being used.

Activity

Select four empirical papers (they can be on any topic – you can select some of the examples listed in Chapter 3, or use papers you have collected to design your study or for other assignments/purposes). Taking one paper at a time, read through the introduction. After reading the introduction carefully, highlight in one colour any places where the authors *describe* a study or theory (e.g., 'Brown and Sleath researched police officers' views of X', or 'many research studies have been conducted to examine offenders' abilities to be empathic'). In another colour, then go through and highlight the places where the authors have been critical about the studies or theories (e.g., 'however, the sample size was small and there were no female police officers in the sample', or 'all these studies have been conducted in the USA, raising issues about the generalizability to other countries'). Finally, go through and underline all the places where the authors make arguments that develop the rationale for the study. You might find here that it is easier to start near the end of the introduction, where the rationale is often stated fairly clearly and then work back to find all the points that were made in building up to the rationale. You will probably find that some of the critical text that you highlighted will also be underlined. You should also see that the underlining will be sporadic during the critical review parts but that it increases towards the end. This exercise should help you see how arguments are formed to develop a clear rationale for a research study and also illustrate visibly how the use of the literature in an empirical paper introduction is different from its use in literature reviews. Once you have done this, you can start to think about how you will structure your own introduction.

Method

The method section is normally split into a number of subsections. Empirical papers need to be concise, and you will see that this section needs to be clear and focussed. Strictly speaking, the aim of the method section is to enable another researcher to replicate your study. You should assume that anyone who wishes to do this has research knowledge, so you do not need to explain methodological and statistical terms/approaches. You will see that the information included in the section is quite 'dry' (i.e., stick to the specific details about the measure or the design, for example: 'A quasi-experimental design with two between-groups variables') and it is not too 'chatty' (i.e., avoid something such as: 'We considered an experimental approach but decided we would use a quasi-experimental approach and then we thought . . .'). The sections required for quantitative studies, which are also often used for some qualitative papers (e.g., where thematic analysis has been used), are quite rigid (see below). There is specific information that should be included in each subsection, so you will need to outline the relevant information in each section without repeating this information anywhere else. There is more flexibility with qualitative papers, so as discussed previously, find some published papers to use as guides. Remember to use the past tense.

Design

This subsection is more commonly used for experimental and quasi-experimental studies. You should state the overall design that you used and then outline your variables; see the following example for case study one.

Case study one

Design

An experimental vignette study was used with two between-groups independent variables: type of abuse (physical violence or nonphysical violence) and sexuality of victim (heterosexual or lesbian). The dependent variables were four questions (from reference) measured using ten-point Likert scales assessing the degree of agreement that the scenario indicated intimate partner violence.

Participants or data

In this section, you describe the participants who took part in your study or the data that you used. Do not confuse this section with the procedure section, as you do not need to say here how you contacted participants or what you asked them to do; you simply describe your sample and the sampling method used (see the following example for case study one).

Case study one

Participants

A convenience sample of 139 police officers (30% female; 65% male; 5% declined to give their gender) from one police force in the UK took part in the study. The average age was 26.2 years (SD = 5.4); 94% identified as White-British and 1% British-Asian; 5% declined to provide their ethnicity. The officers had between 6 months and 15 years of experience (M = 60.25 months; SD = 8.23).

Common confusion

Some journals have introduced policies to encourage authors to use language that focuses on behaviours rather individuals (e.g., we say 'individuals who have convictions for sexual violence' rather than 'rapists', or 'children who have engaged in harmful sexual behaviours' rather than 'child sex offenders'. We have included this here because it relates to journal policies; however, this is a good habit to follow for writing throughout the research process. For example, in a PIS it is better to say, 'You have been selected to take part in this study because you have committed a sexual offence' rather than 'You have been selected to take part in this study because you are a rapist'. If you are not sure of the different impact of this form of wording, think about the following example. Imagine that we want to conduct a study to examine what type of feedback is most effective for students who have failed an assignment. In the PIS we could say: 'You have been selected to take part in this study because you failed one of your assignments', or we could say: 'You have selected to take part in this study because you are a failure'! This should highlight how the use of language and labelling is important. Much has been written about this in the criminological, desistance and forensic psychology literature, and you can research this further if you wish. The main point to note here is that although the phrasing is more cumbersome and uses more words, it is better to identify people as individuals who have engaged in particular behaviours. There are similar debates about whether individuals who have been victims of crimes should be referred to as victims, or survivors, or other terms, and you should carefully consider the most appropriate wording if you are conducting research in this area.

Materials

In this section, you should describe the materials that you used in your study so that readers of the paper have a very good idea about the resources you used to collect your data. You do not need to describe the PIS, consent form or debrief information. Do not confuse this section with the procedure; you do not need to say here that you gave participants first one measure and then another to complete. If you used psychometric tests or scales, you should list these (see the following example for a fictional test). You should describe how you developed any materials (e.g., vignettes or mock case information) for your study and how they were piloted. Since journals are very space conscious, you would not normally include questionnaires or interview schedules in an empirical paper; however, you can include example questions or one version of a vignette, explaining how these materials were varied according to condition. Materials that are more than two to three paragraphs should be summarised, rather than included verbatim.

Example of details of a psychometric test included in a materials section

Interpersonal Anger Scale (IAS). This ten-item scale was designed to measure anger towards others (reference). Each item is measured using a five-point Likert scale (1 = does not describe me, 5 = describes me very well). Scores range from 10 to 50, with higher scores indicating high levels of anger. The IAS was validated on a sample of 250 offenders imprisoned in the UK and discriminated between individuals convicted for violent offences or nonviolent offences (reference). Similar findings have been observed in imprisoned offender samples in the USA (reference) and Australia (reference) and in community samples in the UK (reference). The scale is internally consistent with Cronbach's alphas ranging from .78 (reference) to .82 (reference). Test-retest reliabilities range from .65 (reference) to .75 (reference).

Procedure

In this section, you summarise the procedure in terms of what you asked participants to do or how you collected your data. You should start the section by stating the ethical approval and permissions that you obtained to conduct the study. Make it clear how participants were asked to take part in a study and what they were told about it. Do not forget to mention the ethical procedures that you followed (e.g., 'Participants were given full details about the study, assured their data would remain confidential and that they had a right to withdraw from the study. When they had provided their consent to take part in the study they were asked to. . . . The study took around 20 minutes to complete and participants were thanked and debriefed'.) You should end this section by summarising the analysis you conducted and any software (e.g., SPSS) you used. Where you do not have participants, state how you selected and obtained the

266   Dissemination of your research findings

data you used, and any other procedures that readers need to know in order to understand the key details of how you conducted the study.

In qualitative studies, it is common to have a smaller number of sections, for example, (1) Participants, (2) Interviews and Data Analysis. See the 'Further reading' section for guidelines in reporting qualitative studies. The aim of the method section remains to outline your study such that another person could replicate it. You will see that in order to do this, compared to quantitative papers, more information is provided about how the analysis was conducted. In addition, since it is important to understand the potential influence of the researchers on the analysis, more information about them is required.

Results

QUANTITATIVE PAPERS

There are conventions and guidelines (e.g., APA, see Chapter 14) regarding how you should report quantitative data and analyses (see the 'Further reading' sections in this chapter and in Chapter 12). Broadly speaking, in this section you should list the findings of your study in the appropriate format, and you should not be discursive. If you had to remove the data of any participants, then you should state this first along with the procedures for dealing with missing data. It is important that you describe your data (e.g., include a table of the means and standard deviations of participants responses to the DVs, according to each level of the IVs) appropriately. If your data is interval and meets the assumptions of parametric tests, then you should report means and standard deviations. For other types of data, you should report the frequencies or the range and median or mode, as appropriate. You should describe whether your data met parametric assumptions and any transformations you performed (as per the processes outlined in Chapter 12). Then you can report the outcomes of the analyses you conducted. When you have done a number of analyses and/or have complex data sets, you will need to decide how to structure your results so that it is easy for the reader to follow your analyses. If you identified research hypotheses at the end of your introduction, it is important that you state in the results section whether the results support the hypotheses or not.

QUALITATIVE PAPERS

It can be difficult to present qualitative data in a concise report, and you might need to consider presenting only a small proportion of the findings or a summary/overview of a model, theory or framework that you have developed (see the information on publishing ethics in the 'Further reading' section). It is common to include extracts/quotes from the data to illustrate your findings. For concision, include only the text that is needed to illustrate the point, and select extracts carefully so that you only include the most appropriate. You do not need to show all the extracts where the issues are discussed. Make sure that the information you include will not identify participants (watch out for unusual or distinctive phrases, or for characteristics of small groups, e.g., reference to a female offender when there are few in the population might identify an individual). Most authors use a method of labelling extracts to indicate which participants said what without identifying them. You might want this label to include key characteristics such as gender or age (e.g., you might label an extract as 1F23 to indicate participant 1, who is a female, aged 23). It is important that you explain to the reader, in an appropriate place, how you have labelled the extracts, and use the labels clearly and consistently throughout the results section.

It is relatively common in qualitative papers to link your findings to relevant literature as you outline them (for an example, see Brown, Walker, Gannon and Keown, 2013); the extent to which you do this will determine what you include in the discussion (or conclusion) section. It is important that you do not repeat information, so you will need to look at published papers (particularly papers published in your chosen journal) and decide the approach that is most appropriate for your study.

TABLES AND FIGURES

You should present information in a table or figure if it makes the information easier to understand (see Chapter 14 for the way in which tables/figures should be formatted). If you display information in a table or figure, you should not then also describe it in the text; however, you should tell the readers what key features they should note (e.g., 'Table 1 shows that posttreatment means for the treated groups were lower than the untreated group for all measures apart from denial, where the scores of the groups were similar').

Discussion

The discussion should be a similar length to the introduction, and where the introduction funnels information from a relatively broad perspective to the specifics of your study, a discussion works in the opposite direction (see Figure 15.1). You should start by summarising your findings in a nonstatistical/ methodological way (e.g., for case study one: 'physical violence was more frequently recognised as intimate partner violence by police officers than nonphysical violence'). This is followed by a comparison of your findings with those of the studies that you reviewed in the introduction. As the name of this section suggests, you should discuss the similarities and differences in the findings, and where there are differences, consider why this might be the case.

As an undergraduate, you were probably told to compare your results to the literature, then discuss the weaknesses of the study and then make recommendations for future research. In an empirical paper, however, you can blend these components; for example, if there are differences between the findings of your study and others, and you think that one reason for this might be that your sample was more homogeneous than in the other studies (i.e., a limitation of your study), then you can outline this in the same paragraph and also suggest research to investigate this further. You might then move on to consider another aspect of your findings. Where it is most appropriate, you should make some recommendations for future research. Make sure that these are grounded in your findings and the other aspects of the discussion. For example, it is always the case that you could have a larger sample size, or that the study could be conducted in other countries/settings and so on, so only make such recommendations if there is a specific reason to do so (e.g., your analyses had insufficient power, or your findings are different from studies conducted in other countries).

There are differing views as to whether you should include literature in the discussion that was not considered in the introduction. Some argue that this is simply not appropriate and should not be done. Others argue that if reports are presented logically, as per the development of the study, then new studies can be included in the discussion if, for example, something unexpected was found. You will need to take an approach that is appropriate for your study and discuss this with others if you are not sure how you should tackle this issue. This issue tends to be less apparent in qualitative studies, where it is more common to discuss studies that are linked to the analysis of the data.

In a logical place in the discussion (often after the comparison with the literature), you should consider the limitations of your study. The purpose behind this is to frame your findings within the context of the methodological rigour of your study (i.e., to what extent can we rely on your findings, what factors do we need to take into account when we consider them). The aim should not be to list every tiny problem with the study (if there were many issues, such as spelling mistakes, issues with participants or the way the study was completed, then the study should probably not be published as it is unreliable and/or not valid). As we said in Chapter 3, there are many trade-offs and compromises that have to be made in designing a study, and no study is perfect; therefore, in the discussion, you should outline these decisions/issues, so that your results can be considered with a clear understanding of the methodological issues that are present.

The final aspect of the discussion is to consider the implications of the results. This is often presented at the end of the section, though there is scope to be flexible about where this information is discussed. The implications are likely to be linked to the purpose of the study; (e.g., if you conducted an evaluation, what do your results imply for the intervention and other similar interventions? What might need to be changed?). Be careful not to overstate your results (the findings from one evaluation are unlikely to have implications for all interventions around the world!) and ensure that the implications are grounded in your study (e.g., if you found that there were no problems in police officers' perceptions of IPV, recommending training to improve perceptions is clearly not appropriate).

eferences

All sources should be cited appropriately in the paper, and you should list all the sources that you have cited in the reference list. It is important that you carefully and consistently follow the referencing guidelines specified by the journal.

Appendices

Given journal space restriction, the inclusion of appendices in empirical papers is rare; the PIS, consent form, debrief, data, transcripts and SPSS (or other types of software) outputs should not be included. It might be appropriate to include the vignette you used or a psychometric measure or scale that you developed, provided you are happy for other people to use it (publishing it in a paper results in the scale being publically available for use). Speak to your supervisor/line manager for advice if you are unsure (and see what is and is not included in published papers). Note that you might be asked to include such information by your university if you are submitting an empirical paper as an assignment. Copies of all the materials you used (PIS, consent form, interview schedule etc.) might be required for dissertations; check your university's requirements.

Summary and final checklist

In this chapter, we have outlined the structure of empirical papers and the types of information that should be presented in each section and subsection. In combination with the information provided in Chapters 13 and 14, you should now be able to select an appropriate journal and draft an empirical paper for it. When doing this, make sure that you are clear about each of the points in the following checklist.

1   Identify a journal and read the author guidelines carefully.
2   Agree upon the authorship of the paper and identify whether acknowledgements are required.
3   Find published papers that are appropriate for your study, as well as guidelines for publishing studies of your type and for formatting (e.g., APA guidelines). Use these to guide you throughout.
4   Draft your study, taking time to complete each section carefully.
5   Ask someone with good grammar and writing skills to proofread your draft.
6   If possible (e.g., if it is not an assignment where review of a draft is not permissible), give to your supervisor or co-authors to read and revise or recommend changes.
7   Revise, review and revise until all authors agree that it is ready to submit.

Examples

See the examples section of Chapter 3, where you will find a large number of examples of published empirical papers by design type. Listed here is one paper for each case study, in which a similar study has been conducted that will give you an idea of what an empirical paper might look like for each.

Case study one

Basow, S.A., & Thomson, J. (2012). Service providers' reactions to intimate partner violence as a function of victim sexual orientation and type of abuse. *Journal of Interpersonal Violence, 27*, 1225–1241. doi:10.1177/0886260511425241

Case study two

Laxminararayan, M. (2013). The effect of retributive and restorative sentencing on psychological effects of criminal proceedings. *Journal of Interpersonal Violence, 28*, 938–955. doi:10.1177/0886260512459385

Case study three

Palmer, E., Hatcher, R., McGuire, J., Bilby, C., Ayres, T., & Hollin, C. (2011). Evaluation of the addressing substance-related offending (ASRO) program for substance-using offenders in the community: A reconviction analysis. *Substance Use and Misuse, 46*, 1072–1080. doi:10.3109/10826084.2011.559682

Case study four

Charron, A., & Woodhams, J. (2010). A qualitative analysis of mock jurors' deliberations of linkage analysis evidence. *Journal of Investigative Psychology and Offender Profiling, 7*, 165–183. doi:10.1002/jip.119

Case study five

Burns, M., Bird, D., Leach, C., & Higgins, K. (2003). Anger management training: The effects of a structured programme on the self-reported anger experience of forensic inpatients with learning disability. *Journal of Psychiatric and Mental Health Nursing, 10*, 569–577. doi:10.1046/j.1365-2850.2003.00653.x

Further reading

Publishing advice or guidelines

See 'Further reading' section of Chapter 14.

Qualitative studies

*Tong, A., Sainsbury, P., & Craig, J. (2007). Consolidated criteria for reporting qualitative research (COREQ): A 32-item checklist for interviews and focus groups. *International Journal for Quality in Health Care, 19*, 349–357. doi:10.1093/intqhc/mzm042

Empirical papers 271

Randomised controlled trials

*Schulz, F.F., Altman, D.G., Moher, A., & The CONSORT Group. (2010). CONSORT 2010 statement: Updated guidelines for reporting parallel group randomized trials. *Annals of International Medicine, 152*(11). Retrieved from http://annals.org/

Nonrandomized evaluations of behavioural and public health interventions

*Des Jarlais, D. C., Lyles, C., Crepaz, N., & The TREND Group. (2004). Improving the reporting quality of nonrandomized evaluations of behavioral and public health interventions: The TREND statement. *American Journal of Public Health, 94*, 361–366. (Note that although these are written for public health interventions, many of the guidelines are appropriate for evaluations of forensic interventions.)

Cohort, case-control and cross-sectional studies

*von Elm, E., Altman, D.G., Egger, M., Pocock, S.J., Gøtzsche, P.C., & Vandenbroucke, J.P., for the STROBE Initiative. (2008). The strengthening the reporting of observational studies in epidemiology (STROBE) statement: Guidelines for reporting observational studies. *Journal of Clinical Epidemiology, 61*, 344–349. doi:10.1016/j.jclinepi.2007.11.008 (Note that although these are written for epidemiology, many of the guidelines are appropriate for forensic studies.)

*These guidelines have been published in a number of journals, so you might find slightly different references for them. They might be updated and guidelines might be produced for different types of studies, so make sure that you search for the most up-to-date versions and for guidelines that are relevant to your study's design.

Publishing ethics

Editorial: Duplicate publication and 'salami slicing': Ethical issues and practical solutions. [Editorial]. (2008). *International Journal of Nursing Studies, 45*, 1257–1260. doi:10.1016/j.ijnurstu.2008.07.003

See also the publishing ethics 'Further reading' section of Chapter 14.

Reference

Brown, S.J., Walker, K., Gannon, T.A., & Keown, K. (2013) Developing a theory of empathy and cognitions in sex offenders. *Journal of Sexual Aggression, 19*, 275–294. doi:10.1080/13552600.2012.747223

Chapter 16

Conference presentations

Presenting your work at a conference can be an effective way to disseminate your findings. This can also offer you an opportunity to network with others such as academics, practitioners, policymakers, or representatives of organisations that are relevant to your research. This is an important opportunity for you to showcase your work. In this chapter, we will explain the different types of conference presentations that you may make and advise you on the best approaches for presenting the project that you have completed. Presenting your work can often be a nerve-wracking experience; however, ensuring that you have prepared your presentation materials to the best of your abilities will go some way to addressing these nerves and providing you with a little more confidence about this process. Once you have read this chapter, you should be able to:

- distinguish between the different types of conference presentation formats;
- appreciate the process for submitting a paper to a conference;
- understand how to develop an oral conference presentation;
- identify the best method for producing a poster presentation; and
- apply this knowledge to your own research project.

Types of conference presentations

There are several different types of conference presentations (see the following box for the range of sessions included in conferences). In disseminating your research early in your career, you are most likely to outline a research study in an oral presentation (with other research presentations or in a symposium) or in a poster.

Conference sessions

Keynote presentations are usually *plenary* sessions, in that everyone who attends the conference will be encouraged to attend –nothing else will be scheduled at the same time. The conference organisers usually select the keynote presenters on the basis of their expertise, eminence, research publications and so on. Keynote presentations in some ways are like lectures (and are as long as lectures), with presenters talking about a number of studies or developments in a research and/or practice area. There can be a variety of plenary sessions (e.g., 'debates' on issues of relevance to the attendees).

Symposia are usually sessions in which a collection of presentations is given. The presentations are normally linked in some way (e.g., they might outline a number of studies on a linked topic, or perhaps they are research studies in which the same method or design was used). In some conferences, the link can be based on organisations or locations (e.g., a university might be asked to form a symposium of student research papers). Symposia usually have a chair (i.e., the person who invited the speakers), who during the conference will introduce the speakers and manage the timing of the session. Some conferences might invite individuals to organise symposia on a particular topic, or a call for symposia may be included in the call for presentations (see the 'Planning to attend a conference' section). A symposium is usually scheduled for 60 to 90 minutes, and the timing of the presentations within it will be determined by the chair with each of the presenters. Symposia are normally parallel timetabled, in that there will be a number of symposia (and research sessions) held at the same time, and attendees select the sessions they wish to attend, either prior to the conference or during it.

Research presentations are usually 15 or 20 minutes in length. Like symposia, research sessions are usually parallel timetabled, and attendees select the presentations they wish to attend. Conferences normally invite researchers to present abstracts in a call for presentations (see the 'Planning to attend a conference' section). When the presentations have been selected for the conference, they will be grouped into sessions on the basis of similarity (usually by the topic of the research). Conferences vary in terms of the number of research presentations included in a single session and the number of sessions. A session chair, whose role is to introduce each speaker and manage the timing of the session, may or may not be appointed.

Posters include an outline of a research study. The ways in which posters are managed vary by conference. In some, posters will remain on display throughout the conference; in others, one group of posters will be display on one day and a second group in the next day. Some conferences have timetabled sessions where attendees are encouraged to view posters, and some may expect poster authors to stand by their posters during this time in order to answer questions about their research.

Workshops vary by conference and tend to have more of a 'training' aim. The sessions are at least 90 minutes, and the purpose is to develop a skill (e.g., working with child victims or conducting research using a particular method or design) or to gain knowledge on a topic (e.g., key things that practitioners should be aware of when conducting risk assessments). Some conferences have pre- or postconference workshops with training aims and additional costs.

274 Dissemination of your research findings

An important factor in good conference presentations, no matter what the format or type of session, is careful consideration about the audience (as discussed in Chapter 13). Conferences vary considerably in their attendees; some conferences can be focussed at practitioner audiences, others at academic audiences, and others at a blend of the two. Some conferences might be focussed on different groups within these audiences; for example, the British Psychological Society has conferences targeted towards students and others targeted towards mixed practitioner/academic audiences. Conferences also vary on the extent to which they attract international presenters and/or attendees. All these factors should have an impact on your presentation. Practitioners will most likely be more interested in your findings and their implications than the methods and literature context. International attendees might not have English as a first language, so care will be needed in presentations to account for this. You can often find out who attends a conference by reading the conference web pages, in which the typical audience might be specified. You can read the conference programme to see who else will be presenting. This usually includes the affiliation of the presenters (i.e., university or an organisation). It is also a good idea to seek advice from people with experience attending the conference. This will ensure that you produce the most appropriate presentation for your audience.

Planning to attend a conference

If you decide that you want to attend a conference, then you need to engage in some prior planning. Most conferences release a 'call for papers' in advance of the conference. Note that the deadline for such calls can be several months prior to the conference, so you need to think ahead and submit within the closing date. Obviously, you also need to make sure that you will be able to attend all (or the majority) of the conference. It is difficult for conference organisers to put together a conference timetable, especially for large conferences, and so there may not be flexibility in when your presentation or poster will be scheduled.

Common confusion

If you are accepted to present at a conference, you will need to pay a conference registration fee to attend. There will also be travel and accommodation costs. Some conferences include discounted rates for presenters and/or for students (or those with lower incomes), but this varies by conference. There may also be day rates. Bear in mind that you might not be a student by the time of the conference, so you will need to examine all these details prior to submitting a proposal. It is not good practice to submit a proposal on the off-chance that you might be able to attend, and then to withdraw a presentation/poster once it has been accepted, unless there are exceptional, unforeseen circumstances. If you wish to present at a conference, you need to investigate the costs of this and either be

> prepared to pay these yourself or find some means of funding. You might find that your organisation is prepared to fund this, or there might be some funding that you can apply for from the conference organisers or a more general conference attendance funding scheme.

As with research papers, it is important that you agree upon the authorship of presentations and posters (you can include co-authors, even if you are the only person who will attend the conference), and you must get the approval of all the individuals involved in the research prior to submitting abstracts.

Submitting a proposal

Most conferences ask that you submit an abstract of your presentation or poster. Each conference will have its own format for submitting an abstract, and this often includes a word limit. It is important to note that this abstract will be published on the conference web page and/or in the conference program. Your poster or presentation should be in line with the abstract that you submitted. Therefore, if you are at the start of a project and you have no idea what you will find, whether the research has approval and so forth, then it is too early to submit an abstract because you have no idea what you will be able to present. The abstract should generally be written/structured as per the outline in Chapter 15. Note, however, that conferences might specify the format of the abstract and/or other information that is required. The decision about whether your proposal will be accepted at the conference will be determined on the basis of your abstract, so it is important that this gives a clear overview of your study and that it is well written.

Prior to the conference

If you are accepted to complete a presentation or poster, read all the guidance regarding registration and the format of presentations/posters at the conference. Be clear about the length of time you will have to present and whether that time includes an opportunity for people to ask you questions. Make sure you know what size the poster should be and whether it should be portrait or landscape. Be clear on whether you will be expected to provide handouts. In addition to checking the procedures for your presentation or poster, check the procedures for registration. Closing dates for registration can be prior to the conference, and there are often early-bird rates for early registration, so it is good if you can take advantage of this.

Ethics

It is important to note that your abstract will be publically available, and it is becoming more common for presentations (and in some instances posters) to be made available on conference web sites. Recently, we have noticed a number of individuals taking pictures of presentation slides and posters at conferences; hence, you need to make sure that everything in your abstract, presentation and poster complies with the promises that you made to participants and gate-keepers in respect to confidentiality and anonymity. Remember the warnings we gave in Chapter 13 about not inadvertently revealing the location of your research and participants via social media; the same applies to conferences. For example, it is very easy in a presentation to say that you chose a location because it was the closest XX type of organisation to you, without realising that from this information, many listeners can identify the organisation and thereby also the participants.

Individual oral presentation

The key principles of dissemination that were outlined in Chapter 13 are important to consider when planning your presentation. Think about the key messages that you wish to convey, as well as your audience. Although there are fewer published presentations than journal articles, you can find conference presentations on web sites (e.g., of the conference or the presenter's organisa-tion). Some academic networking sites also include presentations; for exam-ple, many members of ResearchGate (see 'Further reading' section) post their presentations, as well as their peer-reviewed papers. You can use these to get a sense of the range of presentations styles/formats and to choose an approach with which you are comfortable. If your organisation has a template (e.g., with a logo), then it is normally okay for you to use this.

Structure

Generally speaking, a format that is similar to an empirical paper (introduction, method, findings and implications) is a good structure to follow; for most audi-ences it might be better to think of this as:

- Why I did the research
- My aims in conducting the research
- What I did
- What I found
- What this means for research, theory and/or practice.

Remember that the audience is most interested in *your* research. So while it is important to set your research in context, this should be brief and you should not spend huge amounts of your presentation time outlining other people's research.

As previously discussed, think carefully about the level of statistical or meth-odological detail that you provide. While it is important to outline what you did in your study, so people can make some assessment of the relevance of the findings for their purpose, you do not need to go into a great amount of detail. You should say that ethical approval was granted and briefly indicate that ethical procedures were followed, but you do not need to be detailed about this (e.g., outlining what you included in the PIS). Similarly, in terms of presenting your findings, you do not need to present all the details of the statistics (e.g., t and F values are not needed). Saying something like: 'statistically significant differences/relationships were noted between. . . .' is sufficient and will allow you to focus on the key points of your research and the key messages. Think carefully about whether you need to present data in a table; most often people cannot read the numbers in these on the screen or handout, so it is not the best approach. A graph of some type might be more appropriate for a presentation, provided it is clear for the audience.

Case study five presentation outline

You have been given 15 minutes to present the research in case study five to a conference in which the attendees are mostly clinicians/practitioners who deliver interventions to individuals or groups in a range of settings. The following is a suggested plan for the structure of such a presentation.

Intervention (2 mins, 1–2 slides)

Outline the intervention in terms of: (a) the target population for which it was developed/is used; (b) the context in which it is delivered (e.g., one-to-one for self-referrals); and (c) the theoretical background to the intervention.

Background to research (1 min, 1 slide)

Describe: (a) the context in which the research came about (i.e., were you asked, are you a treatment provider?) and (b) the aims of the research.

What you did (3 mins, 2–3 slides)

Briefly describe in layperson terms why a small-N experiment ABA design was used. Explain that you tested three participants prior to the start of treatment, during treatment and after the end of treatment. Outline clearly what you measured; although you can put the full names of the measures on the slides, you should explain what you measured so that people unfamiliar with the measures can understand (e.g., you measured anger using the XX scale, which is a measure of YY). Explain the characteristics of the participants and why they were selected, being careful not to identify them.

What you found (4 mins, 3–4 slides)

Outline the findings of your study without using statistical jargon; for example: 'There was a significant reduction in anger from before the start of treatment to during treatment. However, the level of anger increased posttreatment, though not to the original pretreatment level.' This could be presented in a bar chart (or similar). Do the same for the other measures and describe any other findings.

What this means (2–3 mins, 1–2 slides)

Here you should outline the conclusions that you have drawn from the research and the implications of your study. It might be helpful to think of the implications for different groups or people; for example, you might want to outline first what the implications are for the specific programme, moving on to consider if there are any wider implications (perhaps that the study shows that interventions can be effective with self-referred individuals) or if there are implications for the general one-to-one approach or theoretical background of the intervention.

Thank you/any questions/contact details (2–3 mins, 1 slide)

It is a good idea to have your contact details (e.g., an email address) on view while you ask people if they have any questions and respond to them.

References (1–2 slides for handout purposes only)

If you include references in your slide (and they might not be appropriate for this presentation), then bear in mind that people will not take in reference information in the main part of a presentation; however, it can be useful to include them in slides at the end of the presentation (which you do not show and will only appear on your handouts). Ensure that the references are legible (if you cram lots of references in size 8 font on a single slide, these will not be readable in the handouts).

Timing

It is important that you note the time that you have for your presentation and do your best to stick to this time. For example, if you write a 25 minute presentation, but only have a 10 minute presentation slot, this is going to reflect very poorly on you, and your project will not be adequately presented. This may seem like simplistic advice, but it is easy to overlook such a simple step to take, and the impact on your presentation (and stress levels) can be significant. If there is a session chair, this person might give you an indication of when you are close to the end of your time and/or when you are out of time. Note that you might be stopped at the end of your allotted time whether you have finished your presentation or not. Unfortunately, experienced conference presenters are not always the best role models in this regard; however, it is disrespectful to other presenters in your session to run over time, so it is important to ensure that you prepare a presentation appropriate to the time you have been allocated.

Slides

Think carefully about the information presented in each slide. The rooms in which research presentations are held vary in size, so you need to select a font that you are confident that people can read in a small or large room. Remember, the purpose is not to dazzle people with your presentation slide skills (e.g., with information whizzing in from here or there, or pictures, moving images etc.), but to convey a clear message about your study. For example, it is better to have more slides with larger clearer information on each, than fewer slides crammed full of text. Note that the information on the slide should just provide some visual reference while you are speaking; you do not need to include everything you say on the slides (or in the handouts).

If you wish to present extracts from text data (e.g., interviews), think about how you present this; it can be difficult to read a quote and listen to someone saying something different. So if you wish to present a quote, either leave people to read this (and remain silent as they do so), or read the quote exactly, before moving on to another point. There are no 'hard and fast' rules about these issues; it is about thinking things through and imagining how others can listen/view your presentation for maximum benefit.

Note that the conference may want you to send the slides in advance of the presentation and/or they may have a deadline for this. Make sure that you have a copy of your presentation with you (on a memory stick), and be clear about whether you need to take equipment (e.g., bring your own laptop) or whether all the equipment you need will be provided.

Handouts

Some conferences expect or recommend that you provide handouts. Think about the format of these, since they are no use if people cannot read the information contained within them. As per the electronic version of the presentation, the conference organisers may require you to provide the handouts in advance, or they may ask that you bring copies with you. Either way, you need to plan ahead to make the relevant arrangements.

Dress code

Think about the clothing that you will wear during the conference, as this can vary considerably according to the conference type. If you are in doubt, you can ask others who may have attended the conference before, but you will frequently find that the clothing tends to be smart casual (or business casual). However, for your presentation, it is often appropriate to dress more formally, usually business attire.

Giving your presentation

General advice about giving presentations applies to conference presentations. Remember, many of the most experienced lecturers/presenters get nervous about giving presentations; hence, people will not be surprised if you are nervous and will be understanding of this. We recommend that you practice your

280 Dissemination of your research findings

presentation prior to the conference; it helps if you practice in front of people as well as on your own. Try to make sure that you:

- speak clearly;
- make eye contact with your audience;
- do not rush;
- do not shout but project your voice, so that you can be heard;
- do not read verbatim from your notes or slides; and
- avoid use of acronyms, jargon and other language that the audience might not understand.

Questions

In answering questions, do not be afraid to ask someone to repeat the question or to clarify what he/she wants to know if you do not understand. Essentially, you should give an honest answer to the questions. Be careful not to reveal information that breaches ethics; if you are not able to provide the information that has been requested, explain that you cannot give it for ethical reasons. If you do not know the answer (e.g., if someone asks about the findings of a comparison/difference/relationship that you have not tested), then say something like: 'That's an interesting question; I have not done that analysis but will look into this after the conference'. If it is not possible to ascertain something from your data, explain this and why it is not possible to tell from your study. You can always say that it would be interesting for someone else to look into this in a future study.

Postconference

If during the conference you said that you would send someone copies of your presentation, then try to remember to do this as soon as you can once you are able to after the conference. Do not be surprised to get requests for copies of your presentation slides and/or handout (normally by email). Again, respond to such requests promptly and politely; remember that the people who are making these requests might wish to use your research in some way, which was the aim of you presenting your study in the first place!

Poster presentation

Poster presentations are essentially brief or abridged versions of empirical papers, with similar sections to those outlined in Chapter 15. It is important to pay close attention to the conference instructions. If the conference requests a landscape format and yours is the only portrait poster, you will draw more attention to your study than you had anticipated, and not for the best reason! Similarly, note the size specifications; you might not be able to display your poster if it is too big. Some conferences require that poster authors produce handouts to accompany the posters; some poster authors bring these even if it is not specified as a requirement. If you wish to produce a handout, consider that a small A4 version of your poster is only appropriate if it can be easily read with a microscope! Therefore, you will either need to consider how to present the poster in a readable format or how to produce a handout in a completely different style/format.

When producing a poster, it is important to think about how it looks (e.g., make best use of colour to distinguish between sections and make your poster look good), but try not to include lots of pictures or images, or too many colours. A chart or graph summarising your results is a good idea. Posters presented at conferences tend to have a reasonable amount of text. When developing a poster, it is a good idea to set your Word or presentation software to the size of the document and the orientation required for the poster. This means that you will easily be able to print the document onto the appropriate size of paper. You will probably need to get the poster printed by your organisation or at a shop/ facility or online service that provides printing services. This might take time, so you need to include this in your planning.

When you have selected the appropriate size and orientation, think about breaking the space into smaller sections. The title and the names of the authors would normally be presented across the top of the poster (like a banner), with appropriate logos on one or both sides of the title. You can then include sections in line with empirical papers, or as per the headings previously outlined above for oral presentations (background context; aims, research question or hypotheses; method; findings; implications and conclusions; and references or selected references). It is a good idea to include your email address so people can contact you if they want more information; remember that you probably will not be standing near your poster for the entire time that it is on display.

It is important to consider the perspective of the reader when you write a poster. The readers will not have a great deal of time to read each poster, so you need to convey the key points clearly. Although the font does not need to be as large as would be appropriate for presentation slides, select the size of your font carefully; readers need to be able to easily read your poster standing a little way back from it. Focus on the key points rather than the details. If it helps, think of your poster as a large abstract, rather than a short empirical paper, so that you include only the most important points.

As with oral presentations, the readers will be more interested in your study, so you should keep the context information to a minimum. It is important to state the aims of your research and/or research question(s), and you might have space to include the hypotheses, if appropriate. Think about the audience at the conference and summarise your method in a relevant style/language. Given the visual nature of posters, graphs and bar charts (or similar) are better ways of summarising your findings than large tables with numbers in small fonts. Consider whether you need to include all the statistical values (t and F values,

282   Dissemination of your research findings

for example), or whether it is better to indicate in some way (perhaps with an asterisk) which differences or relationships are statistically significant (you can indicate somewhere on the poster what the asterisk indicates). With text-based data, you will need to choose your extracts carefully; readers will not be able to read things presented in a small font, so choose a small number of important quotes, even if this means that you have to include information on only some of your themes or subthemes.

Although it sounds obvious, think through how you will carry the poster (particularly if you are travelling by train or plane), preferably before the day you embark on your journey to the conference. There are poster tubes/holders that you can buy or perhaps borrow. Similarly, check whether the conference will provide fixings to attach your poster to the display board, or whether you need to provide these.

Summary and final checklist

In this chapter, we have outlined the processes for submitting your research to a conference and the key issues that you need to consider in giving an oral presentation or producing a poster. In combination with the information provided in Chapters 13, you should now be able to write a conference presentation and poster. When doing this, make sure that you are clear about each of the points in the following checklist.

1   Read and follow all the conference instructions carefully.
2   Consider the costs of attending a conference and apply for funding if appropriate.
3   Determine your audience and think about the key messages that you wish to convey.
4   Draft your presentation or poster.
5   Ask someone with good grammar and writing skills to proofread your draft slides and poster.
6   Print your poster or handouts and, if applicable, send your slides/handouts to conference organisers prior to the conference.
7   If applicable, practice your presentation and ensure it meets the conference time limits.
8   Make sure that you have your poster/handouts and/or copy of your presentation when you travel to the conference.
9   Attend the conference, try not to be too nervous, and remember that you will not be the only presenter who is nervous.

Further reading

ResearchGate: http://www.researchgate.net/

Index

Page numbers in *italic* indicate figures and tables.

abstracts 245, 255–7
access to participants and data 98–102, 108
acknowledgments 258–9
aims of review section 18–19
American Psychological Association (APA) publishing guidance 240
analysis of variance (ANOVA) 216
AND (Boolean logic operator) 23
anonymity 171–2
appendices 247, 269
assumption testing 212–14
audience 227–30, 241–2, 274
authorship 238, 249, 254

balancing practitioner/researcher roles 131–3
Barter, C. 36–7
behaviours, language focusing on 264
benefit, maximising 119
between-groups design 33, 34
binary variables 69
Boolean logic operators 23–4
Braun, V. 47
British Psychological Society (BPS) 118–19, 121, 127–8, 128–9

case study one (intimate partner violence): about 2; abstract 256; audiences for 227–8; data and research materials types 81–3; data collection 194; debriefing 124–5; design 263; discussion section 267; ethical guidance/codes of conduct/legislation 165; literature search 80; participant information sheet 172–4; participants 264; practicality and feasibility issues 97, 110; project implementation with external organisations 184; research design, choosing 81; research details 110; research proposal 142–6; research question, designing 80–1; risk assessment *156*, 157; similar study, example of 270; summary of results 231–2; title 255
case study two (sentencing of offenders): about 2; audiences for 228; data and research materials types 85–6; data collection 195–6; literature search 83–4; missing data 211–12; practicality and feasibility issues 97, 110–11; research design, choosing 84–5; research details 111; research question, designing 84; similar study, example of 270; vulnerable participants 131
case study three (intervention delivered to offenders): about 2; balancing practitioner and researcher roles 132; data and research materials types 87–9; data collection 202; informed consent 120; literature search 86; practicality and feasibility issues 97, 111–12; research design, choosing 87; research details 112; research question, designing 86–7; similar study, example of 270
case study four (juror evaluation of DNA evidence): about 2; abstract 256; data analysis 219; data and research materials types 90–1; data collection 197; data transcription and analysis 210; introduction 259–60; literature search 89–90; practicality and feasibility issues 97, 112–13; research design, choosing 90; research details 113; research question, designing 90; similar study, example of 270; title 255

284 Index

case study five (intervention effectiveness):
about 2; abstract 256; balancing
practitioner and researcher roles 132–3;
confidentiality 123; data and research
materials types 92–3; data collection
198–9; data collection, planning 188–9;
dissemination strategy 229; literature
search 91; practicality and feasibility
issues 97, 114; presentation outline
277–8; research design, choosing 92;
research details 114; research question,
designing 92; similar study, example of
270
categorical data 69–70
children, as vulnerable population 129–30
Clarke, V. 47
clinical single case studies 49, 50
Code of Human Research Ethics (British
Psychological Society) 118–19, 127–8
codes of conduct 118–19, 127–8, 162–4,
165
competence, in informed consent 120
competency, as ethical value 118
conclusions section 247
conference costs 274–5
conference presentations: about 272;
audience for 274; planning conference
attendance 274–82; poster presentations
273, 280–2; summary and final checklist
282; types of 272–4
confidentiality 121–4, 171–2, 233–4
confounding variables 32, 67
consent, informed 120–1, 128, 129–30,
131–2
consent forms 175–6
content analysis 68
contingency plans 107–9, 154–5, *156*, 157
cooling-off period 126
copyright 234
correlation 215
corresponding authors 249
cost-benefit analyses 54–5, 59
courts, and ethical approval 168
cover letters 248
criterion variables 64–6
critical qualitative research 47
critical stance toward literature review 25–6
cross-sectional methods 42–3, 57

data: access to 98–102; cleaning 207–12;
evaluation 72–6; extracting 21, 25–7;
falsifying 204–5; interval 71, 214;
keeping track of 202; management

of 124; missing 211–12; missing at
random 211–12; missing completely
at random 211; missing not at random
211; nominal/categorical 69–70; ordinal
70–1, 214; ratio 71; text-based 71–2;
transcribing 208–10; transforming
213–14; *see also* data analysis; data
collection
data analysis: about 207; assumption testing
212–14; qualitative 218–20; quantitative
215–18
data collection: about 193; confusion,
common 205; contingency plans for 109;
difficulties, common 200; ethics 202–5;
planning 188–9; recruiting participants,
difficulties in 199–201; summary and
final checklist 205–6; with participants
193–9; without participants 201–2
data sample/participants and research
locations section 140–1, 144
datasets 44
data types: case study one 81–3; case
study two 85–6; case study three 87–9;
case study four 90–1; case study five
92–3; confusion, common 65, 66, 70,
71; difficulties, common 67, 69, 72;
evaluation data 72–6; measurement,
levels of 69–72; qualitative methods
67–9; summary and final checklist 76–7;
variables 63–7
debriefing 124–5, 126–7, 128, 176–7
deductive content analysis 68
dependent variables 31–2, 64
design and methodology section 140,
143–4, 263
Dictaphones 190
disabilities/difficulties of potential
participants 102
discussion section 247, 267–8
dissemination of research: about 225; aims
and importance of 225–7; audiences,
identifying and understanding 227–30;
copyright 234; defined 225; dissertation
235; methods 230–4; summary and final
checklist 235
dissertations 235
distress 130–1, 197–8
DNA evidence case study *see* case study
four (juror evaluation of DNA evidence)
dress codes, conference 279
drop-outs 87–8, 125–6
dual roles 131–3
Dworkin, S. L. 105

Index   285

ecological validity 32

effectiveness of intervention case study *see* case study five (intervention effectiveness)

effect sizes 217–18

emails to gatekeepers 200

empirical papers: about 253; examples 270; findings, synthesising 13; introduction section 259–62, *260*; key words 257–8; method section 262–9; preparation 254; research highlights and other journal-specific summary sections 258–9; structure of 254–7, *260*; summary and final checklist 269; writing 253–69

epistemology 47

equipment 190

ethical approval: about 161–2; applications for 177–80; confusion, common 171–2; constructing ethical information 168–77; contingency plans for 108–9; ethical guidance/codes of conduct 162–4; legislation 164–5; processes 165–8; summary and checklist 180; *see also* ethics

ethical dilemmas 164

ethical guidance/codes of conduct 118–19, 127–8, 162–4, 165

ethical values 117–19

ethics: about 117; access to participants and data 102; conference presentations 275–6; confidentiality 121–4; confusion, common 123; data collection 202–5; debriefing 124–5, 126–7, 128; difficulties, common 124; ethical values 117–19; informed consent 120–1, 128, 129–30, 131–2; integrating into research 134–5; online research methods 127–8; participants as vulnerable populations 128–31; publishing 248; randomised controlled trials 52; researcher, protecting 133–4; roles, dual 131–3; social media and 233–4; summary and checklist 135–6; withdrawal 125–6; *see also* ethical approval

evaluation data 72–6

evaluation methods 50–5, 58–9

experiential qualitative research 47

experimental methods 31–8, 56

external organisations: communicating with 185–7; project implementation with 182–4

facet theory 41–2, 57

falsifying data 204–5

feasibility issues *see* practicality and feasibility issues

feedback, responding to 179–80, 249–50

Field, A. 213

figures and tables 247–8, 267

findings section 246–7

focus groups 196–7

Gantt charts 150–2, *151*

gatekeepers 168–70, *169*, 182–4, 200

Giles, D. 186–7

G★Power 104

grounded theory 49

handouts 279

harm, minimising 119

homoscedasticity/homogeneity of variance 213

hypothetico-deductive designs 68

IAS (Interpersonal Anger Scale) 265

impact, research 226–7

impact factors 240

implementing study *see* setting up and implementing study

inclusion/exclusion criteria 20–1

independence, testing for 212

independent variables 31–2, 64–5, 66

individual oral conference presentations 276–80

informed consent 120–1, 128, 129–30, 131–2

innovation and originality 11–13

Integrated Research Application System (IRAS) 166, 167

integrity 118

Interpersonal Anger Scale (IAS) 265

interpretative phenomenological analysis (IPA) 49

interrupted time series design 39–40

interval data 71, 214

intervention case study *see* case study three (intervention delivered to offenders)

intervention effectiveness case study *see* case study five (intervention effectiveness)

interviews 196–7

intimate partner violence case study *see* case study one (intimate partner violence)

introduction section 245, 259–62, *260*

IPA (interpretative phenomenological analysis) 49

IRAS (Integrated Research Application System) 166, 167

286 Index

journal, selecting 238–40, 254
journal article publishing 237–43
journal decisions 249–50
jurors 100–1; *see also* case study four (juror evaluation of DNA evidence)

keynote presentations 272–3
key words 257–8
knowledge: in informed consent 120–1; on topic/intervention, understanding breadth of 9–10

language 187–8, 264
legislation 164–5
literature, searching the: case study one 80; case study two 83–4; case study three 86; case study four 89–90; case study five 91; confusion, common 12, 26; critical stance toward 25–6; data, extracting 21, 25–7; defined 7; difficulties, common 8, 9, 10; examples 28–9; number of studies/articles needed 10; process 21–5; process for 17–27; reasons for conducting 7–13; research protocol, writing 17–21; strategy for 19–20; summary and checklist 27–8; types of 13–17; *see also* literature review papers
literature review papers: about 237; journal article publishing 237–43; journal decisions and responding to feedback 249–50; narrative reviews 244–8; submitting 248–9; summary and final checklist 250–1; systematic reviews 243; writing 243–8; *see also* literature, searching the
longitudinal methods 43–4, 57

manipulation checking 34
materials, research *see* research materials
measurement, levels of 69–72
meta-analyses 16–17, 28–9
meta-synthesis 17, 29
methodologies, exploring previous 11
methods: confusion, common 32, 34, 37–8, 38–9; cross-sectional 42–3, 57; difficulties, common 34–5, 45–6; evaluation 50–5, 58–9; examples 56–9; experimental 31–8, 56; facet theory 41–2, 57; longitudinal 43–4, 57; qualitative 46–9, 58; quasi-experimental 38–41, 57; single case 49–50, 58; summary and checklist 55–6; survey/questionnaire 45–6, 57–8

method section 245–6, 262–9
missing at random (MAR) data 211–12
missing completely at random (MCAR) data 211
missing data 211–12
missing not at random (MNAR) data 211
mistaken word/phrase errors 209
mixed design 33
multivariate normality, testing for 212–13

narrative reviews 13–15, 28, 244–8
National Health Service (NHS) 166
National Offender Management Service (NOMS) 166, 167
nominal/categorical data 69–70
non-equivalent control groups (NEGCs) 40
normality, testing for 212–13
NOT (Boolean logic operator) 24

offender populations, access to 99
offender sentencing case study *see* case study two (sentencing of offenders)
omission errors 209
online research methods 127–8
online submission of papers 248
ontology 47
OR (Boolean logic operator) 24
oral conference presentations, individual 276–80
ordinal data 70–1, 214
originality 11–13
outcome measures 73–5

participant checking 219–20
participant information sheets (PISs) 171–5, 264
participants: access to 98–102, 108; communicating with 185–7; disabilities/difficulties of potential 102; keeping track of 198–9; recruiting difficulties 199–201; research findings, giving 126–7; as vulnerable populations 128–31; withdrawal of 87–8, 125–6
participants or data section 263–4
peer review 242–3
Percy, C. 186–7
pilot studies 37–8, 190–2
planning: contingency 107–9, 154–5, *156*, 157; data collection without participants 201–2; data collection with participants 194; *see also* project planning
plenary sessions 272–3
police 100, 167–8

Index 287

poster presentations 273, 280–2
power analysis 103–4
practicality and feasibility issues: about 96–7; access to participants and data 98–102; case study one 97, 110; case study two 97, 110–11; case study three 97, 111–12; case study four 97, 112–13; case study five 97, 114; contingency plans 107–9; sample size, calculating required 102–5; summary and checklist 114–15; time 97–8; variables, operationalising 105–6
predictor variables 64–6
presentations 232–3
prison/probation/young offenders' institutions 167
procedure section 265–6
process evaluation 55, 59
professional reports 232
progress, monitoring/maintaining 152–3
project planning: about 147; progress, monitoring and maintaining 152–3; project schedule/timetable 147–52, *149*; risks and risk management 153–5, *156*, 157
project schedule/timetable 147–52, *149*, *151*
project titles *see* titles
proposals, submitting conference presentation 275; *see also* research proposals
proposed analysis section 141, 144–5
psychology students 101–2
psychometric tests 265
publishing ethics 248

qualitative research: data analysis 218–20; data cleaning 208–10; data types 67–9; evaluation methods 53–4, 59; grounded theory 49; interpretative phenomenological analysis 49; methods 46–9, 53–4, 58, 59, 67–9; results section 266–7; sample size, calculating required 104–5; thematic analysis 48–9
quantitative research: data analysis 215–18; data cleaning 210–12; results section 266; sample size, calculating required 103–4
quasi-experimental methods 38–41, 52–3, 57, 58
questionnaire methods 45–6, 57–8, 66–7
questions, answering 280
quotation mark errors 209

randomised controlled trials (RCTs) 50–2, 58
rapport, building 195–6
ratio data 71
rationale, aims, research questions and hypotheses section 140, 143
rationale for proposed study, establishing 10–11
RCTs (randomised controlled trials) 50–2, 58
recidivism, as outcome measure 73–5
recruiting participants, difficulties in 199–201
references section 142, 145–6, 247, 269
regression 216
related design 33, 34
repeated measures design 33, 34
reports, professional 232
research context/background section 139–40, 142–3
research design, choosing 81, 84–5, 87, 90, 92
research details, case study 110, 111, 112, 113, 114
researcher, protecting 133–4
research highlights and other journal-specific summary sections 258–9
research impact 226–7
research materials: case study one 81–3; case study two 85–6; case study three 87–9; case study four 90–1; case study five 92–3; empirical papers 264–5; ethical approval, gaining 170; as term 46
research presentations 273
research proposals: about 138–9; case study one 142–6; confusion, common 141; data sample/participants and research locations section 140–1, 144; design and methodology section 140, 143–4; example 142–6; project title 139, 142; proposed analysis section 141, 144–5; rationale, aims, research questions and hypotheses section 140, 143; references section 142, 145–6; research context/ background section 139–40, 142–3; submitting 146–7; timetable section 142, 145
research protocol, writing 17–21
research question, designing 80–1, 84, 86–7, 90, 92
respect 118
responsibility 118, 119
results 231–2, 266–7, 268

288 Index

Reynold, E. 36–7
risk-benefit analysis 134–5
risks and risk management 153–5, *156*, 157
roles, dual 131–3

safety, researcher 134
sample size, calculating required 102–5
saturation 105
scales, development of 46
scientific value 119
searching the literature *see* literature, searching the
search terms 22–5
security approval 189–90
sensitivity *versus* specificity 22
sentence structure errors 209
sentencing of offenders case study *see* case study two (sentencing of offenders)
setting up and implementing study: about 182; communicating with supervisors/external organisations/participants 184–8; data collection, planning 188–9; difficulties, common 185, 187–8; piloting your project 190–2; project implementation with external organisations 182–4; summary and final checklist 192; vetting/security approval 189–90
single case methods 49–50, 53, 58, 59
slides 278–9
social care 166
social media 233–4
social responsibility 119
specificity *versus* sensitivity 22
specific research questions section 19
speech, overlapping 210
staff, access to 100
stress, minimising for participants 130–1
students 101–2, 129
supervisors, communicating with 184–5
survey/questionnaire methods 45–6, 57–8, 66–7
symposia 273
synthesising empirical research findings 13
systematic reviews 15–16, 28, 243

tables and figures 247–8, 267
text-based data 71–2
thematic analysis 48–9
Thomson Reuters Social Science Citation Impact Factor 240
time issue 97–8
timetables 142, 145, *149*
titles: of people 187–8; of projects/papers/proposals 18, 139, 142, 245, 255
transcribing data 208–10
transforming data 213–14
treatment change measures of effectiveness 75–6
triangulation 220
t-tests 216
type one error 103
type two error 103

undergraduate students 101–2, 129
unrelated design 33, 34

validity, ecological 32
value, scientific 119
values, ethical 117–19
variables: binary 69; confounding 32, 67; criterion 64–6; dependent 31–2, 64; independent 31–2, 64–5, 66; operationalising 105–6; predictor 64–6; in survey/questionnaire methods 66–7
vetting/security approval 189–90
vignette-based studies 36–7, 56, 82
volition, in informed consent 121
vulnerable populations, participants as 128–31

wildcard symbols 22–3
withdrawal of participants 87–8, 125–6
within-groups design 33, 34
Wood, C. 186–7
workshop presentations 273
writing skills 241

young offenders' institutions (YOIs) 167